EDUCATION REFORM AND SOCIAL CHANGE
Multicultural Voices, Struggles, and Visions

EDUCATION REFORM AND SOCIAL CHANGE
Multicultural Voices, Struggles, and Visions

Edited by
Catherine E. Walsh
University of Massachusetts, Boston

LEA LAWRENCE ERLBAUM ASSOCIATES, PUBLISHERS
1996   Mahwah, New Jersey

Lawrence Erlbaum Associates, Inc., Publishers
10 Industrial Avenue
Mahwah, New Jersey 07430

Cover design by Gail Silverman

Library of Congress Cataloging-in-Publication Data

Education reform and social change : multicultural voices, struggles,
    and visions / edited by Catherine E. Walsh.
        p. cm.
    Includes bibliographical references and index.
    ISBN 0-8058-2251-8 (alk. paper). — ISBN 0-8058-2252-6 (pbk. :
alk. paper)
    1. Critical pedagogy—United States.   2. School managementand and
organization—Social aspects—United States.   3. Multicultural
education—United States.   4. Educational equalization—United
States.   5. Minorities—Education—United States.   I. Walsh,
Catherine E.
    lC196.5.U6E38   1996
    370.11′5—dc20   95-49702
                                                                      CIP

Books published by Lawrence Erlbaum Associates are printed
on acid-free paper, and their bindings are chosen for strength
and durability.

Printed in the United States of America
10 9 8 7 6 5 4 3 2

Contents

IV: NEW CONCEPTUALIZATIONS AND VISIONS

Preface

Twenty-three years ago I began my career as a teacher. My discomfort with the raced, classed, and gendered practices of most schools led me to question, to read, and to become involved in the communities of my students in ways that university courses and professors had never discussed or suggested. It was from these students and their parents that I began to understand how schools are integrally connected to the cultural, linguistic, economic, and political realities of people's daily lives.

Through my work with schools, I also began to understand that the privilege I carry in being a White educator affords me access to the system. I have interpreted this understanding of privilege and access as responsibility. I have thus come to shape and define what I do as activist educational work. It is about addressing and changing the structures, policies, and practices of schools that differentially advantage White, middle-class, native English speakers over students of color for whom English may be a second or additional language. It is also about helping people to think critically about what it is schools do and to consider more democratic, participatory, and equitable approaches. This means working inside and outside the educational institution, working alongside educators, advocates, students, and parents, and working through the so-called democratic system, including legislation and litigation.

This text is a reflection of this work. It began several years ago as a way to document and share on a wider scale the thoughts and experiences that some of the authors herein had presented at a New England conference that I had organized on issues of educational reform and social change pertaining to bilingual students and communities. Since then, the collection has greatly expanded to now include first-hand documentation of the voices, struggles, and visions of students, parent activists, advocates, attorneys and educators—all of whom are involved in educational and social change processes.

So much of today's daily life seems to be permeated with an ever growing conservatism, further fueled and licensed by the 1995 elections. Within the current context, educational and social change work is both more difficult and more essential. I believe this text offers a ray of hope by chronicling real-life efforts of people challenging the status quo and working to build a more participatory, equitable, and transformative future. My hope is that the commitment exemplified by many of the authors here will serve as an example and as a challenge to more actively assume the social, moral, and human responsibility that each and every one of us carries.

My thanks go to the authors for their patience in seeing this book through to its fruition and to Naomi Silverman, editor at Lawrence Erlbaum Associates, for her stalwart support.

Catherine E. Walsh

Introduction

Catherine E. Walsh

Let me give you a word on the philosophy of reform. The whole history of the progress of human liberty shows that all concessions. . .have been born of earnest struggle. The conflict has been exciting, agitating, all absorbing. . .It must do this or it does nothing. If there is no struggle there is no progress. Those who profess to favor freedom, yet depreciate agitation, are men [sic] who want crops without plowing up the ground. They want rain without thunder and lightening. They want the ocean without the awful roar of the waters. This struggle may be a moral one; or it may be a physical one; or it may be both moral and physical; but it must be a struggle. Power concedes nothing without demand. It never did and it never will. Find out just what people will submit to, and you have the exact amount of injustice and wrong which will be imposed upon them; and these will continue until they are resisted with either words or blows, or with both. The limits of tyrants are prescribed by the endurance of those whom they oppress.

—Frederick Douglas (Letter to an abolitionist associate, 1849)

If there is one thing that most people in the United States can agree on, it is that there is something drastically wrong with our education system. Agreement, however, on what the wrong is and how to fix it is much less consensual. Education reform occupies a central yet conflictive space in the current education arena.

Since Reagan-era reports like *A Nation at Risk*, and government-funded task forces like Bush's "America 2000," educational reform has been a hot item with the press, legislatures, state departments of education, and local schools. Virtually every state and every school district in the nation is now undertaking or considering some type of reform. What is the meaning and substance of *reform* in this present-day context? Who makes this determination—in other words, who are the principle actors that shape the direction and the process? Who and what are the reforms directed toward? Who stands to benefit? Why?

Questions such as these are crucial in helping to illuminate the true intent of reform in a society where race/ethnicity, class, language, and gender continue to structure access and opportunity. In fact, as McPartland and Slavin suggested, "there is rising concern that the school reform movement may serve to widen the already substantial gap between the achievement of majority students and those for minority groups unless special steps are taken" (cited in Rivera and Zehler, 1990, p. 2). Such "special steps" are not occurring. A close examination of the substance and focus of most current, system-based and organized reforms, indicates that few prescribe radical change; the structures, policies, and practices that advantage some and disadvantage others remain overwhelmingly stable. An examination of who directs, controls, and envisions most of these reforms is similarly demonstrative. Education reform is overwhelmingly top–down, institutional rather than grassroots and community-based, and homogeneous in terms of race, class, politics, and gender.

Communitites and students of color, now the majority in urban centers and the majority who are failed by the nation's schools, are noticeably and, I believe, intentionally absent in the product and process of most of today's federal, state, and local educational reform efforts.[1] This is because the philosophy, purpose, and act of "mainstream" educational reform in all of these contexts is not about democratic participation or social transformation, nor is it born of or even interested in earnest struggle. It is about further legitimizing the powerful through a process of reforms or compromises that, as Apple (1993) pointed out, take the concerns of the less powerful into account but are defined, decided, and designed to favor those in power. As he explained:

> These compromises occur at different levels: at the level of political and ideological discourse, at the level of state policies, at the level of knowledge that is taught in schools, at the level of the daily activities of teachers and students in classrooms, and at the level of how we are to understand all of this. (p. 10)

Within this context, the actual substance of mainstream reform has come to be directed more at meeting the needs of business and industry than at

---

[1]Exceptions are in Chicago where African American and Latino parents and community activists and organizations have played a major role in shaping the reform agenda, process, and focus (see O'Connell, 1991) and in Philadelphia with the work of the Philadelphia Schools Collaborative (see Fine, 1994).

addressing the human and moral concerns of a culturally diverse society. For the most part, efforts are aimed at change for the sake of competitiveness; business leaders and corporate executives assume a central role in the search for educational recipes that will improve the economy (e.g., see Cuban, 1992), whereas large city school boards seek superintendents with experience in big business rather than in education. The focus of reform is directed at making schools more efficient businesses where accountability, standards, and controlled shared decision making (e.g., school-based management) establish a sense of cohesiveness and involvement that effectively mask the difference, conflict, and tensions within. When racial, cultural, and linguistic diversity are recognized, they are treated as problems that must be "managed," controlled, and, if at all possible, solved. The sad reality in all of this is that, as McLaughlin, Irby, and Langman (1994) pointed out, "those who need the most in terms of services and resources typically get the least, and what they do get often misses the target" (p. 215). As has traditionally been the case, it is the students who already have more economic and social resources who benefit the most; it is they who will be the most trained and prepared for and will have the most access to the future economy. Reform, in this sense, means little more than improving on the status quo.

Douglas' words at the beginning of this introduction, spoken at another place and time, position reform in a different way, that is, within the realms of power and oppression. In so doing, his words provide a historical framework in which to understand contemporary reform issues. Although some progress has been made from Douglas' time until now, the tumultuous struggle for liberty, equality, and justice in all aspects and institutions of daily life remains an unresolved and open battle. Educational reform as spoken about in this text is a present-day manifestation; it is a political, social, and cultural project replete with the conflicts, injustices, contradictions, and varied forms of struggle that have permeated the lives of people of color and other marginalized populations in the United States for generations. As the chapters herein make evident, schools cannot be looked on as isolated institutions, reform cannot be considered as a top–down reshuffling of the same elements, nor can the White political and cultural hegemony of this society be denied. Educational reform and social change must be interwoven. Anyon (1995) made clear how educational reform and social change are traditionally posed as opposites:

> The often unacknowledged predisposition to oppose micro and macro social spheres has unduly influenced how we think about educational change. Thus, educational reform activity assumes an opposition, and therefore a qualitative difference between educational and societal change. It should be acknowledged that both kinds of change are mutually interdependent. Far-reaching social change would be influenced by changes in the educational system, and substantial educational change will be supported by structural changes in the institutional contexts from which schools emerge. (p. 67)

Acknowledging the necessity of the educational and social change connection can help one see beyond the current educational reform rhetoric, raise critical questions about what the substance, purpose, and process of real reform should be, challenge the bureaucracies that limit change, and recognize the necessity of personal and collective involvement.

In recent years, there has been a growing body of educational literature in what is referred to as the field of critical education or pedagogy. Many of the chapters in this text reflect a grounding in critical pedagogy-oriented theories and beliefs. McLaren (1989) offered a clear overview of the theoretical and social tenets that frame this field:

> Critical pedagogy is founded on the conviction that schooling for self and social empowerment is *ethically prior* to a mastery of technical skills, which are primarily tied to the logic of the marketplace. . . . In their attempts to explode the popular belief that schools are fundamentally democratic institutions, critical scholars have begun to unravel the ways in which school curricula, knowledge, and policy depend on the corporate marketplace and the fortunes of the economy. They suggest that schooling must always be analyzed as cultural and historical processes, in which select groups are positioned within asymmetrical relations of power on the basis of specific race, class, and gender groupings. . . . In short, educators within the critical tradition argue that mainstream schooling supports an inherently unjust bias resulting in the transmission and reproduction of the dominant status quo culture. (pp. 162–163)

Although radically changing educational institutions is the focus of much of the critical pedagogy literature, there are few texts that afford concrete examples of how or document actual efforts of the change process. This text helps meet this practical application need.

The real-life efforts of people making educational reform within a critical pedagogy or social change framework are the subject and focus of the volume. The specific project of the book is twofold: (a) to consider the structures, policies, and practices that shape and limit educational change, and learning and teaching; and (b) to document the collaborative and creative efforts of parents, students, educators, activists, and advocates to change them. As such, the text offers a critical framework for both conceptualizing and actualizing educational change. Its intent is to challenge the reader to act and, in so doing, to carefully consider the power, relevance, and immediacy of Douglas' message.

Unlike texts that merely talk about reform, this volume brings together the voices, struggles, and visions of racially, culturally, and linguistically diverse educators, advocates, high school students, parents, and community activists—real people doing something to change their lives and to change educational conditions, structures, policies, and practices in ways that are participatory, collaborative, democratic, and empowerment-oriented. It is the varied nature of who the authors are, the different voices they bring, and the grassroots focus of much of their work that makes this text both unique and powerful. As in real life, the people herein do not speak with a single voice nor do they speak only within the confines of academic discourse. Poetry and reflective prose intermingle with more traditional chapters; yet, illuminated throughout is a sense of urgency, activism, and commitment.

Although the issues and concerns of people of color are generally absent from the education reform discourse, practice, and literature, the issues, concerns, and realities of ethnic communities of color for whom English may not be the native or sole language (e.g., Latinos, Asians, Haitians, Cape Verdeans) are particularly absent. They are the central focus of this text. The intention is not to exclude other communities – in fact, alliances between these communities and African American communities are the subject of two chapters – but rather to give attention to the specific educational concerns, needs, perspectives, struggles, and experiences of these populations that are the least discussed (in positive terms) and the fastest growing.

As the chapters in this book make evident, bilingual and multicultural communities throughout the country are actively working for educational and social change. This work is, for the most part, neither recognized nor documented.

The exclusion of the realities and educational needs of Latino, Asian, Haitian, and Cape Verdean students as well as other immigrant and refugee students and students who may have been born in the United States but speak a language other than English at home is not just a recent phenomenon. It is particularly critical when we think, however, that one in seven students nationwide are now referred to as "language minority"; 41% of public school students in New York, 36% of those in Boston, and 30% in Providence, Rhode Island speak a language other than English at home. In California, such students number more than 1 million and are the majority.[2]

When mention of ethnically and linguistically different students does occur with regard to reform, it is only within what is generally seen by those in charge as the problematic and confined space of bilingual education. Preconceived notions about what these students need replaces any dialogue or informed attention to equitable, quality, and multicultural education. It also masks these students' place within the broad societal and political contexts in which the battle for educational equity occurs. Learning English thus becomes construed as the central and only issue; bilingualism is conceived as temporary, a deficit state in need of remediation that bilingual programs, seen as Hispanic political strongholds (e.g., see Porter, 1990), only impede. Although a different vision and understanding of bilingual education is necessary within the discourse and practice of educational reform, it is important that the educational needs of

---

[2]Statistics come from a talk given by Congressman Jack Reed at the Sixth Annual New England Superintendents' Leadership Council Summer Institute, July 1, 1994 and the Boston Public Schools.

bilingual students and the educational participation of bilingual parents and communities not be limited to program placement or designation. In other words, Asian, Haitian, Latino, Cape Verdean, and other communities have a central role in the overall reworking of schools, in the naming of the problems, issues, and concerns that must be addressed, and in the envisioning and constructing of something different.

This text views the educational needs, concerns, and struggles of multicultural and bilingual students and communities in this broader sense. Its attention is to the general concerns of equitable education in a culturally diverse and unjust society. As a whole, it considers the following questions:

- What are the critical educational concerns in multicultural/bilingual communities and schools?
- How do these concerns manifest in specific situations?
- What are students, communities, educators, and advocates doing about these concerns and situations? What can you learn from their struggles, activism, and experiences? How can you apply this to your own context?
- What fundamental changes are needed to address the reality of culturally diverse schools and society? How can you become actively involved in this change process?

THE ORGANIZATION OF THE TEXT

The text is organized into four sections: "The Social Construction of Policy," "Collaborations for Change," "Transforming Classroom Pedagogy and Practice," and "New Conceptualizations and Visions." This organization affords a theoretical and practical framework for thinking about educational reform and social change—one that moves from the broader structural concerns that are embedded in policy, to case studies that document activism and collaborative efforts to change school, city, and state policies, to classroom-based directions and initiatives, to the construction of personal and collective visions for a more democratic, equitable, and just education—visions that can both frame a different kind of education reform and that shape a more grounded transformational practice.

An introduction to each section provides an overview of the chapters and when necessary, some background information to help the reader contextualize what follows. These introductions help make clear the connection the chapters hold, both individually and together, to the overall theme of the volume. Guiding questions to consider as you read the chapters are provided at the end of each introduction; these questions encourage reflective thought and engagement with the text and invite personal linkages and a thread of action.

As the compiler and editor of this volume, I had a reason and purpose for the book's development, focus, organization and substance, much like a movie maker has when he or she makes a film. The principal difference between this text and a film is that the text should not end when you have finished it. Similarly, the quality and effectiveness of the text should not be measured solely by how much you enjoyed reading the chapters herein but rather, and more importantly, by how much it engaged you intellectually and practically, in how it encouraged you to apply the content, contexts, process, and possibilities to the contexts in which you are (or could become) involved and to your own life. In order to encourage and enable this further involvement, two additional resource sections are included at the end of the volume. The material provided in these sections affords a way for you to extend your understanding on some of the issues and perspectives presented in the text and to become more actively involved. A suggested reading list offers bibliographic information on books and articles in both the theory and practice of critical pedagogy and radical educational reform, particularly from a multicultural perspective. A national network list follows that gives the names and addresses of critical pedagogy-oriented and educational activist organizations.

REFERENCES

Anyon, J. (1995). Inner city school reform: Toward useful theory. *Urban Education, 30*(1), 56–70.

Apple, M. W. (1993). *Official knowledge: Democratic education in a conservative age.* New York: Routledge.

Cuban, L. (1992, October). The corporate myth of reforming public schools. *Phi Delta Kappan,* pp. 157–159.

Fine, M. (Ed.). (1994). *Chartering urban school reform: Reflections on public high schools in the midst of change.* New York: Teachers College Press.

McLaren, P. (1989). *Life in schools: An introduction to critical pedagogy in the foundations of education.* New York: Longman.

McLaughlin, M. W., Irby, M. A., & Langman, J. (1994). *Urban sanctuaries: Neighborhood organizations in the lives and futures of inner-city youth.* San Francisco: Jossey-Bass.

O'Connell, M. O. (1991). *School reform Chicago style: How citizens organized to change public policy.* Chicago: Center for Neighborhood Technology.

Porter, R. (1990). *Forked tongue: The politics of bilingual education.* New York: Basic Books.

Rivera, C., & Zehler, A. (1990). *Assuring the academic success of language minority students: Collaborations in teaching and learning. Report of the Innovative Approaches Research Project.* Arlington, VA: Development Associates.

I

THE SOCIAL CONSTRUCTION OF POLICY

This first section considers how and why educational policies have been problematic for students of color, particularly bilingual students in U.S. schools.

The section begins with Puerto Rican poet Martin Espada's depiction of language struggles and policies as lived in an urban high school. In its humorous but direct style, this poem provides a window into the administrative xenophobia and fear of loss of control that has accompanied changing school demographics in many school districts. The poem also raises broader questions about how school policies are made and why, by whom, based on what criteria, and in whose interest.

As Roger Rice and Catherine E. Walsh point out in chapter 1, two decades of public discussion and political activity focused on the crisis in our nation's schools have done little or nothing to address the continued disparities in educational performance between native English-speaking, White, middle-class children and children who are poor and culturally, ethnically, or linguistically different. Rice and Walsh argue that state as well as federal education reforms, in terms of both their approaches and substance, threaten to perpetuate existing educational inequities. Through a discussion of some of the sources of inequality in school performance, Rice and Walsh illustrate how cultural disconnections, teacher attitudes and curricular access, fiscal resources, and parental participation continue to serve as barriers to success for linguistic and racial minority students. They then go on to examine how the key components of systemic state and federal reform efforts—standards and tests, the measurement of teacher quality, and accountability—suggest a re-forming of more of the same; attention

1

to the formulation of equitable policies and practices that address the continued failure of schools for the new majority in a growing number of U.S. schools remains absent. Rice and Walsh's chapter makes clear that unless drastic changes in government occur, the struggle for a more just and equitable education and society cannot be left to policymakers and politicians. As such, the chapter provides an important framework and backdrop for the chapters in this and other sections of the book that follow.

Over the years, numerous educators, researchers, and politicians have argued that the problems and inequities in public education, particularly in urban schools, cannot be addressed without critically examining and changing the way that public education is funded. Alan Jay Rom (chapter 2) investigates school financing formulas and funding distributions and their impact on equal educational opportunity, particularly for students in bilingual education programs. Through a discussion of school financing in a number of states, Rom illustrates that current funding formulas work to support and maintain unequal education and a class system by ensuring that the funds to support public education (and, as a result, educational services and resources) are significantly greater in more highly educated and more economically well-off towns than in poorer urban areas. Further, Rom provides evidence to show that although additional educational funds are both necessary and mandated for bilingual education, many cities and towns actually spend less on bilingual students. He documents legal struggles to change the funding system to provide more equitable funding alternatives.

Language policy is a crucial concern in the design and implementation of educational programs for linguistic minority students. In chapter 3, Georgette E. Gonsalves addresses this concern in general and discusses its particular significance for Cape Verdean students, a seldom discussed group that has settled in large numbers in the Northeast, primarily in Massachusetts. Although Cape Verdeans speak Creole, education in Cape Verde continues to be in Portuguese, the language of its colonizers. The educational result of this legacy is continued high rates of illiteracy and school failure. Using the example of Boston which has the largest Cape Verdean student population in the nation and which has the oldest and most developed Cape Verdean bilingual program, Gonsalves describes how continued tensions among educators and parents around the educational use of Creole stem from internalized colonial beliefs that Creoles (including that spoken by Haitians) are somehow "substandard" and explains how, absent a clearly articulated language policy, such beliefs can negatively impact classroom instruction.

Gonsalves' chapter not only makes clear why language policy needs to be much more closely examined and considered within educational reform but also illuminates how the reality of colonialism, in its historical and present-day manifestations, must be taken into account in educational policy decisions. As such, this chapter serves as a reminder that bilingual students and bilingual communities are not monolithic.

Chapter 4 takes a critical look at the policy implications of school–community collaboration and parental and community involvement in educational reform from a perspective that has not been previously considered in any of the educational reform rhetoric or literature. Tony Baez and Eva Mack, community activists and educators from Milwaukee, argue that public school educational reform has not only failed to create a meaningful connection between schools, communities, and parents but it has also failed to give meaningful attention to the educational needs of school noncompleters, adult basic education students. Drawing from their work in Milwaukee, Baez and Mack argue that in order for educational and community transformation to occur, adult members of communities that have been relegated to a marginalized and dependent status need to become empowered with academic experiences and reflective opportunities that promote an active involvement in and a reclaiming of the institutions that have failed them. Baez and Mack maintain that by reinventing and reclaiming schools as community institutions, parents can come to connect with the educational process in ways that capacitize and empower them and advance the community. Through the establishment of what they refer to as "Community Advancement Schools for Adults"—educationally and community transformative schools in poor and minority neighborhoods that prepare adult learners (the parents of school-aged children) to be active participants and leaders ("knowledge workers") in community development and educational reform—Baez and Mack offer a concrete way to shape, connect, and direct adult education and K–12 policy and reform and make clear the fact that educational, community, and social transformation are interrelated.

The last chapter in this section details the challenge students of color, particularly Latinos face in the U.S. educational system. The author, Beatriz McConnie Zapater, has a long history of community-based organization work with Puerto Rican/Latino youth and adults; the chapter emanates a belief, shared by many other authors in this text, that educational reform must involve community responses and solutions.

Using Boston as a case study example, McConnie Zapater chronicles the sad reality of urban schooling for Latinos and names both the barriers—racism, economics, and bureaucracy—and their practical school-based manifestations that prevent these students from realizing their full potential in public schools and in higher education. Although these barriers may, as McConnie Zapater points out, seem insurmountable, community responses and recommendations that have evolved in Boston as well as in other parts of the country afford a guide for examining and redirecting practice in order to provide a quality, equitable education for all students. The 16 recommendations detailed here provide an excellent entry into the collaborative and community-based struggles for educational reform in the section that follows.

As you read the varied policy-related chapters here, you may want to consider the following questions:

- How is educational policy formulated? Who makes the decisions? Whose interest do these policies support and represent?
- What is the relationship between educational policy and broader political, economic, and social concerns?
- If social justice and democracy are the aims, how should educational policy be rethought? What should be the role of educators, students, parents, and communities in this process?

The New Bathroom Policy
at English High School*

Martín Espada

The boys chatter Spanish
in the bathroom
while the principal
listens from his stall

The only word he recognizes
is his own name
and this constipates him

So he decides
to ban Spanish
in the bathrooms

Now he can relax

Nueva norma para el baño
en la English High School

Los muchachos cacarean español
en el baño
mientras el principal de la escuela
los oye desde el inodoro

La única palabra que reconoce
es su propio nombre
y esto le da estreñimiento

Por tanto decide
prohibir el español
en los baños

Ahora puede relajarse

---

*From: "Rebellion is the Circle of a Lover's Hands" by Martín Espada. Permission to reprint from the author and Curbstone Press.

1

Equity at Risk: The Problem with State and Federal Education Reform Efforts

Roger Rice
Catherine E. Walsh

In the decade since *A Nation at Risk* became part of the national public consciousness, it has become a widely shared article of belief that U.S. public education is in a state of unique crisis, a crisis so pervasive as to threaten the economic survival of the United States itself.

Although some have questioned whether, in fact, U.S. schools as a whole really are lagging their counterparts in the industrialized world, there is little question that the schools attended primarily by children who are poor, are of color, or of other than English home backgrounds very often do not function equally well with schools whose students are predominantly well off, predominantly White, and predominantly English-speaking (e.g., NCES, 1992; U.S. Department of Education, 1991, 1992). Whether or not there is a whole nation at risk, surely there are communities at risk.

The response to this perception of crisis in the educational system has been nearly two decades of political activity known as "educational reform." Virtually every state legislature has enacted some aspect of educational reform measures and Congress has passed into law a "systemic reform" approach that in essense synthesizes the disparate state level reforms and projects them forward for the next decade.

What is most striking about this intensely public discussion of plans for school improvement is the near absence of solutions that address the sources of disparity in educational performance between what continues to be considered as "mainstream" U.S. children (i.e., children who are native English-speaking and White) and children who are culturally, ethnically, or linguistically differ-

7

ent. On its face this would seem to be illogical. If the U.S. overall educational performance is being pulled down by its difficulties in educating poor and minority children, it would seem that educational reform would demand an intense analysis of why schools particularly fail that group of children and what to do about it. Instead, the needs of those who need education reform the most are largely ignored or subsumed in overall generic process-oriented approaches to educational improvement.

In part, this stems from the nature of the education reform movement itself. Education reform could be a process initiated by parents and students at the school level (as numerous chapters in this text make evident). The operant concept of that kind of reform is "initiated by" the primary educational stakeholders according to their own perceived needs and timetable. What has come to be known as education reform is a much different sort of animal. Education reform in its most prominent forms consists of proposals by politicians at state or national levels who not only have little or no contact with schools but, worse yet, are totally divorced from the reality and needs of most students and parents. Thus, we have "education governors" or "education presidents" who push to enact proposals called *education reform*. To be sure, some of these proposals mandate so-called school-based management aspects or local planning requirements but in their top–down structural process approaches, the role of local initiative is constrained and the chance for true organic change involvement by parents and students is severely limited.

The result is that rarely does educational reform, at least in its public policy variations, seriously address widely acknowledged manifestations and sources of inequality in school performance. As a recent study by the Educational Testing Service (ETS; 1991) points out, more than a decade of reforms targeted at increasing student achievement have had no significant effect in closing the gap between the performance of Whites and students of color, particularly Latinos. Moreover, although school completion rates have improved for Whites and Blacks, they remain static for Latinos; Latino college enrollment continues to decline (De LaRosa & Maw, 1990; ETS, 1991).

INEQUALITY: IDENTIFYING SOME OF THE SOURCES

By way of illustration of some of the sources of inequality in school performance, we might consider issues around cultural disconnection between students and schools, administrator and teacher attitudes toward poor and different students and the effect of those attitudes on teaching, limited access to challenging curriculum, lack of fiscal resources enjoyed by schools attended by poor and minority students, and the practical exclusion of parents and community members from school life.

Cultural Disconnection

Cultural disconnection or cultural gap refers to the obvious fact that most schools reflect the attitudes, styles, and life understandings of the middle class, and usually (although not necessarily) of the administrators and teachers who work in them. Students who come from homes where languages other than English are the medium of communication, who share customs and beliefs unique to their cultural community and/or home countries, or who face the range of challenges posed by economic insecurity will not often find much of their family, community, or national existence reflected in the school setting. Often these students feel that school is itself foreign, alienating, and unrelated to their beliefs and concerns (e.g., see Marcelino, this volume; Walsh, this volume). Well-meaning teachers find that they cannot connect with these "different" students, indeed many may literally not be able to understand them at all. In turn, the students may reject the school setting precisely in order to maintain the sense of identity they hold outside of school. This rejection or what is increasingly referred to as *resistance* represents, as numerous studies have documented, a survival response to cultural disconnection and exclusion (Fine, 1987, 1990; Polite, 1994; Walsh, 1991).

Teacher Attitudes and Curricular Access

In the 1970s, researchers showed that teacher expectations of and attitudes toward students varied by perceptions of student social class and determined the instructional practices directed toward those students (e.g., Rosenthal & Jacobson, 1968). Put simply, children who were thought to be unteachable were not taught, or at least not taught much. Practices such as tracking and ability grouping have become widespread examples of this phenomena. And although it has been shown that such ability sorting denies equal education to those students who are presumed to be less teachable (e.g., see Oakes, 1985; Oakes, Orsmeth, Bell, & Camp, 1990; Slavin, 1986), these practices continue as commonplace in every state in the nation.

Linguistic minority students particularly suffer from lack of equal access to curriculum. Moreover, education for these students continues to focus excessively on English acquisition to the detriment of academics. Often, school districts do not have bilingual programs or teachers who can afford the range of course offerings available to English speakers.[1] Although "sheltered" or content

---

[1] The growing need for bilingual teachers has also not been addressed by educational reforms. Increased course requirements for certification, the introduction of new licensing exams, and other state certification initiatives weigh heavy on language minority candidates. For a discussion, see Gandara (1994) and Murnane, Singer, Willet, Kemple, and Olsen (1991). Moreover, although one in five school-aged children are now language minority—almost 10 million students (see Waggoner, 1994)—state and university efforts to prepare bilingual teachers remain sorely lacking.

English as a second language (ESL) methodologies are sometimes employed in lieu of academic instruction with bilingual teachers, the net result can be a dumbed or slimmed down version of what mainstream students receive. So too, linguistic or other racial minority students tend to be given "basic" or "fundamental" variations of the full academic curriculum (Berman et al., 1992).

It is thus not unusual to find that in many high schools, bilingual students (as well as many other students of color) are not enrolled in algebra or calculus but in basic or practical mathematics. Access to laboratories, computers, and other technology as well as texts, supplementary resources, and library materials also tends to be severely limited. As a report by the Stanford Working Group (1993) points out, "This amounts to a two-tiered system of education, with challenging curriculum for some and mediocrity for the rest" (p. 19).

A recent California study by Minucucci and Olsen (1992) found that limited English proficient high school students have been frequently tracked into courses that not only do not yield credit for university admittance but do not even count for graduation. Walsh discovered this reality to be true in a Boston-area high school; she and her limited English-speaking son discovered at the end of a school year that the bilingual courses he had taken could not be considered for college admittance and would have to be repeated in the "mainstream" program.

Fiscal Resources

Students can also be seriously disadvantaged by the lack of adequate financial resources. Schools attended by poor students and by mostly students of color may receive only a fraction of the fiscal support enjoyed by affluent suburban school systems. For example, an analysis of per pupil expenditures of Massachusetts school systems in June 1993 found as much as a $4,000 per pupil expenditure difference between several White, wealthy suburban towns and the city of Holyoke where almost 80% of the student body receive free or reduced lunch and 78% of the students are "minority," primarily Puerto Rican.[2]

In his book *Savage Inequalities*, Kozol (1991) painted a realistic picture of the dismal blight and the inherent financial neglect that characterizes most urban schools. Although some researchers have at times questioned whether bare measures of per pupil expenditure do themselves express any important educational quality differences (e.g., see Hanushek, 1981, 1989), there does not seem to be much serious debate that money can make a difference in providing some critical aspects of educational quality.

Inequities in financing of schools is not simply an urban versus suburban

---

[2]For an analysis of Massachusetts per pupil expenditures by district, see *Boston Globe*, June 17, 1994. A detailed analysis of how city budget cuts in Holyoke have impacted Puerto Rican students can be found in Walsh (1992).

phenomenon. In fact, inequities can be found within many districts in terms of the dollar amounts that White middle-class students and poor and minority students receive as evidenced across a number of indicators. One such indicator is teachers, specifically the amount of experience teachers have that is demonstrated and rewarded at their salary level. Commonsense and research evidence both support the proposition that it is better to have a reasonably experienced teacher than a novice. Yet many poor area urban school classrooms are staffed by either novice teachers or worse, by a series of substitutes and tutors throughout the school year; at the same time, schools within the same school district attended by more affluent students enjoy a stable and experienced faculty. In other words, within the same school system more money may be spent to provide a higher quality faculty for the relatively wealthy at the expense of poor and minority neighborhood students.

Parental Participation

Finally, we can consider the inequality in parental interaction with schools at all levels of input and governance. It has become fashionable of late to realize that parents have a critical role to play in educating their young and that parental involvement is an important dimension of educational reform. Yet here, too, there are real barriers to meaningful school participation by parents who do not speak English, who work two or more jobs, or who have to face the hard edge of daily life concerns with basic housing, medical care, food, and safety. Schools can take steps to overcome these barriers by, for example, employing bilingual–bicultural outreach workers who visit with parents in their homes at times the parents find convenient, by linking important social and educational services desired by the parents directly to the school setting, or by utilizing existing community structures as the locus of school-related activity. More often than not such measures are not in place. In sharp contrast are the many schools in more advantaged neighborhoods that are truly neighborhood schools in that their middle-class parent clientele can and do participate freely and often.

THE PROBLEM WITH STATE AND FEDERAL REFORM

The question then is to what extent education reform as it is currently being conceived seeks to reform these sources of educational inequality. We worry that it is not. To be sure the game is far from over. There is still much education reform fervor at all levels and many of the educators involved in education reform policy development are doubtless very much aware of the sources of inequality we have mentioned. Yet flawed by its top–down, process-focused, and politically driven direction, much of what is already enshrined as education reform either fails to address these equity concerns or actually exacerbates inequalities.

Standards and Tests

Symptomatic of the problem has been the stillborn notion of equity standards as part of federal education reform efforts. This is most notable in what the Senate has referred to as the "blueprint for revitalizing education," Goals 2000: The Educate America Act. As with earlier state education reform efforts, Goals 2000 emphasizes the articulation of curricular standards and tests as its main engine of educational change. Early on in the policy debate, advocates for confronting the sources of inequality in schooling argued that real educational reform was not simply a matter of requiring students to pass mastery tests. Rather those concerned with equity have maintained that along with raised outcomes standards should come equality in inputs standards that schools would have to attain before students could be held accountable to pass any newly devised tests. Without equality in inputs standards, mastery tests threaten to serve as gate keeping mechanisms, effectively pushing out those who don't make the grade. Furthermore, as Darling-Hammond (1994) pointed out,

> Testing students will not provide accountability in education while some students receive only a fraction of the school resources that support the education of their more privileged counterparts. For all students to receive high quality instruction from highly qualified teachers, financial investments in schooling must be equalized across rich and poor communities. (p. 25)

Although the final chapter on federal equity standards has not yet been written, there is little doubt that equity of opportunity is not going to be a central feature of federal concepts of education reform. At first, the retreat was symbolic. In place of concepts such as equity or equal educational opportunity, the politically acceptable description was one of "opportunity to learn standards." The thinking of liberal democrats in Congress was, as Peterson (1994) pointed out,

> that it is unfair to hold children and schools to content or performance standards if the "opportunities" they have in terms of resources, funding and physical facilities are inadequate. Thus it is reasoned, the government should institute "opportunity to learn" standards bringing all people up to an equitable playing field. (p. 6)

However, political pressure from conservatives resulted in such standards becoming voluntary and as a result virtually meaningless, with no federal funds allocated "to prod states reluctant to take up the issue of equitable resources" (p. 6). And in the wake of the 1994 Congressional shift, even voluntary standards are thought to go too far in nudging schools, however slightly, toward equity. No federal sanction such as loss of eligibility for federal funds would be suffered by a state or school district that chose to ignore the vague invitation to articulate these opportunity to learn standards. Moreover, nothing in these standards requires any state or school district to frontally address equitable resources or such issues as prenatal care, childhood poverty, developmentally appropriate preschool for all children, or issues such as tracking, lack of bilingual teachers, and barriers to parental involvement.

As Peterson noted:

> The most important question is not the existence of standards, but the meaning-fulness of those standards—an issue that must be resolved in practice. The key question is, who is defining the standards and for what purpose. Creating standards at a national level holds particular dangers, given the top–down nature of such a process and the disproportionate lobbying power of business interests. While various national curricular associations have a number of helpful and exciting ideas, it is unclear whether developing curricular goals should be closely linked to a process of developing "national standards"—a process having as much to do with political as educational agendas. Further, there must be flexibility in how local districts, parents, and teachers are able to decide how they want to use such curricular goals. (p. 6)

To be sure there is a sense in which the articulation of specific educational goals and standards (usually described as "world class" or "next century" standards) can be a help toward ensuring that all students are exposed to the same learning content. But without specific attention being paid to the equity barriers, it is difficult to see how new or higher standards by themselves will compensate for years of ingrained unequal treatment.

In Texas, for instance, students have been required to pass a rigorous examination before they can graduate high school. As a result, a dispropor-tionate number of Latino and African American students do not graduate even though these students have passed all their courses. During this time, there has been no system in place to ensure that those students ever received exposure to the material being tested; even the former state education commissioner has acknowledged that many Latino and African American students did not receive that exposure. Nonetheless, Texas proceeded to require test passage of material not taught to the students because the political imperatives of educational reform demand that the state not be seen as retreating from its commitment to world class standards. In other words, standards alone do nothing to ensure equal access to those standards.

The Measurement of Teacher Quality

Another problem with education reform proposals is in terms of their teacher quality or staff development components. In some cases, teacher tenure laws are replaced by requirements that teachers re-apply periodically for certification. In other instances, teacher candidates and even incumbent teachers are required to pass competency tests. Here, too, the politically popular short cut rules the day. In vogue is the easily grasped slogan that we don't want as teachers people who cannot "pass the test." Of course, parents of linguistic minority and other disfavored students want their children's teachers to be competent. At issue, however, is how competency is defined and who defines it. The linguistic and cultural competency that we and many others believe is necessary to teach students of color and students who speak a language other than English at home are not typically considered.

Given that disproportionate numbers of Latino and African American teachers or teacher candidates tend to do poorly on standardized tests, the net effect of quality control testing of teachers has been to drive minority teachers out of the teaching pool at the very time more and more students enter the schools from nonmiddle-class, non-White homes. It is thus no surprise that approximately 88% of U.S. teachers are White.

In one illustrative instance of which we are personally familiar, an unusually gifted South Texas Mexican American kindergarten student teacher was removed from a graduate teaching program because she faired poorly on a timed multiple-choice test, this despite her high undergraduate grade point average and rave reviews from supervisors and parents alike. Experienced educators in her school district stated that they would gladly have hired her but could not under the state's education reform law that required this test.

Apart from the irrelevance of teacher testing to ensure a teacher crop that is truly equipped to teach poor and minority students, nothing we are aware of in the prevalent education reform proposals guarantees that the schools of the poor will be staffed by experienced and competent teachers instead of revolving substitutes and tutors. Teachers who pass the test can continue to opt for assignments far away from schools attended by those who most need experienced and competent teachers.

Resource Equity

Despite the fact that the children most in need of help are in poor, urban and rural schools, the education proposals have little to say on the subject of resource equity. Generally, redistribution of state and local wealth has come about, if at all, as the result of protracted court cases. And, as Schwebel (1994) pointed out in The Nation, many of these cases have been undermined.

In New Jersey, for example, a class-action suit known as *Abbott v. Burke*, claiming that the state operates two separate and unequal school systems, was filed in 1981. The Superior Court judge's decision in favor of the plaintiffs was handed down in 1988. New Jersey's Supreme Court affirmed the lower court's decision in 1991 and, saying "the children have already waited too long," ordered that funding for the state's 30 poorest districts must equal that of the wealthiest by 1995–96. In 1993 a Superior Court judge found that the legislation to satisfy that requirement was inadequate. So here we are, thirteen years later, and nothing fundamental has changed except that the longstanding disparities between the rich and poor districts have widened. (p. 592)

Accountability

Accountability is the last piece of the education reform package. On the federal level, accountability seems to be a systemic process. Local schools submit school improvement plans to their school districts, school districts submit plans to the state department of education. If all planning documents are in order, eligibility for federal funding is improved. The mere fact that schools are unequal in dollars, employ tracking and ability grouping practices, fail to develop or employ teachers with multilingual or multicultural abilities, or fail to engage the parents of their students as partners does not lead to a loss of funding or other notable sanction.

At the state level, three common types of accountability mechanisms are school choice, school-based management, and state intervention authority. How much can any of these forms of accountability do to even the educational playing field?

School Choice. The marketplace notions behind school choice are commended mainly by the simple idea that if parents do not like the school's "product" they will go elsewhere. This would mean that ineffective schools would be forced to improve or close. Although choice notions have the virtue of simplicity, they are illusory to address the problems discussed previously. Parents who are new to the United States, who do not speak English, or who work several jobs, are not equally equipped as consumers to vie for the best schools for their children. Without a massive effort to inform those parents of the differences between schools, their right to choose is meaningless. Equally important would be the guarantee of free transportation to whatever school might be chosen. Although transportation will not be of much concern to middle-class car poolers, it can be a prohibitive concern to the poor. This problem is exacerbated when there are multiple siblings attending schools, when neighborhoods are unsafe, and when parents do not have cars and there is no public transportation.

Since Massachusetts adopted a limited-choice program as part of its education reform law, 90% of all students electing to move interdistrict have been White, middle-class students leaving districts with large minority enrollments. With these students goes a substantial portion of the school budget. Macedo (1994) offered an example of the potential impact of "choice" in one urban school district.

> At the same time that Brockton Public Schools in Massachusetts terminated the contract of 120 teachers owing to a draconian budget cut, the system shifted approximately $1 million to support Brockton middle-class students who chose to enroll in the more affluent Avon Public Schools. (p. 166)

In the end, choice as a remedy only works if there are a sufficient number of readily available and accessible choices. For culturally, ethnically, or linguistically different children, the reality is that there are not a range of good alternatives. As the Chicago-based Designs for Change argued, in many instances, public school choice is becoming a new form of segregation, creating multitiered and unequal educational opportunities (Moore, 1989).

School-Based Management. School-based management may be seen as another variation on accountability reform. The idea is that those most directly involved with running schools at the schoolhouse level should be given the authority to make significant decisions about what goes on the school building. Rather than having distant central office or state administrators making critical educational decisions, it is thought that the frontline building personnel who know best should be responsible for educational improvement.

Whatever intrinsic value school-based management may have as an educational management reform, it is close to meaningless as a guarantor of more equity for students. As a prior consideration, no case has been made that central office administrators, for example, are the source of inequity in the first place. In fact, there is a concern that school-based management can mean diluting whatever weak equity or civil rights monitoring that now take place in many systems. The more basic limitation of school-based management is that by definition it does not seek to correct the sources of inequality. If building staff who are culturally or linguistically distant from their students or who prefer regressive forms of tracking become the official decision makers at the school, little can be gained from an equity perspective. Systemic fiscal inequities are also beyond the pale of school-based management. At best, school-based management committees can reallocate existing funds that in many poor area schools amounts to reslicing the same small pie.

Moreover, school-based management committees are rarely reflective of the student clientele of the schools. In many instances, the committees are made up solely of teachers and administrators without any requirement that bilingual or other teachers of linguistic minority children be represented. If there is room for parent representation at all, it is unlikely that parents will be represented in meaningful numbers. In a western Massachusetts school, for example, parent representatives were school employees who happened to have children attending the school. The only one of these "parent" representatives who was Latino (in a school where Latino students were the majority) said that he had to be careful what he said in the meetings because he could lose his job if he spoke up too loudly on behalf of Latino students and the community.

Most often, no mechanisms exist in state reform proposals or in district school-based management plans to ensure that parents represent the diversity of student populations or that meetings be multilingual. More to the point, it is often unrealistic to think that the parents of the most excluded children will have the time to commit to endless meetings and reviews of turgid educational budgets and data that would be required to bring them up to speed with teacher and administrator committee members particularly when important decisions like administrative hiring and program direction are seldom the purview of school-based management committees. Of course, as Lee and Brugge (this volume) argue, with a concerted effort at outreach and training over time, such parents could and have become full contributors to school-based management committee discussions. Unfortunately, few schools have demonstrated the inclination or wherewithall for such efforts.

Chicago serves as a contrary, unique example of parental inclusion and serious school-based management. There, real community empowerment has been achieved through widely supported local elections for school governance councils. Parents have organized themselves to take part in these elections because their participation on the school councils is not token. Rather, the councils exercise real authority in setting the school's direction and in choosing its management.

State Takeovers.   Finally, and at the other end of the spectrum, are provisions in some state education reform laws that provide for state takeovers of failing school districts or failing schools. In theory, these drastic administrative measures could be employed to force attention to equity concerns. In practice, however, such takeovers are the exception, whatever the statutory authority that might exist to support them. After all, state department of education officials are frequently former local school officials who have a great deal of sympathy for their colleagues, share their basic opinions about the teachability of ethnically, culturally, and linguistically diverse students and therefore find it difficult to move forcefully to displace local school officials who fail to achieve equity in their districts. Where state-level authority is exercised, the situation is usually one of allegations of massive fiscal mismanagement or other school board or administrative misconduct. We are aware of no instance where there has been an imposed state-level monitor or receiver solely because, for example, a school district failed to involve linguistic minority parents, had a school-based council unrepresentative of the parent community, did not adequately implement bilingual or multicultural programs, persisted in negative ability grouping practices, or had a majority White staff for a majority "minority" student body. These equity issues are simply not the stuff of drastic state takeover remedies.

CONCLUSION

Education reform as it is being conceived and practiced at local, state, and federal levels suggests a re-forming of more of the same; the policies and practices that have systematically denied a quality education to linguistic and racial minority students in U.S. schools are neither the subject nor the focus. Equity is truly at risk.

Bilingual students and other students of color already constitute the majority in many urban schools and soon will constitute the majority in the nation. Attention to the multiple factors that have contributed to inequality in school performance as well as to the formulation of equitable federal, state, and local policies and practices is now imperative. Certainly this would offer a new, innovative, and historic direction for U.S. education and for education presidents, governors, commissioners, and officials.

As individuals long involved in promoting educational change at the community, school, district, state, and national levels, we believe that equity-based reform must involve the active participation of bilingual parents, students, and teachers and parents, students, and teachers from other traditionally excluded populations. The voices and experiences of those the schools have failed most should guide the shaping and framing of a new, equitable and inclusive education. Such equity-based reform must take as its central focus the real significance of "all children can learn" by addressing the conditions that we have mentioned here among others that have prohibited or limited learning for large segments of the U.S. population.

The chronicled accounts in this text make clear that the struggle for a more just education and society is in fact underway in numerous schools and communities throughout the nation. The question that we leave you to ponder is how these real, equity-based reform efforts can influence, shape, and/or be connected to state and federal education policy.

REFERENCES

Berman, P., Chambers, J., Gandara, P., McLaughlin, B., Minicucci, C., Nelson, B., Olsen, L., & Parrish, T. (1992). *Meeting the challenge of linguistic diversity: An evaluation of programs for pupils with limited proficiency in English*. Berkeley, CA: BW Associates.

Darling-Hammond, L. (1994). Performance based assessment and educational equity. *Harvard Education Review, 64*(1), 5–30.

De LaRosa, D., & Maw, C. (1990). *Hispanic education, A statistical portrait.* Washington, DC: National Council of La Raza.

Educational Testing Service. (1991). *The state of inequality.* Princeton, NJ: Author.

Fine, M. (1987). Silencing in public schools. *Language Arts, 64*(2), 157–174.

Fine, M. (1990). *Framing dropouts.* Albany, NY: SUNY Press.

Gandara, P. (1994). The impact of the education reform movement on limited English proficient students. In B. McLeod (Ed.), *Language and learning: Educating linguistically diverse students* (pp. 45–70). Albany, NY: SUNY Press.

Hanushek, E. A. (1981). Throwing money at schools. *Journal of Policy Analysis and Management, 1*(1), 19–41.

Hanushek, E. A. (1989). The impact of differential expenditures on school performance. *Educational Researcher, 18,* 45–51.

Kozol, J. (1991). *Savage inequalities: Children in America's schools.* New York: Harper.

Macedo, D. (1994). *Literacies of power: What Americans are not allowed to know.* Boulder, CO: Westview.

Minucucci, C., & Olsen, L. (1992). *Meeting the challenge of language diversity. Vol. V. An exploratory study of secondary LEP programs.* Berkeley, CA: BW Associates.

Moore, D. (1989). *The new and improved sorting machine.* Chicago: Designs for Change.

Murnane, R., Singer, J., Willet, J., Kemple, J., & Olsen, R. (1991). *Who will teach?* Cambridge, MA: Harvard University Press.

NCES. (1992). *Are Hispanic dropouts related to migration?* (OERI Education Research List). Washington, DC: U.S. Department of Education.

Oakes, J. (1985). *Keeping track.* New Haven, CT: Yale University Press.

Oakes, J., Orsmeth, T., Bell, R., & Camp, P. (1990). *Multiplying inequalities: The effects of race, social class, and tracking on opportunities to learn mathematics and science.* Santa Monica, CA: RAND Publication Series.

Peterson, R. (1994). Equity absent in Goals 2000. *Rethinking Schools, 8*(4), 6.

Per pupil expenditures in Massachusetts schools. (1994, June 17). *Boston Globe,* pp. 17–19.

Polite, V. C. (1994). Reproduction and resistance: An analysis of African-American males' response to schooling. In M. J. Shujaa (Ed.), *Too much schooling too little education: A paradox of Black life in White societies* (pp. 183–202). Trenton, NJ: Africa World Press.

Rosenthal, R., & Jacobson, L. (1968). *Pygmalion in the classroom: Teachers expectations and pupils intellectual development.* New York: Holt & Reinhart.

Schwebel, M. (1994). Goals 2000: Educational pie in the sky. *The Nation, 258*(17), 591–592.

Slavin, R. (1986). *Ability grouping and student achievement in elementary schools: A best-evidence synthesis.* Baltimore, MD: Johns Hopkins University.

Stanford Working Group. (1993). *Federal education programs for limited-English-proficient students: A blueprint for the second generation.* Stanford, CA: Author.

U.S. Department of Education. (1991). *Indian nations at risk: An educational strategy for action.* Washington, DC: Author.

U.S. Department of Education. (1992, February). *Language characteristics and educational achievement: A look at Asian and Hispanic eighth graders in NELS.* Washington, DC: Author.

Waggoner, D. (1994). Language minority school-aged population now totals 9.9 million. *NABE News, 18*(1), 1, 24.

Walsh, C. E. (1991). *Pedagogy and the struggle for voice: Issues of language, power, and schooling for Puerto Ricans.* New York: Bergin & Garvey.

Walsh, C. E. (1992). *A report on the consent decree implementation of HPAC v. Holyoke for the Federal Court.* Boston, MA: Author.

2

School Finance and Equal Educational Opportunity

Alan Jay Rom

School funding is cited as one of the major concerns not adequately addressed in current education reform efforts (Rice & Walsh, this volume). Examining how school finance works and how funds are presently allocated, particularly for bilingual students and others considered "different" from the mainstream, is important for critiquing current policy and working toward a more equitable distribution of resources. The reality is that state funding schemes for elementary and secondary education are highly complicated and difficult to understand. The starting point is the recognition that in the United States, history and tradition has found the funding of elementary and secondary education to be a product of local decision making, also known as local control. Local funding of schools, as well as other municipal services, such as police, fire, water and sewer, libraries, and so on, has come from the only source of local fundraising capacities—revenue from the property tax. Very few cities and towns have the legal authority to impose income or sales taxes.

The level of financial support for competitive municipal services is dependent on the ability of communities to raise money from the property tax. The amount of money a community can raise depends on the value of the property within its borders and the tax rate it decides to impose on property owners. Where property values are high, more than sufficient funds are raised from relatively low tax rates. Conversely, where property values are low, and even where a community taxes property within its borders at a high rate, sufficient funds can never be raised to meet its basic municipal necessities.[1] Most states have statutes that contain for-

---

[1]The tax rate imposed by a community per $1,000 of property value is also known as "local effort."

mulas for aid to cities and towns. How these formulas translate to aid for public schools is a separate question. How aid that actually translates to aid to education is apportioned to competing educational demands is still another question. It is these latter two questions that this chapter seeks to address.

EQUALIZATION AND OTHER FUNDING EFFORTS

The reason why state funding schemes are difficult to understand emanates from states' attempts to "equalize" funding in their cities and towns. *Equalization*, in this context, means the provision of additional funds to make up, in part, for the lack of funds a community can raise for its schools locally through property tax revenues. State equalization efforts often have not been initiated out of any sense of any educational or moral obligation; rather, most have resulted from litigation brought on behalf of children who reside in property-poor communities.

Since the 1970s, almost half of all the states have revised their funding schemes for public schools, often in response to litigation that held previous funding schemes to be unconstitutional (see Henderson, 1991).[2] For example, between 1971 and 1995, 13 states found their school funding schemes to be unconstitutional[3] and, because of litigation, subsequently passed legislation to revamp the manner in which public schools were funded (see Theobald & Picus, 1991). In 16 states, state constitutional challenges to the manner in which public schools were financed have not succeeded.[4] Decisions on how school finance schemes operate to distribute funds raised for different educational needs, such

---

[2]The reason these cases are litigated state by state, with different results, is because in 1973, the United States Supreme Court ruled that there was no fundamental right to an education and therefore, the Fourteenth Amendment was not violated due to the inequality of a state school funding scheme. *San Antonio Independent Sch. Dist. v. Rodriquez*, 411 U.S. 1 (1973). Ever since then, litigation has been limited to challenges based on each state's "education" and/or "equal protection" clause(s) to determine if equality in funding is required.

[3]Arkansas, Arizona, California, Connecticut, Kentucky, Massachusetts, Montana, New Jersey, Tennessee, Texas, Washington, West Virginia, and Wyoming. In addition, in December 1993, the New Hampshire Supreme Court held that there is a fundemental right to education under the New Hampshire Constitution, but there needs to be a trial to determine whether, on the facts, the state has denied that right. A trial is scheduled for April 1996.

[4]These included Colorado, Georgia, Idaho, Maryland, Michigan, Minnesota, Nebraska, New York, North Carolina, North Dakota, Ohio, Oregon, Pennsylvania, South Carolina, Virginia, and Wisconsin.

However, new challenges have been initiated in Maryland, New York, North Carolina, Pennsylvania, Ohio, and South Carolina.

Litigation has begun, but there is no final state supreme court decision on the merits in Alabama, Alaska, Florida, Illinois, Louisiana, Maine, Missouri, New Mexico, Rhode Island, South Dakota, and Vermont.

Litigation was initiated, but the cases have either been withdrawn or lie dormant in Indiana, Kansas, and Oklahoma. Litigation has not been initiated in Delaware, Hawaii, Iowa, Mississippi, Nevada, and Utah.

as bilingual education, special education, and occupational/vocational education, as to what is sometimes called the "regular day" or "standard curriculum" are varied. At a minimum, there needs to be a recognition that different educational needs require additional funding just in order to achieve equal educational opportunities. For example, because bilingual education requires the utilization of two languages, the home language and English, to give classroom instruction, and because of the challenge of tailoring dual-language instruction to the wide range of language abilities of the students, bilingual classrooms need to be of lower class size than standard curriculum classes. Often bilingual classes have bilingual aides. Also, there are additional costs for books, materials, assessment instruments, and tests associated with dual-language teaching, costs that have increased over the past years as the number of students speaking languages other than English has increased in the nation's public schools. A survey of the funding schemes adopted by the courts and legislatures in some states, and the impact on linguistic minority students, provides a useful tool for understanding some of the problems.

California

In California, the desirability for local control over school funding decisions was rejected by the state Supreme Court as a justification for the gross inequities in the schools resulting from disparate tax bases. The court instead mandated a "minimally adequate and uniform system" that would increase state control of funding and equalize spending across the state. The net result was that there was a minimum funding guarantee for education that was combined with a property tax limitation statewide. Although equalization across the state improved dramatically, there is still competition among state programs and services for an ever-shrinking state budget.

Texas

The public school funding scheme in Texas was held to be unconstitutional in 1989, when the state Supreme Court determined that the system did not ensure the "general diffusion of knowledge." It was ordered that, like California, there must be a base level of revenues for education, and that varying local wealth would be compensated for by the state. Since the 1989 decision, the state Supreme Court has had to pass on funding schemes four more times. In a January 1995 decision, the court upheld a new finance scheme. The new scheme is silent on the funding of particular programs such as bilingual education, but an earlier scheme was more specific.[5] How the new statute will allocate funds for these specific programs is as yet unclear.

---

[5]The earlier formula, after the 1989 decision, used to determine the appropriate level of funding was based on weighted average daily attendance, or "weighted ADA." Funding allocated per pupil was set by assigning the same base level for each student and weighting it for various factors to

New York

The state of New York provides a different perspective for analyzing this issue, particularly with regard to bilingual program students, since the state is not statutorily required to provide these services. Like many states, New York uses a weighting system to calculate levels of funding on a per pupil basis. Aid for bilingual programs and other aid is tied to the operating aid formula, which comprises approximately 65% of all school funding.

Basic funding was set at $3,761 per pupil, which is multiplied by the number of pupils' average daily attendance (ADA), and a wealth measure reflecting the local property tax. Assuming the total operating aid turns out to be $1 million, the total is divided by the number of pupils, with each bilingual program student earning an additional 15% in funding.

For bilingual education program students, then, the basic funding is augmented by 15%, but in order to qualify for those funds, the school must submit a comprehensive plan.[6] Once a comprehensive plan is submitted, the school then becomes eligible for more than $10 million in categorical funds. The state is currently reshuffling its aid formulas in an effort to increase accountability for the spending of bilingual program funds.

Florida

Florida, like New York, is operating under a constant decree to provide funding for bilingual program students. According to the Florida Department of Education, the state is trying to achieve school-based management of funding, moving toward greater discretion within each district to fund bilingual and other programs.

Florida's funding formula operates on a weighted full-time equivalent (WFTE) basis. Bilingual program students are allocated additional weighting of 1.64 (elementary level) and 1.69 (secondary level). There is an additional weighting for students participating in dropout prevention programs, special education, and gifted programs. The legislature adopted a 3-year averaging method in

---

calculate the necessary additional funding. The requisite additional funding was administered through two separate programs which contemplated these factors: 1. vocational and/or special education needs; and 2. low income and/or bilingual needs.

Vocational or special education funding was weighted between 2.3 and 7.11, but was based on the notion that these programs would replace the traditional ADA program (known as the "instead of" program). Low income or bilingual education was weighted at 2.0 and 1.0 respectively, but these were "in addition to" funds which follow the student and don't replace other programs.

[6]The consent decree now in place in New York City, resulting in litigation brought by *Aspira of New York, Inc.* against the Board of Education of the City of New York in the early 1970s, constitutes a comprehensive plan for the purposes of bilingual categorical funds.

computing these cost factors in order to protect districts from rapid changes in their budgets due to changing program costs.

In order to be eligible for bilingual program funding, each district must submit a bilingual program plan to the state that, if approved, is valid for 3 years. The state then performs routine monetary audits of the program.

New Jersey

The Quality Education Act of 1990 (QEA) represents New Jersey's new funding system for public schools. Under QEA, the state determines a basic amount to be spent per pupil, then provides additional aid based on property wealth and aggregate income (the previous funding formula considered property wealth only).

Like many states, New Jersey districts then receive additional aid for other costs not included in the basic, or "foundation" budget. These include categorical aid, which encompasses bilingual education aid. To determine the amount of a district's bilingual eduction aid, the state multiplies the number of students enrolled in bilingual education programs by the foundation amount for categorical aid ($6,835) and the cost factor for bilingual education (.18).

Massachusetts

The Massachusetts Supreme Judicial Court ruled on June 15, 1993 that "the provisions of . . . the Massachusetts Constitution [Part II, c.5, §2] impose an enforceable duty on the magistrates and Legislatures of this Commonwealth to provide education in the public schools for the children there enrolled whether they be rich or poor and without regard to the fiscal capacity of the community or district in which such children live." The Court found education to be a fundamental right by tracing the history of public education in Massachusetts back to the establishment of the Massachusetts Bay Colony in 1630, through the writing of the Massachusetts Constitution in 1780 and in case law development since then. The Court found abundant evidence that "The bleak portrait of the plaintiffs' schools and those they typify, painted in large part by the defendants' own statements and about which no lack of consensus has been shown, leads us to conclude that the Commonwealth has failed to fulfill its obligation" (McDuffy v. Robertson, 1993, p. 617).

In this case, the Supreme Judicial Court followed the rationale of the Kentucky decision that the issue is about more than money; it is about how the money is spent (i.e., results). The Court related seven capabilities from the Kentucky decision that children must receive as part of their constitutional right to a public school education:

(i) sufficient oral and written communication skills to enable students to function in a complex and rapidly changing civilization; (ii) sufficient knowledge of economic, social, and political systems to enable students to make informed choices; (iii) sufficient understanding of governmental processes to enable the student to understand the issues that affect his or her community, state, and nation; (iv) sufficient self-knowledge and knowledge of his or her mental and physical wellness; (v) sufficient grounding in the arts to enable each student to appreciate his or her cultural and historical heritage; (vi) sufficient training or preparation for advanced training or preparation for advanced training in either academic or vocational fields so as to enable each child to choose and pursue life work intelligently; and (vii) sufficient level of academic or vocational skills to enable public school students to compete favorably with their counterparts in surrounding states, in academics or in the job market. (p. 618)

Neither the aid formula that brought about *McDuffy* nor its aftermath has solved the inequities of appropriate school spending for bilingual education. The problem lies less with the formula than in the failure to require its implementation.

In 1978, Massachusetts converted its state aid for education formula from a "reimbursement for costs" to a "state aid" system, that created a WFTE system for counting the number of students (on which aid is based) and weighting the aid based on particular student groups. For example, for every $1 in aid given for a regular data FTE student, Massachusetts decided that $1.40 should be given for the education of bilingual program students who are enrolled (full time) in bilingual education programs. Similarly, an additional $1 is given as aid for each student coming from homes defined to be in poverty, with additional weights given for students enrolled in occupational/vocational education programs and special education.

THE "RIP-OFFS"

Regardless of the calculations that take into account the perceived needs of different students in order to provide equal educational opportunities, two financial diversions, or rip-offs, occur in each of these states, as well as in others.

The first diversion, or rip-off, occurs because, when all is said and done concerning the needs of different students in the public schools, the aid for "education" is sent by the state to cities and towns that can use the aid for police, fire, water and sewer services, libraries, filling potholes, and so on. No "strings" are attached requiring that these funds be spent on school children. What is allocated to the schools depends on the relative strength, stature, or importance education plays in the political life of the city or town. Obviously, the better educated the community is, which often has a relationship to the income of its residents and where they choose to live, the higher the priority that is given to public support for education.

The poorer the community, the more important other life issues such as food, clothing, and shelter will be, and the time and effort required to produce them. Despite the great concerns these parents have for the education of their children out of the cycle of poverty, the ability to apply sufficient political pressure and produce sufficient funds to support public education is not great. Since most of the funds for education come from the property tax, and since poor people do not tend to live in property wealthy communities – they can not afford it. They live where property values are low. Despite great efforts to raise funds (i.e., high property tax rates), not enough money is raised to support all of the needed municipal services. When education is competing with police, fire, and other services, it does not fare too well in this marketplace.

It is not too surprising to learn that most of the students with special needs, most bilingual program students, and most children from homes with incomes below the poverty level, are enrolled in these poorer school districts. They are the very students that require additional effort to provide equal educational opportunities. By equal educational opportunities, we mean that children are given what they need to provide a level playing field so that in later years they can compete for jobs in the marketplace.

A second diversion, or rip-off, occurs after the city or town has determined the school system's budget when the school board determines the allocation of those funds. In a number of school districts in Massachusetts, for example, the requisite of $1.40 for bilingual program students was not being spent; in fact, all too often, less than $1 of state assistance was spent on these students' education (assuming that funds raised locally from the property tax were spent dollar for dollar on an equal basis between bilingual and regular program students). It is not surprising then to learn that the mandate for bilingual education, Chapter 71A, is not being implemented according to this state statute and regulations.

In order to understand how money that should be spent on bilingual program students is not being spent according to their needs, the case of Massachusetts is illustrative. For example, an analysis of the 1987–1988 reports of the Bureau of Data Collection and Reporting of the Massachusetts Department of Education (MDE) showed an average per pupil expenditure of $4,123 for students in the bilingual programs and an average per pupil expenditure of $4,071 for students in the standard curriculum. If the formula had been implemented correctly, more than $1,500 more than was actually spent would have been allocated to each bilingual program student. In 22 school districts that enrolled 59% of all bilingual program students, the per pupil expenditure for bilingual program students was less than the per pupil expenditures for those in the standard curriculum. In the 1988–1989 school year, the average amount spent on bilingual program students was actually more than $200 less than what was spent on regular day students and almost $1,700 less per pupil than should have been expended. A similar pattern of less than adequate expenditures also held true for the 1989–1990, and 1990–1991 school years.[7]

The practical implications of the underfunding of bilingual education are obvious to educators. Because all too often other educational voices are louder and carry more political clout than those advocating for the needs of bilingual education students, the budget allocated for bilingual education is lower than it should be. The mechanics of achieving this result comes through an annual spring undercount of the number of the number of bilingual students projected for the fall. The school system budget is usually determined in the late spring/ early summer. If there are fewer bilingual program students projected for the fall, then more funds can be allocated elsewhere. The result is that each fall, with regularity, there are bilingual program students without teachers, aides, books, materials, and so on. School administrators then act surprised, say they will do something about it immediately, and it may be December – or later – of the school year before the needed teachers, aides, book, and materials are in place.

Complaints about these underestimations to school boards fall on deaf ears, as these matters are left to the administration's expertise; school boards sometimes say they do not want to micromanage the system, and this is one example of where they mean it. Similarly, once city hall has allocated the school budget, such complaints are similarly referred to the school administration. There are no effective controls anywhere to ensure that funds get spent on what should be the intended beneficiaries.

CONCLUSION

As this brief review demonstrates, Massachusetts has at least given the issue of funding for bilingual education more thought than most other states having significant limited English proficient student populations. In its brief to the Supreme Judicial Court defending the statutory funding scheme relating to bilingual education, the attorney general argued that the "existence of statutory rights for vulnerable populations, including . . . bilingual students . . . demonstrates the Legislature's provision for education, in accordance with, and far exceeding, what the Education Clause [of the Massachusetts Constitution] could be construed to require" (*McDuffy v. Robertson*, 1993, Defendant's Brief at 101). But, at least in the case of vulnerable bilingual program students in poor cities and towns, the statutory structure operates as a sieve through which the

---

[7]The Legislature "resolution" to the problem of the $1.40:$1.00 ratio not being spent was to eliminate the ratio in the Education Reform Act of 1993, enacted three days after the Court's decision in *McDuffy*. In its place is a complicated mathematical equation that, while the number is different for bilingual program students, there is no pretense that the difference ought to be spent on the bilingual programs. The effect is the same; the $1.40 wasn't spent on bilingual program students, and the Education Reform Act's new formula doesn't require it either.

legislature's provisions for the education of bilingual students pass, never the while reaching their intended beneficiaries. The challenge of *McDuffy* is to not only ensure that more resources reach the schools, but that the right of students to a public education defined by the Court reach this population too long ignored. This is a challenge that must be waged nationwide.

REFERENCES

Henderson, R. L. (1991). An analysis of selected school finance litigation and its impact upon state education legislature. *Journal of Education Finance, 17,* 193.

McDuffy v. Robertson, 415 Mass. 545 (1993).

Theobald, N. D., & Picus, L. O. (1991). Living with equal amounts of less: Experiences of states with primarily state-funded school systems. *Journal of Education Finance, 17,* 1.

3

Language Policy and Education Reform: The Case of Cape Verdean

Georgette E. Gonsalves

One salient problem in the current schooling of language minority children is the lack of a coherent language policy by which educators can guide their planning and approaches. A language policy is important because it gives validity and direction to instructional language use and because it helps make clear to teachers the fundamental role of language in education of students who may speak a language other than English at home. Language policy is a particu- larly key concern for Cape Verdeans, a seldom discussed creole-speaking population, who are from an archipelago located off the coast of West Africa. In the United States, Cape Verdeans are concentrated in Massachusetts, mainly in cities such as New Bedford, Brockton, and Boston. This chapter discusses the critical importance of establishing a language policy for Cape Verdeans (as well as other linguistic minority groups) as part of a broader effort at educational reform.

THE BILINGUAL EDUCATION MANDATE IN MASSACHUSETTS

In 1971, Massachusetts passed the first state bilingual education law in the nation, breaking new ground in the education of language minority students. Chapter 71A made an important statement about the role of a child's language and culture in learning, making clear that these were positive and essential elements in children's ability to fully participate in school. Legislation in and of

31

itself, however, does not insure quality appropriate education. Chapter 71A requires that school districts with 20 or more students from a given language group use these students' native language to teach academic subject matter while, at the same time, students are developing English. However, this law leaves wide discretion on how the local school district will design the programs, including the implementation of a coherent language policy, and related aspects like the management of actual time spent teaching both languages, instructional materials, and other pedagogical considerations needed for achieving successful schooling for language minority children.

Although there is variation in linguistic groups served among the 50 districts that offer transitional bilingual education programs in Massachusetts, one common area of need in Massachusetts and elsewhere is the articulation of programmatic language policies. Such policies should (a) clearly define the language of the students (e.g., Cape Verdean creole and not Portuguese for Cape Verdeans), (b) determine how this language will be used in academic instruction, (c) address how literacy development will be fostered, and (d) articulate the relationship between the native language and English at different stages of childrens' linguistic development and at different levels of the educational process. The lack of articulation has led to inconsistencies in educating these populations. In general, there is such emphasis on the teaching of English that the teaching of the native language of the student is largely ignored. School administrators, teachers, and some parents are yet unaware of the research that demonstrates the importance of the native language in the learning of a second language. Old assumptions about the need to "get the language as soon as possible," meaning English, continue to drive educational decisions made for these students, often to their disadvantage.

THE CASE OF CAPE VERDEANS

Cape Verdeans have been immigrating to the United States since the 18th century. In 1975, Cape Verde, along with several other colonies (Angola, Moạmbique, São Tomé and Guinea-Bissau), gained its independence from Portugal. The legacy of colonialism continues to weigh heavy on Cape Verde, despite its "independence." Fundamental problems including those of education continue to plague the government. As with most Third World emerging nations, operationalizing all aspects of a sovereign state has made heavy demands on the knowledge, preparedness, and political will of a people who have never governed. Issues of economic development where there are very few natural resources overshadow the educational needs of a population that has been largely illiterate, put at 60% shortly after independence.

Why is the rate of illiteracy so high and what implications does this have for language policy? It is well known among current second language theorists and pedagogues that successful second language acquisition and learning depends, to large degree, on the level of knowledge of one's first language. The skilled second language teacher understands the role of the students' native language and builds on it. In Cape Verde, such is not the case. Although every Cape Verdean speaks the Cape Verdean language, the language of schooling has always been Portuguese.

Under colonial rule and under sovereignty, the Cape Verdean language has been largely ignored in formal instruction; it is viewed as a slang or dialect that has no academic value in the classroom. Although the language is a creole based on a Portuguese lexicon, all other aspects of language such as syntax and grammar are not understandable to Portuguese speakers. Similarly, Cape Verdean creole speakers do not understand standard Portuguese. Current rates of academic failure (about 73%) in Cape Verdean elementary schools suggest a direct correlation between instructional language use and school achievement. The large majority of children do not learn because the language of instruction is not comprehensible to them. Additionally, they do not learn because teachers do not employ second language teaching methods, this based on the long-standing, colonial assumption that there is no "first language" for Cape Verdeans.

Cape Verdean children who immigrate to the Boston, Massachusetts area are indeed among the more fortunate. Of the estimated Boston bilingual student population of 10,000, Cape Verdeans in bilingual programs number 700. The Boston school system began implementation of a Cape Verdean Bilingual Program in 1973, shortly after passage of the new legislation and 2 years before Cape Verde became independent. It was a very exciting time for those of us whose parents had immigrated to the United States in earlier years. Our own language and identity would emerge along with those of other groups who have long lived in the shadow of colonial oppression. A consequent ruling in the Massachusetts House of Representatives called for the recognition of the Cape Verdean language as a Modern Language, thereby supporting its validity as a language for purposes of public interest, and most especially in education. As such, Massachusetts moved beyond the limits of Cape Verdean political independence, and became the first place in the world to support the opening of linguistic independence for the Cape Verdean people!

To date, the Boston school system is the only one offering a comprehensive bilingual kindergarten through Grade 12 program for Cape Verdean-speaking children in the United States and, so it seems, in the world. Measurable successes have been achieved in these 20-plus years, this despite the lack of a coherent districtwide language policy that was to have been elaborated alongside the Massachusetts mandate of 1971. Given that passage of the legislation preceded planning for program design, teacher training, materials preparation, and the education of the larger community of Boston, the task of implementing the mandate has been, in large part, left to those few teachers and administrators who understand and embrace the intent of the law: that all children whose first language is not English should be provided comprehensive instruction in their own language while acquiring the necessary English language skills in preparation for academic success in the mainstream classroom.

Immediate steps were taken to hire bilingual teachers for the large number of distinct linguistic groups. In the mid-1990s, there were 13 such groups/programs in the schools, numbering more than 10,000 children. Each of these groups differs greatly in the quality of native language and culture education across the system. Some of the disparity is due to uneven interpretations by the teachers regarding their role as bilingual educators for the group that they purport to serve; some disparity is related to the lack of appropriate curricula for all grades and for all subjects; some is because of the lack of textbooks and other didactic materials in the targeted languages and cultures; some is due to the resistance of administrators to mandated aspects of the legislation, viewing this as an economically unfeasible imposition on school resources (i.e., that bilingual education is not essential schooling, is "un-American," and does not help children to learn American ways, etc. toward full compliance of the Massachusetts Law).

CAPE VERDEAN LANGUAGE POLICY
AND THE BOSTON PUBLIC SCHOOLS

Among the 40 Cape Verdean-speaking teachers, paraprofessionals, and support staff who currently work in Boston's bilingual program, there is a wide variety of educational experience, social class background (real or perceived), attitudes toward race, and attitudes toward the roles of Portuguese, Cape Verdean, and English. Differences also exist in the degrees of understanding of the U.S., Massachusetts, and Boston mandates relating to the education of linguistic minorities. All of these divergencies have effectively inhibited the articulation of a coherent language policy to date. This means that, in practice, teachers tend to use language as they see fit. In 1994–1995, a series of meetings with central office staff, the entire teacher component of the Cape Verdean program, and parent representatives resulted in major steps toward the elaboration of a written native language policy for the system.

Despite these initial positive steps, arriving at an agreed on language policy for Cape Verdeans is both complex and controversial, given the fact that the language is a "creole" (i.e., the result of prolonged contact made between differing linguistic groups). European colonizers had over five centuries encountered and subjugated a variety of peoples whose local languages were gradually fused with theirs. Although the Cape Verdean lexicon is mainly Portuguese in origin, as are other creoles such as Haitian and Papiamento, aspects of grammar are radically different from the European source and contribute to their definition as languages, not dialects, as has been the popular view. Despite the fact that creoles are languages in their own right, many educators (including native Creole speakers) continue to believe that bilingual programs should be in the colonial language, the language of "prestige." One problem contributing to this belief has been the general absence, until recently, of written literature and educational materials.

A very recent development in the arena of language policy from the Cape Verdean Ministry of Education should help enable language policy efforts here. A group of seven linguists, all Cape Verdean, has recently elaborated a coherent creole orthography or writing system that is fundamentally a compromise of vowel and consonant sounds and symbols that lends itself toward a unified writing system. The lack of a unified writing system has been a sticking point for some educators who see language in terms of an agreed on set of letters or symbols.

There are two principal reasons why unification has taken so long: (a) the varieties in oral language expression among the nine inhabited Cape Verde Islands; and (b) the fundamental issue of *attitude* toward a language that was considered to be inferior to the superstate, the Portuguese, and described by the colonizers as an African bastardization of the Portuguese language and culture, not worthy of serious consideration in educated society. For Cape Verdean educators in the United States, this orthography will help facilitate our efforts in developing curricula and materials for Cape Verdean-speaking students.

Despite this major advance, officially eliminating the vestiges of old world thinking among many Cape Verdean staff, there remains a necessary element for the establishment and implementation of a local language policy. Many teachers continue to maintain that the Cape Verdean language does not have a grammar suitable for educational purposes, some insisting that they, even as teachers, are unable to read or write a language they "only speak"; and that Cape Verdean parents do not accept the language in any written communication with the home (although many cannot read either Portuguese nor English). Others perceive a "political cabal" emanating from Cape Verde or from Boston School officials as the basis for any decisions that further diminish the role of Portuguese in Cape Verdean schooling. Finally, some educators say they are pressured to focus only on English because of the unfavorable school climate toward bilingual education.

Boston's language policy meetings have forced Cape Verdean teachers who have resisted the understanding that any creole language can be taught, can be read, and can be written to reassess their thinking on the role of the Cape Verdean language in schooling. As part of this process, they have also begun to confront the reality of their colonial history where their language was spoken but never heard in schools. Indeed, many still recall the kneeling on stones or the slapping on the hands with a heavy wooden stick, this the punishment for not being able to perform accurately in Portuguese. Coming to terms with this past and constructing an educationally appropriate as well as socially, culturally, and linguistically liberating instructional policy and practice are essential if we are to reform U.S. schooling for Cape Verdean students.

CONCLUSION

Teachers are now asked to face the newest challenge in their role as advocates for educational reform. Although excuses for refusing to fully implement the bilingual education mandates are many, the most fundamental is directly connected to an unwillingness or inability to empower students, to allow them to fully express who they are and what education can potentially mean for change in their communities and in the larger society. Cape Verdean teachers have themselves been victimized by a system that denied the existence of their history and culture. They have been well trained in how to continue the victimization of their own students. A clear and honest language policy may contribute significantly to the breaking of this cycle.

Finally, what appears to be a simple reference to language policy is actually a major challenge to the status quo in the education of language minority students in U.S. schools. Overarching calls for change in local, state, and federal school reform do address the importance of a citizenry who are competent in at least two languages. Those who are intelligent and understanding of the demographic changes and momentum in U.S. society today must see and support the role of languages and languages for all. Language minority students may easily acquire a second language without jeopardizing their first, thus becoming bilingual and bicultural.

4

Reclaiming and Transforming Community Through Adult Education

Tony Baez
Eva Mack

As we explore ways to expand educational options and work opportunities for people of color and the poor in preparation for the 21st century, we must promote the enactment of social and educational policies grounded in the belief that every child and every adult has the ability and human right to acquire the critical tools needed for full participation in this evolving knowledge-based society. For this to happen, we need to rethink public education. New policy is also needed to promote and support authentic school and community collaboration on behalf of education that is individually and community transformative, enriched in its content by the language and sociocultural experiences of its old and new partakers, supported in its delivery by empowering technologies, and accessible along a learning continuum that begins in childhood and continues into adulthood where it is available for the purposes of college and work preparation and lifelong learning.

After reflecting on the condition of adult basic education in our local community of Milwaukee, Wisconsin, we discuss a new paradigm for adult education in which adult learners, many of whom are parents of children in public schools, can be involved in a process of community-based and socially transformative learning.

It's squarish, brickish, two to three storyish; it could be newish, but more likely it's oldish. It has an American flag flying in front, on top, or from it, and a large cyclone fence enclosed cement area in back, to the side, or around it.

Public schools are surely the most recognizable structures to be found, "plopped down" almost, in the middle of urban neighborhoods. It is their

37

noncharacter, their clearly "other" quality, that allows K–12 alumni from vastly different regions, neighborhoods, and circumstances within this geographically disbursed and demographically diverse "nation of immigrants" to instantly know them. Amidst the rich texture of our differences, schools, unlike the other institutions that have glued communities together, have dared to be generic and unabashedly government-issued. Although the corner stores, record shops, bakeries, gas stations, churches, and parks have thrived to the extent that they have "fit in" to their neighborhood surroundings, emitting indigenous sounds, smells, and colors, and hurrying to announce themselves in the local idiom or language, public schools have typically been funded, planned, and administered from without. In appearance, but also attitude, they have assumed a defiant stance in the host communities that have received them with high expectations.[1]

In accordance with the functionalist philosophy that has held sway in public schooling since Horace Mann made his first proposal for curing society's ills through the construction of the "common school," everything about the school (teachers, curricula, codes of dress and conduct, holidays, lunch menus, textbooks) has been imposed and deemed superior to any resources that could possibly come from the presumed-to-be problem ridden communities that surround them. For 150 years, assimilation and patriotism have been the main threads around which public school curricula have been woven; curricula that have relentlessly told the children from poor, immigrant, and minority families that their futures lie with befriending the likes of Dick, Jane, and Sally, and disavowing their cultural, linguistic, familial, and neighborhood ties.

If, in the process of "mainstreaming," the schools stop to consider that their student bodies are derived from young people who are, in fact, also members of families and communities, this insight is often lost beside a list of (government-generated) detractors: dysfunctional, illiterate, single parent, at risk, nonverbal, disadvantaged, culturally impoverished, and so on. If, in their roles as sons, daughters, brothers, sisters, grandchildren, neighbors, or playmates, these children speak other languages, hold other allegiances, pursue other pastimes, conduct themselves according to codes neither comprehended nor condoned within the school, they are not considered possessors of valid, albeit different, knowledge, but instead to be disadvantaged.

On the conveyor belt that schools presume (but too often have not proven) to be, there is only room for the individual. Although the rhetoric of public education casts a wide net, by design or default they quickly become narrow

---

[1]In *Critical Teaching and Everyday Life*, Shor (1980) described community colleges, the schools with which he is most familiar, as "monuments to class bias and bad taste." In discussing the reasons for this, he provided some insight regarding K–12 school construction and design: "The stark aesthetic functionalism was merely the product of [their] stark economic functionalism. . . . This latest layer of schooling, aesthetically and pedagogically inferior to the rest of academe, appeared as a model of inequality announcing itself as the "great equalizer" (p. 13).

siphons pulling in only the few willing (and perhaps idiosyncratically able) to separate from their family and neighborhood support systems in order to climb out of them, from those whose futures are still integrally connected to that of their communities. According to school standards, this last group has failed. According to school noncompletion data, we may conclude that they have been failed as well.

As public school noncompleters become parents, they too often watch a rerun of their failure in their children. Not, as some would argue, because of some family legacy or cycle of semi-literacy, but because the schools continue to stand apart, above, and in the long run irrelevant to the children who at first eagerly enter their doors. Because of the schools' inability or unwillingness to become a part of their communities, not just individuals but communities are failed; they are deprived of new generations of what Drucker (1994) referred to as "knowledge workers" who, authenticated by their experiences, may be able to connect and advocate and design and create in their communities' collective self-interest. Instead, yesterday's school children become today's scapegoats, blamed and punished for the fact of their, and now their children's, marginalized status.

OUR IMMEDIATE CONTEXT: MILWAUKEE

In our educational advocacy work in Milwaukee, we have seen firsthand the consequences of educational policy that fails, particularly, the children of people of color and the poor. We have also noticed that efforts to reform public education have not included a meaningful connection between schools, communities and the parents of K–12 children, nor have they given any meaningful attention to the educational needs of school noncompleters.

The evidence of this can be readily found in school completion data. For instance, the U.S. Census for 1990 shows that Milwaukee, with a population of 625,000, has 50,674 adults over age 25 who reported completing less than an eighth-grade education. An additional 94,265 said that they had completed between 9 and 12 grades of schooling. To this number (144,929), we can add another 27,000 high school dropouts/"push-outs"[2] and newcomers to the community between 1990 and 1994. From Census information that correlates race with schooling, we estimate that at least 44% of Hispanic adults, and 30% of African American adults do not have a high school diploma or GED. In total, approximately 26% of the city's 18 to 64 age group is in need of adult basic education. What is truly alarming about these figures is that the number of adults in need of basic education is higher than Milwaukee's K–12 public school

---

[2]On an average, the Milwaukee public school system has an 18% to 20% dropout rate, calculated on an annual index.

population (which is currently less than 100,000). More than half of these adults have, or will soon have, children in the Milwaukee public school system (MPS).

In this midwestern city, the statutory responsibility to provide educational services to adult nonschool completers rests with the Milwaukee Area Technical College (MATC). Although some 22,000 (14%) of those in need of adult basic education are now served annually by the college, its network of community-based organizations (CBOs), and/or volunteer tutors in area libraries and other small CBOs where retention and success rates vary. None of these service providers either explicitly connect the education of adults to preparation for higher education, community transformation, or public school educational reform. Most, both because of funding limitations and a lack of pedagogical sophistication, merely offer remedial, deficit-based education and GED preparation.[3]

As to physical facilities, there are about 158 buildings designated by MPS as educational centers for K–12 students, not to mention dozens of other private and religious school buildings, and at least 18 CBOs used for alternative school programs. By contrast, adult learners have limited space at MATC, and access to often no more than one to two rooms per site in some 25 CBOs and church basements, equipped, if they are lucky, with old discarded public school furniture. Some CBOs have computers, but not necessarily the trained personnel to operate them; none of them have science laboratories or libraries designated for adult learners in basic education programs.

As we lick our wounds and scratch our heads while being transformed from an "industrial society" to a "knowledge society," Milwaukee, like other urban communities across the country, is struggling with many challenges. Those who are confonted by the hardest circumstances need to transform their community socioeconomic conditions the most. The leaders of the social and educational struggles of our near future could emerge from these same neighborhoods; many belong to racial/language minority groups, all are poor. Today, their marginalized and dependent status renders them voiceless at a time when the imperative to reclaim the institutions that have failed them is the greatest. In order to become the "knowledge workers" capable of redefining and, indeed, transforming their communities, adult members of these communities need to become empowered with the academic experiences and reflective opportunities that allow for their thoughtful, successful, and persuasive entry into the discourse within and about their communities and institutions, a discourse, as Freire (1994) suggested, about possibilities and hope.

---

[3]The money spent in adult education in Milwaukee in 1994 represented less than .8% of the MPS budget. If one were to compare per student expenditures, the average spending per adult learner in basic education programs in Milwaukee in 1994 was about $300 compared to a $6,451 per student expenditure in MPS.

COMMUNITY ADVANCEMENT SCHOOL
FOR ADULTS

New policy directions in school reform should include the designation of public funds for the building and sustaining of educationally and community transformative schools in poor and minority neighborhoods—Community Advancement Schools for Adults (CASAs)—drawing upon the tradition of community/ popular education as has been interpreted by, among others, the Danish Folkschool, the Canadian Antigonish, and the Appalachian Highlander experiments. In fact, they could borrow directly from the tenets developed by the Antigonish leadership who sought to put their connections to both the University and the Catholic church. Laidlaw (cited in Lovett, 1981) summarized their goals as follows:

- Social reform must come through education.
- Education must be through group action.
- Education must begin with the economic situation.
- Effective social reform involves fundamental changes in social and economic institutions.
- The ultimate objective is a full and abundant life for everyone in the community.

EDUCATIONAL PROGRAM

Conceptualized as a humanities-based leadership development school committed to preparing adults for transformative activity within their communities, precollege, noncredit, and college-level courses, and a variety of seminars related to community development, research, and educational reform would all be offered. These would vary as to their formality, but the goal of all courses and seminars would be to develop strong subject-content knowledge, confidence, habits of academic rigor, including self-directed learning, analytic and divergent thinking, technological literacy, and the art of collaboration. Then, in the contexts of learning projects, these skills would be put to use in the quest for solutions to community and educational problems. In addition to succeeding as individuals, the expectation is that adult learners become ambassadors for socially transformative multiculturalism in the still predominantly White and middle-class colleges and workplaces where they will continue their learning journeys. In order to ease the transition and/or provide greater access to college and quality jobs, some courses and seminars could also be offered by CASA acting as an off-campus location for collaborating universities and technical colleges.

LEADERSHIP DEVELOPMENT

Other courses may follow in the too long vacant footsteps of the People's Universities that emerged during the 1960s: Community members, leaders, and professionals could volunteer to teach or facilitate learning experiences for adult learners who have a need or desire to know more. Thus, parents may need to study education law as they work with teachers and others to develop a community-controlled public school; adults can work with teenagers in projects that serve as an alternative to street life, such as street theater under the professional guidance of members of the Repertory Theater; writing and computer skills must be learned as part of publishing a community newspaper; knowledge of and practice with public speaking and parliamentary procedure can build the confidence for community residents wanting to contribute effectively at PTA, school board, utilities commission, or city council and county board meetings and hearings; neighbors within a community being silently poisoned by the waste products of closed factories can, by acquiring a familiarity with various research methods, gather documentation to support proposals for antipollution effort; small business skills could be taught to help with the development of low-cost child-care cooperatives for working mothers; Urban Homesteading and community rehabilitation could proceed if architects and contractors would share their skills with residents of the community; script writing, video production, and broadcasting skills could be developed to prepare residents to share information and redefine the community to wider audiences. As a result of collaborative efforts between the public schools, the city/county, area colleges, and community-based and parent organizations to realize this learning paradigm, adults could become involved in informed individual and community development projects that hold out the possibility of reclaiming both.

CULTURAL AND LINGUISTIC RECLAMATION

As community institutions with physical and spiritual identities CASAs could become the perfect locations for cultural and linguistic reclamation projects. By drawing on cross-generational resources within the community, traditional art, language, and music could be reinvented and re-incorporated as the community-sustaining force that they are. CASA locations could bring young people and adults together in community-based cultural revitalization projects that have the potential for reinvigorating communities in need of large doses of hope.

ORGANIZATION AND GOVERNANCE

Although the details of organization and governance are yet to be worked out, the notion that poor and/or racial/ethnic communities are inherently incapable, and therefore dependent, must be loudly rejected. On the other hand, capacity is not inherent and must be developed in a way that is mindful of the past. Whereas our communities have been cut off from access to the mainstream, CASA must build linkages, and with them hope. Whereas the members of our communities have been silenced first in classrooms and subsequently in civic life, CASA must provide opportunities to acquire and practice leadership skills. Whereas our communities have been denigrated and decapacitated by the mainstream institutions in their midst, CASA must create the means for authentic and meaningful learning which will produce community "knowledge workers" capable of and committed to their transformation from generic, even parasitic, entities into generative and nurturing ones.

If institutions, like the critically important public schools, are to be re-invented and reclaimed so that they are accountable to communities, parents, and children, then we need places like CASA to adequately prepare community residents to collaborate with those within the schools who are ready to transform them into places that effectively prepare our children and their parents for a better life in the 21st century.

REFERENCES

Drucker, P. (1994, October). The age of social transformation. *The Atlantic Monthly.*

Freire, P. (1994). *Pedagogy of hope.* New York: Continuum.

Lovett, T. (1981). Adult education and community action. In J. L. Thompson (Ed.), *Adult education for a change* (p. 159). London: Hutchinson.

Shor, I. (1980). *Critical teaching and everday life.* Boston: South End Press.

5

Accepting the Challenge, Unleashing the Potential: A Look at Latino Students in Boston, Massachusetts

Beatriz McConnie Zapater

A diverse and fast-growing segment of the youth population, Latino youths represent a critical part of this nation's future leaders and workers. However, the current educational, economic, employment, and family status of young Latinos reveal alarming problems and the need for serious efforts to prepare them adequately for the jobs of the twenty-first century.

—Children's Defense Fund (1990)

A careful look at the Boston school system, the oldest in the nation, affords the opportunity to examine the educational realities of so-called "minorities" enrolled in urban school systems with similar demographics across the country. The Boston Public School (BPS) system is fairly small, with approximately 63,738 students in 117 schools, and its student population is majority "minority" or non-White. Although since the mid-1980s it has introduced a variety of popular reform policies such as revised promotion policies, and centralized curriculum objectives, these have fallen woefully short in reversing the downward spiral in which many students find themselves.

It is ironic that in Boston, known as the "cradle of liberty" and as the home to dozens of world class institutions of higher education, the majority of its public schools' students, namely Puerto Ricans, Latinos, and other underrepresented and disenfranchised children, will not have the qualifications to even knock on these doors. For in the shadows of Harvard, MIT, Boston University, Boston

45

College, and many others, lies a school system that, as a whole, has not fully recognized the potential, nor accepted the challenge of providing the excellent and equitable education required by tomorrow's, better yet, today's workforce.

According to a 1989 New England Board of Higher Education report entitled *Equity and Pluralism,* the chances of Blacks and Hispanics obtaining college educations in New England are severely limited because of racism, economics, and bureaucracy. As of 1989, Blacks and Hispanics represented 6.2% of the population in New England, and yet, they only received 3.7% of all bachelor degrees, 3.4% of master's, and 4.3% of doctorate degrees in the region. These outcome statistics have changed minimally since 1989 even though the Latino population nearly doubled in Massachusetts between 1980 and 1990, according to 1990 census figures. According to the seventh-year report by Simmons College's Fenway Retention Consortium studying patterns of college enrollment and retention of BPS graduates,

> the percentage of non-Whites in the cohorts has increased from 48% in 1983 to 77% in 1989; . . . there has been a 19.9% increase in BPS graduate enrollment at colleges; . . . but, Asian-Americans and whites have consistently higher retention and graduation rates than do blacks and Hispanics, . . . and, financial aid has a strong relationship with first-year completion for black and Hispanic students. . . . Boston's Latino community, taken as a group, did not have much formal education. Only 9.3 percent of Latinos had a four-year college degree, and 44 percent had not completed high school. Most—71 percent—had dropped out of high school or had a high school degree only. (Langer, 1991, p. 1)

THE CHALLENGE: A DEMOGRAPHIC PROFILE

The city of Boston is officially 11% Hispanic. According to the 1990 census, 5% of Massachusetts' population—287,549 individuals—is now of "Hispanic origin," a doubling of the state's Latino population since 1980. Latinos are now the largest "minority group" in Massachusetts. The Latino population in Massachusetts is growing quickly because of continued in-migration and because the birth rate is higher than average for the United States. It will continue to grow faster than other groups because of the relatively young average age of Latinos in Massachusetts, which means that a large percentage still have their childbearing years ahead of them. Statewide, 8% of children under 18 years of age are Latinos, compared to 18.1% in Boston.

The 1990 census data further indicates that the Massachusetts Latino poverty rate (47%) in the late 1980s was the highest Latino poverty rate in the country. Latinos were also the poorest group in Boston with a poverty rate of 46% during this period. Three out of every four (75%) Hispanic children under the age of 6 in Boston lived in poverty in 1989—more than twice the rate for African American children and four times the rate for White children. Nationwide, 21% of Hispanic children are poor compared to 11% of all U.S. children, according to 1990 census data. It is well known that persistent poverty is strongly associated with problems in education, health, employment, housing, civil rights, and access to equal opportunities to succeed.

In a nutshell, these are some of the facts, as they relate to the education of Latinos in Boston and in Massachusetts:

- The number of Latino students in public education in Massachusetts increased by 58% from 1980 to 1988, whereas the number of non-Latinos decreased by 21%.
- In 1988, although almost 7% of Massachusetts public school students were Latino, just over 1% of all public school employees were Latinos (Uriarte, Osterman, & Meléndez, 1992).
- Twenty-three percent or approximately 14,933 students in the BPS are Latinos, yet 8.06% or 360 teachers and administrators are Latinos (Uriarte, Osterman, & Meléndez, 1992).
- Latinos in the BPS are being held back in grade, suspended from school, placed in the lowest academic tracks, and eventually pushed out of the system at rates higher than for other groups (Wheelock, 1990).
- The 1988 cohort dropout rate for Latinos in Boston was 49%, compared to 37% for all students (Horst & Donohue, 1990, 1991).
- Statewide, the projected 4-year dropout rate for Latino students is 45%, the highest of any group.
- In New England, Blacks and Hispanics represent 6.2% of the population, and yet, they only receive 3.7% of all bachelor and 3.4% of all master's degrees (New England Board of Higher Education, 1989).

Far too many times, demographic data is simplistically equated with school failure. Terms such as *cultural* and *language barriers* are oftentimes used by the dominant culture to explain away "minority student" failure and their unpreparedness to enter the labor market. In other words, a "blaming-the-victim" approach becomes the norm in the schooling of our children, thus, giving way to low expectations resulting in self-fulfilling prophecies of nonachievement by large numbers of "minority" children. Demographics, thus, become "barriers." In order to break the barriers that prevent our children from realizing their full potential, first we must recognize what these barriers are, name them, and then face them one by one. In my view, the real barriers placed before these children are racism, economics, and bureaucracy. These barriers manifest themselves through numerous ways, which I attempt to identify here.

Racism

Discrimination-by-Expectation. On the part of educators, discrimination-by-expectation leads to grouping or "tracking" Black and Latino youths in the lowest academic tracks. According to the Mass Advocacy Report (Wheelock & Dentzer, 1990), *Locked In/Locked Out*, these self-fulfilling prophecies translate into placement practices in which these students are placed below their grade level, in low-status courses, or in remedial tracks. At one of the district high schools, for example, "where 33% of the student body is African-American and 26% is Hispanic, of 44 students enrolled in Algebra 1/Trigonometry only 4 (9%) were African-American and none were Hispanic" (p. 53). Latino students are also disproportionately represented in special education classes. As noted by Wheelock (1990), "while Latino students comprise approximately 18 percent of all Boston students, they make up 41.8 percent of the enrollment in substantially separate programs for students with speech and language problems and 30.5 percent of substantially separate programs for students with a severe hearing loss" (p. 19). Moreover, students requiring bilingual programs have virtually no access to Boston's examination schools or magnet high schools. "By seventh grade, only 8 percent of all Latino students are enrolled in Boston's selective examination schools compared to 18 percent of all Boston students" (p. 19).

School Policies. School policies on nonpromotions, tardiness and attendance, and suspension contribute to pushing adolescents out of school. For example, Latinos are more than twice as likely as all students statewide, and three times as likely as White students to be held back in grade; and, schools at all levels may turn tardy students away at the door, thus discouraging attendance (Wheelock, 1990).

Exclusion of Parents. Parents and other community members whose language is not English are often excluded from having meaningful participation in the life of the school. Data show that approximately 10% of all parents of children in public schools are actively involved in their children's education. Dan Rothstein, executive director of The Right Question Project, wrote:

> The absence of active parent participation has left room for stereotypical statements often articulated by school personnel about Latino parents' "lack of interest" in their children's education. Our work with parents has demonstrated that quite the contrary is true. Many Latino parents care passionately about their children's education, they are, however, unsure of how to act on that concern. . . . Enabling parents to learn how to advocate for themselves is the difference between . . . passively and painfully accepting the poor education of their children or advocating on behalf of improving it. (*Nuestros Hijos/Our Children Initiative* Proposal, 1991, p. 2)

Negative Attitudes. Some school personnel present negative attitudes. Teachers are sometimes heard in the school hallways saying, "Puerto Ricans are dumb in two languages. . . ." Students (referring to school counselors or some outside program counselors) often say, "They don't believe in me . . ." or "They tell me what to write in the application or they write it out themselves, instead of teaching me how to do it . . ." According to Cummins' (1986) *Empowering Minority Students: A Framework for Intervention,* many reform measures, although necessary, succeed in "deflecting attention from the attitudes and orientation of educators who interact on a daily basis with minority students. It is in these attitudes that students are disabled" (p. 33).

Twisted Equation. Many believe that lack of English equals lack of intelligence and potential. This was discussed earlier in the section on discrimination-by-expectation.

Absence of the Dominated Minority Students' Language and Culture into the School Program (Cummins, 1986). Several studies point out that "students' school success appears to reflect both more solid cognitive/academic foundation developed though intensive native language instruction and reinforcement of their cultural identity" (p. 25).

Absence of Latino Teachers, Administrators, and Other School Personnel Throughout the System (Beyond Bilingual Programs!). As of 1989, approximately 7% of all students enrolled in public education in Massachusetts were Latinos, whereas only 1% of all school employees were Latinos.

Economics

Since the 1980s, Massachusetts has been in the eye of a budgetary hurricane whose force is having a devastating impact on local aid to cities and towns. Human services and education, in particular, have suffered massive cuts, thus, drastically reducing or eliminating services for the poor and curtailing postsecondary education opportunities for low-income students. As mentioned previously, the poverty rates for Latinos in Boston increased during the 1980s, while they decreased for Whites and African Americans. Approximately 79% of Latino single parents in Boston live in poverty.

In addition, programs for at-risk youth funded by the state have been completely eliminated or vastly scaled down since 1989. For example, Commonwealth Futures, a dropout prevention program jointly funded by the Department of Employment & Training (DET) and the Department of Education (DOE), lost all of its funding in FY91, down from $1 million in FY89, and Chapter 188 dropout prevention funds, administered by the DOE had been reduced by 75% since FY89, from $2,250,000 to $553,000 in FY91 (Massachusetts Youth Policy Council, 1990).

Among programs that have also sustained substantial reductions or full elimination are the McNair program, which provided financial aid to Massachusetts' disadvantaged students, and various other scholarships for disadvantaged students. These facts, coupled with a general decrease in the higher education budget, and effected tuition hikes of up to 32% for state colleges and universities means that students who aspire to attend higher education institutions, must find additional alternatives, scholarships, and loans to meet their full financial need.

Bureaucracy and Admissions Requirements

In addition to all the barriers already mentioned, language minority and other disenfranchised students must overcome the hurdle of admissions requirements such as applications, SATs, TOEFL, and other standardized tests that a majority of aspiring students are not prepared to do. And to top it off, they often have to do this in total anonymity in large university campuses where not too many people speak their language, and where related departments do not speak with each other. In some institutions, for instance, the admissions department does not speak to the financial aid department. And no one speaks to the student in any language!

UNLEASHING THE POTENTIAL: COMMUNITY RESPONSES AND RECOMMENDATIONS

The challenge of opening up the "pipeline" of equity and excellence in education for Latino students in public education is one that cannot be met by school systems alone. On the other hand, community responses and solutions must be recognized and welcomed by the "system."

In the face of so many seemingly insurmountable barriers, I attempt to make recommendations that will not only pave the way to the doors of higher education, but will also help Latinos and other ethno-racial groups succeed in these postsecondary educational institutions. These recommendations concur with those voiced by the Children's Defense Fund, the New England Board of Higher Education, the Hispanic Association of Colleges and Universities, ASPIRA, Jim Cummins, the National Council of La Raza, and the Hispanic Policy Development Project, among others, and have been informed by our own experience through the HOPE Talent Search program.[2]

1. First and foremost, there must be fundamental changes that involve

---

[2]The Hispanic Office of Planning and Evaluation's Talent Search Program, located in Boston and funded by the U.S. Department of Education, is designed to encourage and assist Latino students to advance to postsecondary education.

"personal redefinitions of the way classroom teachers interact with the children and the communities they serve" (Cummins, 1986, p. 18). Cummins suggested that "attempts at educational reform such as compensatory and bilingual education have been unsuccessful because they have not altered significantly the relationships between educators and minority students, and between schools and minority communities" (p. 18).

2. Educators must become advocates for their students. They must promote their linguistic talents, their culture, and their sense of self-confidence and self-esteem.

3. Schools must encourage and welcome parental and community participation. The past decade has yielded numerous reports (e.g., Hispanic Policy Development Project, Schools Reaching Out, Massachusetts Department of Education, NCLR's Project Excel) documenting the impact of parental and community involvement on the school achievement of children. Although all of these studies conclude that there is a strong correlation between strong parental/community involvement and student success, they also agree that community-derived and culturally appropriate interventions prove to be most beneficial to both children and the school community.

In Boston, the Latino Parents Association (LPA), in conjunction with the Right Question Project, recently embarked in developing a grassroots educational program, *Nuestros Hijos/Our Children Initiative*, that will enable Latino parents to advocate effectively for their children's education. According to Antonieta Gimeno, president of the LPA, "Latino parents want and need to be organized consistently, with our agenda, from the base." She believes that their model will "turn the tide around" because their organization speaks in their own voice to their needs, priorities, and goals. After all, their strategy involves parents training and supporting other parents—a marked departure from traditional, court-mandated parent organization strategies.

4. Educators must implement pedagogical approaches that are liberating and additive rather than subtractive and dependence-oriented. We recommend the creation and implementation of a multicultural and comprehensive curriculum that validates children's experience and history; operates from a strengths position rather than a deficit position; creates a climate of caring, respect, and acceptance in the classroom, and; prepares all children to live, learn, and work in a pluralistic and increasingly interdependent world.

5. Educate all teachers to be effective educators for all children; foster multicultural appreciation, and the notion that all children can learn (Children's Defense Fund, 1990). There must be support for on-going professional development, teacher training, and retraining on educational practices that promote excellence for all students by: acknowledging individual strengths and learning styles, practicing democracy in the classroom, and designing a full spectrum learning environment that taps on multiple forms of intelligence (Gardner, 1993).

6. "Earlier introduction to the world of work and higher education, through community service programs, career exploration activities, and college/ secondary school partnerships . . . could improve the school retention, postsecondary enrollment, and school-to-work transition of Latino youth" (Children's Defense Fund, 1990, p. 29).

Both research and experience show that middle schools are important links and critical junctures in the pipeline leading to higher education. The Children's Defense Fund, the New England Board of Higher Education, and the Hispanic Association of Colleges and Universities (HACU), among others, strongly recommend programs of aggressive postsecondary education outreach such as Talent Search and Upward Bound to counsel and place Latino students in postsecondary institutions, particularly 4-year colleges. In addition, they recommend that these programs provide extensive information on financial aid for low-income students, as "the decline in Hispanic college participation rates can be attributed primarily to economic factors."

For the past decade and a half, the HOPE Talent Search experience has taught that, in order for a student to make a smooth transition between high school and college, there must be a set of support systems in place: the earlier, the better. Again, to begin the process toward postsecondary education in high school is oftentimes too late. At minimum this process should begin at the middle school level, if not earlier.

7. Guarantee payment of college costs by providing grants instead of loans, and exploring ways of relieving the burden of student debt. Re-authorizing the Higher Education Act of 1965, and incorporating the Hispanic Higher Education Act of 1991 will alleviate some of the economic burden for many low-income and moderate income Latinos.

8. Waive certain admissions requirements or devise new ones to afford traditionally underrepresented students a chance to demonstrate their potential for postsecondary work.

9. Implement intensive ESL and integrated studies programs that grant credits toward associate or bachelor's degrees.

10. Expand programs to support students academically, financially, and personally.

11. Forge collaborations with other postsecondary educational counseling programs in order to increase outreach and services to all students in need.

12. Replicate effective community solutions and programs that promote youth leadership, and academic achievement such as ASPIRA, Project Excel, and the Valued Youth Program in San Antonio, Texas.[3] Expand program concepts to increase positive peer interactions through tutoring and mentoring.

---

[3]These three programs are national dropout prevention models whose central strategy is to build participants' self-esteem by placing them in positions of leadership and responsibility, such as in peer tutoring, community service, and other educational and civic endeavors.

13. Create more mentoring programs that match youths with positive adult role models.

14. Provide equitable funding for poor communities. In a 1991 Massachusetts Department of Education task force report to the Board of Education, it found that at least $42 million was needed to bail out four nearly bankrupt school communities in Massachusetts: Holyoke, Lawrence, Chelsea, and Brockton. Chelsea, with a Latino school population of approximately 70%, was under receivership. In Holyoke, where Latino students constitute almost 80%, Latino parents sued because of the substandard education; the city is now under court order to provide minimum school funding. The financing of Bilingual Education must be closely reviewed to ensure that funds intended for bilingual education are actually spent on these students' education without stopping at city hall.

15. Build accountability mechanisms for a child's education, from the child's home to the teacher, to the principal, to the superintendent, to the school committee, and to the mayor.

16. Provide clean, safe school buildings.

THE BOTTOM LINE

Educators and policymakers are strongly urged to accept the personal and political challenge of redefining their roles within the classroom, the school, and the community so that these result in interactions that unleash the potential of students, rather than disable them. At the same time, gatekeepers and policymakers are urged to redefine systemwide goals so that the schools "transform society by empowering minority students rather than reflect society by disabling them" (Cummins, 1986, p. 34). To conclude, if we are to prepare the labor force and residents of this state, and this nation, we need to learn by taking a close look at our school systems. In Boston, as in other parts of the country, we cannot afford to continue business as usual. As Latinos continue to grow into the largest "non-White" group in the United States, it behooves us to examine and redirect our practice in order to provide an excellent and equitable education for all students. Finally, if we are to build a sustainable community of learners who provide responsible local and global leadership and participation, we cannot do it without *dignidad, respeto y cariño.*[4]

REFERENCES

Children's Defense Fund. (1990). *Latino youths at a crossroads.* Washington, DC: Author.
Cummins, J. (1986). Empowering minority students: A framework for intervention. *Harvard Educational Review, 56*(1), 21.

---

[4]Spanish terms for dignity, respect, and love.

Gardner, H. (1993). *Multiple intelligences: The theory in practice.* New York: Basic Books.

Horst, L., & Donohue, M. (1990). *Annual and cohort dropout rates in Boston public schools: Focus on programmatic and demographic characteristics.* Boston: Public School's Office of Research and Development.

Horst, L., & Donohue, M. (1991). *Annual and cohort dropout rates in Boston public schools: Focus on programmatic and demographic characteristics.* Boston: Public School's Office of Research and Development.

Langer, P. (1991). *Patterns of enrollment-year seven: The local college enrollment and retention of Boston public school graduates.* Boston: Fenway Retention Consortium.

Massachusetts Youth Policy Council. (1990). *Principles for effective programs for at-risk youth.* Boston: Author.

New England Board of Higher Education. (1989). *Equity and excellence in higher education.* Boston: Author.

Rothstein, D. (1991). *Nuestros Hijos/Our children initiative funding proposal.* Boston: Author.

Uriarte, M., Osterman, P., & Meléndez, E. (1992). *Latinos in Boston: Confronting poverty, building community.* Boston: The Boston Foundation.

Wheelock, A. E. (1990). *The status of Latino students in Massachusetts public schools: Directions for policy research in the 1990s.* Boston: Mauricio Gaston Institute for Latino Community Development and Public Policy.

Wheelock, A., & Dentzer, E. (1990). *Locked in/locked out: Tracking and placement practices in Boston public schools.* Boston: Massachusetts Advocacy Center.

II

COLLABORATIONS
FOR CHANGE

This section chronicles the real-life efforts of people challenging the status quo and working to build a more participatory, equitable, and transformative educational system. The focus is on grassroots work, multicultural alliances, and understanding the practical and theoretical significance of collaborations for change.

By documenting community, school, and university-based initiatives, struggles, and collaborations, the chapters in this section demonstrate the multiple contexts of educational reform. In other words, they help make clear that educational reform does not just happen in administrative offices or school buildings but occurs, amongst other areas, in neighborhoods, communities, community centers, in city and statewide coalitions, and in partnerships between researchers, families, and schools.

The chapters reveal that common concerns regarding the quality of education for Latinos, Asians, Haitians, and African Americans (as well as other groups) can serve as a catalyst for these different communities to communicate and undertake collaborative and collective work, thus challenging the competitive individualism and stark racial/ethnic divisions that, in varied forms, have been promoted and supported in this country, particularly during the Reagan/Bush years and, more recently, under Gingrich and the conservative-controlled Congress. Individualism and divisions are further challenged by the various collaborations across subject position documented here: parents, activists, advocates, attorneys, teachers, students, and university-based educators have joined hands to work for something different.

In chapter 6, Kiang offers a window into the anti-immigrant sentiment, racial violence, and English-only advocacy that have accompanied recent changing demographics in Lowell, Massachusetts. A former textile city built by European immigrants, Lowell now has the second largest Cambodian population in the country as well as Lao and Vietnamese populations and a rapidly growing Latino community. Kiang chronicles how Southeast Asian and Latino parents' demands for educational access, equity, and reform led to organizing and coalition building and, eventually, to demands for political representation and community empowerment. Not only does the chapter engage the reader in the lessons and ongoing process of educational and social change in Lowell, but, even more importantly, it cements the link between educational reform, community work, and political involvement and makes evident the enhanced power that can result when otherwise marginalized groups work together.

Since *Brown v. Board of Education*, lawyers and the courts have played a major role in struggles for equal educational rights. Although litigation has historically shown itself to be an important strategy in moving forward the interests of nonempowered communities, litigation is not generally discussed or considered as a strategy in the literature, discourse, or efforts of present-day educational reform. Perez-Bustillo (chapter 7) demonstrates the educational change and community empowerment that can occur when litigation is used and is tied to sustained community action.

This chapter documents how an educational model for change that incorporated legal challenges and political empowerment evolved in Florida. It speaks to the process by which Mexican, Puerto Rican, Cuban, Haitian, Central American, and African American parents, advocates, attorneys, activists, and organizations have come together to reverse the educational deprivation of these various groups, discusses the focus and outcomes of their work, and describes the creation of an organizational network—the Florida Multicultural Network for Educational Rights—that has helped afford an ongoing institutional commitment to educational change and community empowerment.

Who writes educational reform legislation? Who participates in its construction? Whose interests does it most often represent and serve? Lee and Brugge address these questions in chapter 8 on grassroots educational reform efforts and coalition building among Asian and African American parents and activists in Boston. As in many parts of the country, government, and education officials in Massachusetts have been actively engaged in educational reform discussions, plans, and legislation. Lee, a parent, educator, and community activist, and Brugge, a community activist, describe how the concerns and voices of urban parents of color have been excluded in this top–down reform process. They detail the process by which parents and activists have come together within and across communities to rethink educational reform and to draft parent participation legislation. Through interviews with Chinese and African American parents, the authors document the substance of parents' concerns, hopes, and visions as well as the significance of multiracial coalition work. Their chapter, along with the previous two, offer some important lessons about building cross-community alliances and coalitions and about enabling and supporting grassroots educational reform and community empowerment.

The final chapter (chapter 9) in this section documents collaborations for change from a different contextual perspective. Here, members of *La Colectiva Intercambio*—a group of Puerto Rican researchers and educators from the United States and from Puerto Rico—describe five collaborative projects between students, teachers, communities, and researchers in New York City, Tucson, Arizona, and San Juan, Puerto Rico. In contrast to the grassroots-oriented voices of the previous three chapters, this chapter's authors are more academic in voice. They describe the shared theoretical approach that guides their individual projects and their collective work, identifying five components that, while not named in theoretical terms, were also present in the previous chapters: (a) educational and social change; (b) collaboration; (c) communities as intellectual and cultural resources; (d) pedagogy; and (e) the relationship between theory and practice. By elaborating on their theoretical understandings of these components and explaining how these understandings shape their participatory and ethnographic research approaches as well as their interactions and involvement with communities and schools, the authors afford a generalized framework not just for understanding their work but also for reflecting on the previous chapters, reading that which is to come, and pondering your own theories, beliefs, experiences, practices, and possibilities.

Several key questions might be helpful to consider as the chapters in this section are read:

- How do the authors similarly or differently define collaboration and collaborative work? How does their own involvement in the collaborations and in the underlying struggles about which they write seem to influence their understandings?
- What are the similarities and the differences in the collaborations they detail and in the ways these collaborations engender educational change, collective action, and community and/or student empowerment?
- What made the coalitions that are described work? What lessons can you take from them?
- How do the definitions, practices, and sociopolitical nature of what is discussed here support or challenge your own conceptions and experiences? What do they suggest for your future educational work? For work in your own community?

6

Southeast Asian and Latino Parent Empowerment: Lessons from Lowell, Massachusetts

Peter Nien-chu Kiang

During the 1980s, Lowell, Massachusetts, a city famous in U.S. immigrant and labor history, experienced a dynamic, albeit bitter process of demographic transformation. Like other cities such as Monterey Park, California (Wang, 1989), which underwent dramatic demographic change during the past decade, the rapid growth of Asian and Latino communities in Lowell has tested each of the city's institutions including the hospitals, police, courts, and the public school system. At the same time, a climate of anti-immigrant resentment has developed in Lowell, reflected in racial violence and "English-only" policies within the city.

This case study analyzes the challenge of changing demographics in Lowell as reflected in dynamics surrounding public school education. The Lowell example illustrates how organizing and coalition building by Southeast Asian and Latino parents in relation to issues of educational equity for their children, led to demands for political representation and community empowerment.[1]

LOWELL AS AN IMMIGRANT CITY

The town of Lowell was established in 1826 in the context of America's industrial revolution. Seeking to expand their economic base, Boston-based

---

[1]For a discussion comparing recent Cambodian community development in Lowell with that of the city's Irish community during the mid-1800s, see Kiang (1994).

59

gentry purchased land alongside the Merrimack River and built a chain of textile mills with an elaborate canal-lock system that powered looms with energy generated by the river's current. As Lowell emerged as the country's textile center, teenage girls were recruited from the area's surrounding farms to work in the mills. Paid at half the male wage, yet earning more than they would from farm work, the mill girls lived in dormitory-style housing constructed next to the factories. Harsh working and living conditions, however, led to some of the country's first examples of labor organizing—including mill girl strikes in 1834 and 1836, formation of the Lowell Female Labor Reform Association in 1844, and a petition to the Massachusetts Legislature for a 10-hour workday in 1845 (Cullen, 1987).

As successive waves of European immigrants entered the country throughout the 1800s and early 1900s, cheap immigrant labor entered the booming textile industry and replaced the mill girls in Lowell. The mill girls' dormitories evolved into overcrowded tenement housing for successive waves of Irish, French Canadian, Greek, Polish, and Portuguese new immigrants. As the textile industry reached its height in the 1890s, Lowell became widely recognized as a city built by immigrants.

Labor organizing also continued. The Yiddish-speaking Lowell Working-men's Circle formed in 1900, and Greek immigrants led a citywide strike in 1903 that set the stage for the well-known 1912 Bread and Roses strike in the neighboring mill town of Lawrence.

But by the 1920s, the textile industry in Lowell entered a long period of decline. By 1945, 8 of the city's 11 big mills had closed and unemployment soared. Foreshadowing the decline of many midwestern industrial cities during the 1970s, Lowell and other textile mill towns in the Merrimack Valley region all but died during this period.

In the 1970s, however, a combination of factors, including the emergence of new industries fueled by high-technology research at Massachusetts-based universities and the political muscle of the Massachusetts congressional delegation—which included Speaker of the House "Tip" O'Neil and Senator Edward Kennedy as well as Senator Paul Tsongas who was born and raised in Lowell—led to a turnaround in the state's economic condition. A combination of federal dollars and corporate investment revitalized Lowell's economy, enabling the city to move from 13.8% unemployment in 1978 to 7% in 1982 to less than 3% in 1987. The run-down mill factories were rehabilitated. The city's vacant industrial land area dropped from 100 acres in 1978 to zero in 1987 (Cullen, 1987).

Central to the economic revitalization of Lowell was the decision of An Wang, a Chinese immigrant and chairman of Wang Laboratories, Inc., to relocate the company to Lowell in 1976. Wang purchased cheap industrial land, and with the added incentive of $5 million in federal grants, built new electronics assembly plants and corporate office towers. The timing of the move coincided with Wang's take-off as a company. Corporate sales rose from $97 million in 1977 to $2.88 billion in 1986. As the largest employer in Lowell, Wang's payroll in 1986 accounted for $114 million. Furthermore, the company purchased $25 million worth of goods from local vendors and paid more than $3 million in local taxes (Wilke, 1987) – infusing the city with a strong economic base.[2]

By the mid-1980s, Lowell was cited as the "model city" of the "Massachusetts Miracle" – a city whose legacy included leading America's industrial revolution, becoming home to successive waves of ethnic immigrant groups, and overcoming industrial decline to reemerge as a leading center of the country's high-technology revolution.

RECENT DEMOGRAPHIC CHANGES

People in Lowell talk about it being an ethnic city, but they only embrace that and endorse that as long as they are white. (J. Gonsalves, Lowell Human Rights Commission Planning Committee, cited in Wong, 1987b, p. 9)

Beginning in the late 1950s as part of large-scale Puerto Rican migrations throughout the northeast industrial states, a small number of Puerto Ricans settled in Lowell. In the late 1960s, a large group of Puerto Rican workers based at garment factories in New Jersey were transferred to Lowell. Through the 1970s, Puerto Ricans and growing numbers of Dominicans developed stable Latino communities. By 1987, the Latino community had reached 15,000 or 15% of the city. In neighboring Lawrence, Massachusetts, the Latino population swelled to 40% of the city's population – reflecting significant demographic changes throughout the Merrimack Valley area.

The most dramatic growth in Lowell during the 1980s, however, resulted from Southeast Asian refugee resettlement and secondary migration. The 1990 U.S. Census counted 11,493 Asians in Lowell compared to only 604 in 1980. Highly critical of undercounting by the U.S. Census, however, Lowell city and community estimates showed a growth profile from less than 100 Cambodians in 1980 to between 15,000 and 20,000 Cambodians in 1990. In addition, city and community leaders estimated an additional 1,000 Lao and 1,000 Vietnamese. During the 1980s, Lowell became home to the largest Cambodian community on the east coast and the second largest concentration of Cambodians in the United States after Long Beach, California.

The majority of Cambodians in Lowell are secondary migrants – having

---

[2]Beginning in 1988–1989, however, and continuing through the 1990s, Wang Laboratories faced severe economic difficulties, leading to lay-offs of thousands of employees, drops in quarterly earnings and stock prices, and resignations of many managers, including An Wang's son, Frederick. The socioeconomic impact of Wang's difficulties on the city of Lowell needs further study.

moved there from other states in the United States rather than being resettled directly from refugee camps in Southeast Asia. Many settled in Lowell because of the city's well-publicized economic health and availability of jobs. Some were drawn by the establishment of one of the few Cambodian Buddhist temples in the country in the mid-1980s. Others came because family members or friends were already established there. Still others came, simply because they heard that Lowell was a place where Cambodians live.

As the numbers of Latinos and Southeast Asians expanded rapidly during the 1980s, the city found itself unprepared to address the multiple issues of housing, bilingual services, and civil rights that confront new immigrants. Furthermore, Lowell's economic rejuvenation had failed to refurbish the city's 19th-century housing stock and public school facilities, particularly in neighborhoods such as the Acre where large numbers of Latinos and Southeast Asians had settled. Educational issues and the schools quickly emerged as a primary concern for Lowell's new immigrant communities.

STRUGGLES IN THE SCHOOLS

They don't want our minority children mixing with their white children . . . they are not thinking of the education of all kids, only of their kids. We want to make sure our kids get equal opportunity. (Huertas, Parents United in the Education and Development of Others, personal communication, June 11, 1987)

Lowell has the sixth largest Hispanic student population and the second largest number of Asian students in Massachusetts. In 1975, only 4% of Lowell's school children were minorities. By 1987, however, minorities made up 40% of the school-age population—half of them being limited-English proficient. As Southeast Asians continued to migrate to Lowell throughout 1987, as many as 35 to 50 new Southeast Asian students arrived and enrolled in school each week. Strains on the public school system quickly reached crisis proportions.

In response to the influx, the Lowell School Committee established makeshift classrooms in nonschool facilities such as the Lowell Boys Club and Lowell YMCA. This process segregated 170 Southeast Asian and Latino elementary-age school children in buildings that lacked library and cafeteria facilities as well as principals and supervisory staff on site. Overcrowded, makeshift classrooms accommodated students from Grades 1 to 6. Partitions separated bilingual classes in Spanish, Lao, and Khmer. Special education classes were held in hallways where it was quieter. Other spaces such as the basement boiler room and an auditorium storage area of the Robinson School were also converted into classrooms. A Lao bilingual class in the Daley School met in a converted lavatory with a toilet stall still in the room.

After 3 months of segregation in separate, unequal facilities, minority school children and their parents took action. The Latino parents had already seen the educational system take its toll on their children. Although the Latino high school population had doubled from 200 to 400 between 1982 and 1987, the number of those who successfully graduated had dropped from 76 to 55.

Southeast Asian students had fared no better. Over half of the Lao students who entered Lowell High School in 1986–1987 had dropped out by the end of the year. Given the trauma and sacrifice endured by Southeast Asian parents in order to provide their children with a chance for education and a better future, the conditions in Lowell's schools had become intolerable.

PARENT ORGANIZING

When they say "Americans," they don't mean us—look at our eyes and our skin. We are minorities, but we have rights too. We need to support each other. (Bounphasaysonh, Laotian Association of Greater Lowell, personal communication, June 11, 1987)

For the next 18 months from May 1987 through November 1988, Latino and Southeast Asian parents led efforts to demand equal access and equity for their children in the Lowell public schools. With organizing and technical assistance from Multicultural Education Training and Advocacy Inc. (META), and a statewide bilingual parents network, Parents United in the Education and Development of Others (PUEDO), the parents convened joint meetings in four languages between the Hispanic Parents Advisory Committee (HPAC), the Cambodian Mutual Assistance Association of Greater Lowell and the Laotian Association of Greater Lowell to develop tactics and strategy. Eventually, a coalition of those organizations established the Minority Association for Mutual Assistance (MAMA).

The parents employed a range of tactics that included grassroots canvasing and petition drives combined with outreach to churches and other groups such as Big Brothers/Big Sisters in Lowell. When the Lowell School Committee failed to act, the parents organized press conferences and mass community meetings with state education officials to propel their case forward.

Eventually, the parents and students filed suit in federal district court against the Lowell School Committee and the city of Lowell on the basis of unconstitutional segregation of the Lowell public schools and denial of equal educational opportunities to students of limited English proficiency in violation of Title VI of the 1964 Civil Rights Act and the Equal Educational Opportunities Act of 1974 (HPAC, 1987).

In the process, the parents developed a comprehensive 33-point program of educational reform directed not only at desegregation and upgrading of facilities, but that also targeted issues of personnel hiring and training, curriculum reform, dropout prevention, special education program development, and parent involvement. Furthermore, they demanded compensation and remediation for educational harms incurred by linguistic minority students placed in inappropriate classroom settings between 1984 and 1987 (META, 1987).

On November 9, 1988, after 18 months of organizing and negotiations, the parents won their demands in an historic out-of-court settlement approved in a 6–1 vote by the Lowell School Committee.[3] The settlement represented an unqualified victory for the Latino and Southeast Asian parents and children in Lowell, and set a precedent for educational reform in the interests of linguistic minority students everywhere.

RACIAL VIOLENCE AND ENGLISH-ONLY EXCLUSION

English is our mother tongue and it's the language that's going to be used at our meetings. This is an English-only school committee in an English-only America. (G. D. Kouloheras, Lowell School Committee, June 3, 1987)

The success of the parents had not come without a price, however. Through the course of advocating for their children's educational rights, the Latino and Southeast Asian communities confronted a reality of disenfranchisement within the city's political institutions and a climate of anti-immigrant resentment and racial intolerance.

At a school committee meeting to discuss the crisis on May 6, 1987, 100 Latino and Southeast Asian parents came to voice their concerns about their children's education. After requesting to speak with the assistance of interpreters who accompanied them, the parents were quickly rebuffed by George Kouloheras, senior member of the school committee, who declared that they were in an English-only meeting in an English-only town in an English-only America. Kouloheras then walked out—undermining the quorum needed for the meeting to continue. He later castigated the Latino parents as "those bastards who speak Spanish" (Ribadineira, 1987, p. 17).

While anti-minority and anti-immigrant incidents, including racial harassment, tire slashings, broken windows, job and housing discrimination, were not uncommon in the city, little attention had been paid to minority concerns amidst the Dukakis 1988 presidential campaign's national promotion of Lowell as the model city of the "Massachusetts Miracle" (Wong, 1987b). Once Kouloheras took the offensive from his position as a school committee member, however, public attention toward Latinos and Southeast Asians within the city shifted from neglect and resentment to accusation and attack.

---

[3]The settlement was approved by the court in February 1989, and did not include monetary compensation for educational harms, although $80,000 in attorneys' fees and costs of $5,000 were awarded eventually in November 1989.

In June 1987, under pressure from the parents and threatened with funding cuts by the state, the Lowell School Committee adopted a desegregation plan that Kouloheras and some White residents vehemently opposed because it required mandatory busing to integrate several predominantly White schools. The desegregation plan became the focal point for candidates' campaigns during the fall 1987 school committee and city council elections. Fueled by Kouloheras' hostile, English-only rhetoric, anti-Latino and anti-Asian sentiment escalated throughout the summer.

On September 15, one week after school reopened amidst widespread bitterness and confusion over the busing plan, an 11-year-old White student accosted Vandy Phorng, a 13-year-old Cambodian bilingual student while Vandy and his brothers were walking along the canal near their home. After making racial comments about Vandy's background, the White youth punched Vandy in the face, dragged him down a flight of stairs to the canal and pushed Vandy into the water. Vandy was carried away by the strong current and drowned. The father of the boy charged with killing Vandy Phorng was an outspoken advocate for the English-only movement in Lowell (Tan, 1987a, 1987b; Wong, 1987a).

Like the killings of five Southeast Asian children at the Cleveland Elementary School in Stockton, California,[4] the tragedy of Vandy Phorng's murder was cruelly ironic, given that Southeast Asian refugees have escaped so much war and death in their home countries. The children represent their hopes for the future—they are not supposed to die from violence here. Yet, amidst the climate of anti-minority, anti-immigrant sentiment promoted by English-only advocates, including some of the city's most influential political leaders, racial violence was predictable and, perhaps with different leadership, preventable.

POLITICAL REPRESENTATION AND POLITICAL POWER

We need to protect the civil liberties of the majority . . . let them take the minorities and do what they want with them. (G. Kouloheras, Lowell School Committee on election night, cited in Dabilis, 1987, p. 62)

The death of Vandy Phorng gave little pause to the anti-immigrant campaign of Kouloheras and others who rode its bandwagon to victory in the October 1987 primaries and November city elections. In the school committee election,

---

[4]On January 17, 1989, Patrick Purdy fired more than 100 shots from an automatic assault rifle into the Cleveland Elementary School yard—killing five Cambodian and Vietnamese children. Witnesses observed that Purdy had aimed specifically at Southeast Asian children before firing. An investigation by California state Attorney General John Van de Kamp, concluded in an October 1989 report that, "Purdy attacked Southeast Asian immigrants out of a festering sense of racial resentment and hatred." The report also noted that Purdy, according to his half-brother, often confronted people speaking a foreign language and told them to speak English in America (Kam, 1989; Wong, 1989).

Kouloheras succeeded as the top vote-getter while his protege, Kathryn Stok-losa, came in second. Sean Sullivan, a first-time candidate whose campaign focused exclusively in opposition to "forced busing" was also elected, while George O'Hare, a longtime incumbent who supported the desegregation plan was defeated. The struggle surrounding the schools also affected the city council race as Tarsy Poulios, a vehement opponent of the desegregation plan, received the third highest vote total because, according to a former Lowell City manager, "he got every hate vote out there" (Dabilis, 1987, p. 62).

For the Southeast Asian and Latino parents, the election reinforced what they had begun to recognize. In spite of their growing numbers, they had no political representation or even influence within the city's institutions. The only Hispanic in city hall, as many community leaders were quick to point out, was a gardener (Wong, 1987b).

In the months following the 1987 city elections, the parents continued to press their case forward—united around their common interests and their vision of educational reform. The working relationships they had developed within MAMA continued through the next year as their lawsuit against the city slowly progressed. Finally, in November 1988, the Lowell School Committee accepted most of the parents' demands for reform and agreed to an out-of-court settle-ment of the lawsuit. During that period, Huertas, the most visible leader of the parents, decided the time had come for a person of color to run for office in Lowell.

PARENT EMPOWERMENT AND ELECTORAL POLITICS

The lack of Latino and Asian representation has made our struggle harder. In next year's elections, we need to promote our own candidates. (A. Huertas, PUEDO, personal communication, June 11, 1987)

Lowell is a city of 100,000 residents, but only 40,000 voters. The overwhelming majority of Southeast Asians and Latinos are not registered, and many are not citizens. Numerically, however, they account for roughly 40% of the city's population, and are continuing to grow. Successful candidates in Lowell elec-tions typically receive less than 10,000 votes. Kouloheras, the top vote-getter in the 1987 school committee race, for example, received only 8,400 votes. Al-though not a factor in the most recent election, the political potential of both the Latino and Cambodian vote seems exceptional in this context.

It is useful to remember that in 1854, when the city's population was nearly one third foreign-born, the mayor was elected based on a "Know-Nothing" anti-Irish, anti-immigrant platform.[5] Later waves of European newcomers con-

---

[5]A nativist political party, initially established as a secret society in New York, the Know-Nothing Party dominated Massachusetts politics and controlled the state legislature during the mid-1850s. Millard Fillmore ran for the U.S. presidency as a Know-Nothing candidate in 1856.

tinued to face resentment, exclusion, and exploitation characteristic of the immigrant experience in New England.

Yet, eventually each group achieved some measure of representation and political power. As early as 1874, with nearly 40% of the population being immigrants, Samuel P. Marin became the first French-Canadian to win elected office in Lowell. Under his leadership, the ethnic "Little Canada" community grew and thrived. By the 1950s, most of Lowell's ethnic groups, including the English, Irish, Greeks, and Polish had succeeded in electing their "favorite sons" to the mayor's office and had won basic political representation within the city.

Will the newest immigrant groups of Latinos and Southeast Asians follow this same historical pattern of European ethnics' structural assimilation into the social, economic, and political mainstream of Lowell? Alternatively, does their current state of disenfranchisement reflect their status as urban racial minorities as much as it does their being new immigrants? Recognition of their own minority group membership, in fact, may be essential if they are to strengthen their organizations, develop leadership, promote consciousness, and build coalitions within and between the Southeast Asian and Latino communities that can lead toward empowerment.

TRANSFORMING THE FUTURE OF LOWELL

The Puerto Ricans . . . it's so easy for them to get up and yell, "WE WANT THIS!" For us, we hide our faces and whisper to ourselves, "we want this" . . . But give us a couple more years, we're still learning. (S. Bounphasaysonh, Laotian Association of Greater Lowell, personal communication, June 11, 1987)

Schools have historically served as sites of struggle by minorities and immigrants for access, equity, and democratic reforms. Such landmarks in U.S. legal history as *Lau v. Nichols* and *Brown v. Board of Education* testify to the significance of the fight for educational rights.

Furthermore, for immigrant and refugee parents who have sacrificed their own lives and dreams in order to give their children opportunities for security and social mobility, the schools often represent their single most important investment in this country.

As cities undergo shifts in their ethnic and racial make-up, the schools quickly emerge as one major arena, and often as the initial battleground, where contradictory agendas unfold based on conflicting relations and responses to the demographic changes (First & Willshire-Carrera, 1988).

Anti-immigrant sentiment, racial harassment, and English-only advocacy characterize one set of responses to the challenge of changing demographics currently facing many U.S. cities. These reactions, framed by struggles over turf and the interests of a shifting electorate, lead to divisiveness and segregation as in the case of the Lowell public schools. Typically, this results in violence and tragedy as with the killing of 13-year-old Vandy Phorng.

An alternative set of responses, however, recognizes that when a city's population changes, the city's institutions must also change in order to reflect the needs and interests of its people. An example of this basic demand for access and equity was crafted by Latino and Southeast Asian parents seeking educational reform in Lowell. Typically, however, this approach meets resistance, if not overt hostility, and leads directly to the demand for political representation and political power as exemplified in the initiation of Huertas' campaign for city council.

Huertas withdrew from the city council race in Spring 1989 due to family responsibilities. By taking that initial step in declaring that minorities should run for political office, however, Huertas and Lowell's Latino parents made their aspirations clear.

Although it is difficult to know whether or not the Lao and Cambodian parents would have felt sufficiently inspired to mobilize their communities and participate actively in the elections if Huertas had stayed in the 1989 city council race, it is, nevertheless, clear that empowerment is on the agenda of Southeast Asian and Latino parents in Lowell. Although the Latino parents clearly set the tone for the movement, Southeast Asian parents have learned quickly through the process. A Cambodian community activist, Sambath Chey Fennell, in fact, considered running for school committee. At the time, he could have become the first Cambodian American elected official in the country.

The city's political dynamics, however, are fluid and volatile. Amidst a deepening economic recession in 1989, Lowell's electorate voted on a non-binding referendum introduced by Kouloheras to declare English the official language of the city. The English-only referendum passed by a wide 72% to 28% margin with 14,575 votes for and 5,679 votes against (Crittendon, 1989).

Not unlike the "Know-Nothing" electoral sweep of 1854, the 3–1 English-only referendum vote, galvanized nativist opposition to the rapid demographic changes taking place in Lowell. Yet, as Perez-Bustillo (1992) noted, it was ironic that so many European Americans, whose own families had previously confronted exclusion and harassment as immigrants in Lowell, felt so threatened by the population growth of Latinos and Southeast Asians.

Since 1988, Wang Laboratories and, by extension, the city's economy, faced steady deterioration and severe difficulty. Between 1988 and 1992, Wang's workforce declined from 31,500 to 8,000. With losses of nearly $140 million in fiscal year 1992, Wang Laboratories filed for Chapter 11 bankruptcy in August 1992 (Yenkin, 1992). In March 1993, an additional 500 layoffs were announced for Wang's Massachusetts-based workers as part of their Chapter 11 plans (Hyatt, 1993).

In the wake of Wang's decline and several more years of regional economic recession, drastic cuts in school budgets and social services coincided with increased unemployment, homelessness, small business closings, and youth gang and drug activity among Southeast Asians in Lowell. Local Cambodian community leaders also observed patterns of out-migration, suggesting that as many as 15% of the population had left Lowell to seek a better living elsewhere.

The story of Lowell is unresolved. Yet, the city has already been transformed. The Latino and Southeast Asian parents' successful 18-month struggle for access and equity in the Lowell public schools represented an initial and inspirational step in an ongoing process of organizing and coalition building that may eventually lead not only to the defeat of the city's anti-immigrant, English-only forces but to the election of Cambodian and Latino candidates to city office and to the eventual empowerment of the Southeast and Latino communities. Perhaps then, Lowell will rightfully be considered a "model city" in a "Massachusetts miracle."

REFERENCES

Crittendon, J. (1989, November 8). English referendum passes nearly 3 to 1. *Lowell Sun*, pp. 1, 6–7.

Cullen, K. (1987, October 25). Lowell: The dark side of the boom. *The Boston Globe*, pp. 1, 3.

Dabilis, A. J. (1987, October 7). Lowell desegregation opponents fare well in school, council races. *The Boston Globe*, p. 62.

First, J., & Willshire-Carrera, J. (1988). *New voices: Immigrant students in U.S. public schools.* Boston: National Coalition of Advocates for Students.

Hispanic Parents Advisory Council, et al. (1987). *Complaint*, U.S. District Court District of Massachusetts, Civil Action No. 87-1968 K.

Hyatt, J. (1993, March 16). Wang set to unveil Ch. 11 plan today. *Boston Globe*, pp. 1, 42.

Kam, K. (1989). A false and shattered peace. *California Tomorrow*, pp. 8–21.

Kiang, P. N. (1994). When know-nothings speak English only: Analyzing Irish and Cambodian struggles for community development and educational equity. In K. Aguilar-San Juan (Ed.), *The state of Asian America: Activism and resistance in the 1990s* (pp. 125–145). Boston: South End Press.

META Inc. (1987, May 21). Letter to Lowell School Committee.

Perez-Bustillo, C. (1992). What happens when English-only comes to town? A case study of Lowell, Massachusetts. In J. Crawford (Ed.), *Language loyalties: A sourcebook on the official English controversy* (pp. 194–201). Chicago: University of Chicago Press.

Ribadeneira, D. (1987, May 8). School panelist in Lowell is accused of racism. *The Boston Globe*, p. 17.

Tan, L. K. (1987a, September 23). Family demands justice in teen's slaying. *The Boston Herald*.

Tan, L. K. (1987b, September 24). Police defend arrest of boy. *The Boston Herald*.

Wang, C. C. (1989). Monterey Park: A community in transition. In G. M. Nomura, R. Endo, S. H. Sumida, & R. L. Leong (Eds.), *Frontiers of Asian American studies* (pp. 113–126). Pullman: Washington State University Press.

Wilke, J. (1987, November 9). Wang had key role in Lowell's economic revival. *The Boston Globe*, p. 24.

Wong, D. S. (1987a, September 22). Day of fishing ends in violent death for Lowell boy. *The Boston Globe*, p. 23.

Wong, D. S. (1987b, November 3). Lowell is seen not fulfilling its promise for Asians, Hispanics. *The Boston Globe*, pp. 1, 9.

Yenkin, J. (1992, September 25). Wang Says '92 loss may get worse. *Boston Globe*, p. 66.

7

Rocking the Cradle: A Case Study of Linguistic Minority Educational Rights in Florida

Camilo Perez-Bustillo

NOT KNOWING, IN AZTLAN

the way they look at you
the schoolteachers
the way they look at you
the City Hall clerks
the way they look at you
the cops
the airport marshals
the way they look at you

you don't know if it's something you did
or something you are

—poem by Chicano poet Tino Villanueva in *Shaking Off the Dark*
(1984, p. 64)

This chapter is about the building of a coalition in Florida that served as a leverage of political power for its constituents, about the nexus of the political power of the coalition and legal challenges, and about what this coalition was able to achieve through this nexus in terms of education reform generally. A case study of the Florida coalition is important because of the people and communities it brought together and because of the educational changes it engendered. In a state where ethnic groups have been at unique loggerheads and where there had previously been no successful legal or educational advocacy, the

71

Multicultural Network for Educational Rights offers some crucial lessons for advocates, activists, community members, and educators dedicated to collaborative work and educational and social change.

It began on May 1, 1992 in Orlando, Florida at a weekend retreat of 50 Latino, Haitian, African American, and Anglo advocates, parents, students, educators, and community activists commited to the founding of a new statewide organization, since known as the Multicultural Network for Educational Rights. Two days before, angry Latino and African American youth had begun to rise up in Los Angeles in response to the acquittal of four White police officers in the Rodney King case. Fires were still burning throughout south central Los Angeles as we met, and rocks were beginning to be thrown in Orlando's Black neighborhood near where we had gathered. Throughout the weekend we struggled with the painful counterpoint between our dreams of multiracial unity and the harsh realities of interracial and interethnic hatred, fear, and violence symbolized by the flames of Los Angeles.

The Network grew out of a multiracial and multiethnic coalition that had brought a successful statewide case compelling Florida to, for the first time, set mandatory standards for the identification, assessment, placement, and provision of programming to the state's fast-growing numbers of linguistic minority students. Plaintiffs included the Florida affiliate of the League of United Latin American Citizens (LULAC), State Conference of NAACP Branches, the Haitian Refugee Center, the Florida branch of Aspira (A Puerto Rican education advocacy group based in New York City), the Farmworkers' Association of Central Florida, and three Miami-based organizations: the Spanish-American League Against Discrimination (SALAD), the American Hispanic Educators' Association of DADE (AHEAD), and the Haitian Educators' Association.

THEORETICAL APPROACH

This case study approaches an analysis of this litigation and its impact from the vantage point of legal anthropology, defined as the cross-cultural study of legal processes as social phenomena, and focusing on "how individuals and groups in particular times and places have used legal resources to achieve their ends" (Starr & Collier, 1989, p. 2). Within this framework, "Legal systems are cultural systems . . . legal rules, processes and concepts exist only as they are invoked by people. Legal orders endure because people act as if they do, and people change legal orders by invoking new rules and abandoning old ones" (p. 12). In this sense, as Starr and Collier noted, changes in legal norms imply changes in the various ways that power and privilege are distributed through legal means, and "changes in asymmetrical power relations among groups are treated as the defining feature of legal change" (p. 13).

Educational rights advocacy on behalf of linguistic minority communities is a specialized form of the broader category of "public interest" advocacy in the United States, distinctive for its potential to impact social, cultural, and language policy in schools as well as in the broader society. In fact, the Florida case suggests ways in which language rights litigation can itself become a contributing sociolinguistic factor shaping the terrain that determines the extent of minority language maintenance or erosion.[1] As such, this kind of advocacy fits usefully into Tushnet's (1987) characterization of institutional reform litigation as a social process and as a potential vehicle for the political education of the communities involved.

The broader political and sociolinguistic impact of such advocacy depends, in large part, on the extent to which the advocates and communities involved are conscious of and committed to transcending the legal instrumentalities of purely bureaucratic change. Legal advocacy in general and perhaps litigation in particular, are inherently "conservative" activites in the most functionalist sense in that they necessarily imply a pro forma acceptance of, and entrance into, existing institutional channels of undistributed power. As such, understanding and approaching the dilemmas that legal work and litigation can present for traditionally excluded communities as well as for advocates and attorneys commited to social change is both a theoretical and practical necessity.[2]

The Florida case developed within this framework of looking at legal conflicts as a form of social power. In other words, although it was about getting schools to address the educational rights of language minority students, it was also about promoting a vision and practice of multicultural pluralism and collaboration within a state where racism, cultural separatism, and English-only reign.

THE FLORIDA CONTEXT

The Florida case, *LULAC et al. v. Florida State Board of Education*, filed on August 14, 1990, is an appropriate case study to assess the potential sociolinguistic and political impact of educational rights advocacy because of the size of the state's linguistic minority population and its centrality in the national debate about making English the official language. The state has a combined Deep South and Caribbean flavor, characterized both by its relative marginality during the 1960s civil rights movement and its more recent economic and cultural integration into Latin America.

Many continue to associate Florida with the large Miami-based Cuban immigrant community. Yet Florida also stands out with Illinois as among the

---

[1]For a discussion of language maintenance and erosion, see, for example, Macias (1985) and Brice-Heath (1985). For a contradictory view, see Fishman (1985).

[2]Critical race theory provides a theoretical framework in which to discuss these dilemmas. See, for example, Crenshaw and Peller (1993).

few states with large numbers of Latinos of both Mexican and Puerto Rican origin. Puerto Ricans tend to be concentrated in the Miami and Orlando metropolitan areas. Mexicans, in contrast, are frequently more represented in agricultural areas, working primarily as migrant farmworkers. Florida has the third largest migrant farmworker population after California and Texas. Major farmworker communities include Immokalee, Belle Glade, Apopka, Ruskin, and Homestead in Collier, Palm Beach, Hillsborough, and Dade counties, respectively. Latinos in Florida also include significant numbers of Central Americans, including Nicaraguans, Guatemalans, and Mayans.

The state is also home to the second largest concentration of Haitians in the United States (after Brooklyn, New York). The Haitian community is concentrated primarily in Miami, Fort Lauderdale, and Palm Beach. Haitians also live in large impoverished farmworker communities in Belle Glade, Immokalee, and Apopka.

Miami was the site of the first contemporary bilingual public school in the nation. The Coral Way Elementary School bilingual program, created in 1963 as Dade County's response to the pedagogical needs of thousands of Cuban children new to the school system and the country, served as a model for the development of bilingual programs throughout the country. In April 1973, Dade adopted an ordinance proclaiming the county officially bilingual/bicultural; Spanish was considered the second official language. Concerns about effectively addressing the needs of language minority students and sanctioning the use of Spanish, however, did not extend much beyond Dade. The growing Cuban economic, political, and cultural ascendancy spurred Anglo backlashes in Miami as well as elsewhere in the state. In 1973, proposed statewide bilingual education legislation failed. Tensions began to increase in Spring 1980 with the arrival of the Mariel and Haitian "boat people." These influxes along with the growing conflict beween Cubans and Miami's long subjugated Black community helped pave the way for the repeal of Dade's bilingual ordinance. As of Fall 1989, there were still no mandatory statewide standards in Florida for the identification, assessment, placement, and provision of services to linguistic minority students.

Florida educational policy prior to the successful resolution of our case essentially took a laissez-faire market approach to linguistic minority educational rights issues; compliance with minimum federal civil rights standards depended on the whims of unsupervised local school officials. The long-held, prevalent assumption was that the home languages and cultures were barriers to language minority students' educational and social advancement and, as such, needed to be erradicated as rapidly as possible. The repeal in 1980 of Dade County's status as a bilingual/bicultural county and the passage in 1988 of a statewide referendum amending the state Constitution and making English Florida's "official language," reflected the growing tensions toward the rapidly growing and geographically expanding Latino and Haitian communities. As I discuss later, the statewide referendum and the racist climate that accompanied it had a major role to play in cementing a broad base of support for our case.

COALITION BUILDING FOR A STATEWIDE CASE

The initial educational advocacy work was led by the Orlando affiliate of LULAC. Traditionally a Mexican-American organization, LULAC took on a different character in Florida, working most closely with the Cuban and Puerto Rican communities. The Orlando area affiliate was based in rural Osceola County and was run primarily by Puerto Ricans. The expanding local service economy fueled by nearby Disneyworld made the Orlando area a magnet for direct migration from the island and, eventually, for secondary migration from New York and New Jersey. According to the 1990 census, Osceola County had the single largest growth rate in Latino population of any county in the United States; Orlando had the largest growth in Latino population of any city. By Fall 1990, Osceola County's Latino student population was the fifth in the state, whereas Orlando's Orange County was third. By 1992, more than 20% of Osceola's total student population was Latino—overwhelmingly Puerto Rican.

Multicultural Education Training and Advocacy, Inc. (META), where I worked, was first approached by LULAC in 1984. META is a national public interest nonprofit legal advocacy organization that addresses issues of educational civil rights for language minority and immigrant students. LULAC was referred to META by the director of the National Origin Desegregation Assistance Center at the University of Miami.[3] This was one of the federally funded regional centers set up in the wake of the Supreme Court's *Lau* decision to assist local districts in complying with evolving federal mandates for bilingual and English as a second language (ESL) programs.

At the time LULAC approached META, Osceloa's Spanish speaking students were spending most of the school day in English-only classrooms staffed by monolingual White teachers who had had no training in ESL or in working with language minority students. The only ESL services that students received were by an itinerant teacher once a week for several hours. During this time, the teacher sought to both teach these students some rudimentary English and, at the same time, help make up for the subject matter instruction that had been lost because students did not understand English.

It quickly became clear to me and the other META attorneys that a major obstacle to advancing LULAC's demands for quality bilingual services in the Osceola schools was the lack of mandatory state standards for educating limited

---

[3]The director, Rosie Castro Feinberg, was later elected to the Dade County School Board and played a critical role as an influential expert, public official, and friend in helping shape the successful resolution of the case ultimately filed.

English proficient students. Visits to Ruskin, Belle Glade, and Homestead convinced us that the problem was not in Osceola alone, that, in fact, Florida exhibited a statewide pattern of neglect in the provision of services to these children.

A statewide case brought against the state board and department of education in federal court seemed to be the best litigation vehicle to address the lack of meaningful state standards. We previously had brought similar cases in Texas, Idaho, and California. Given the diversity and potential for divisiveness among Florida's linguistic and racial minority populations, however, we knew no case could be effectively brought unless it was supported by representative sectors from the various communities. It was this reality that led to the formation of a coalition. Key elements of this coalition included local LULAC activists, Farmworkers of Central Florida organizers, and the Haitian Refugee Center in Miami, then led by Gerard Jean-Juste, a member of META's board of directors. We also sought support from the Haitian American Community Association of Dade.

A hearing held in Miami's Little Haiti in 1987, organized by the National Coalition of Advocates for Students to focus on the needs of immigrant children in U.S. public schools, helped bring together much of the anecdotal information we would need to put a statewide case together. It was at this hearing that we learned, for example, from Reine Leroy, a Miami teacher, Haitian parent advocate, and later assistant principal of the Toussaint L'Ouverture Community School, that no one in the Miami public schools actually knew how many Haitian students there were in the system. Reine led a door-to-door, community-based effort to finally come up with the first such count.

Once again, we had stumbled upon a statewide issue: Dade did not count Haitian students as such because the state did not require them to. In fact, Haitian students were typically counted as "Black, non-Hispanic" if they were counted at all. Our focus thus became on literally making Haitian students count in Florida's public schools as well as on assuring appropriate services and staff for them once they were identified.

The efforts of Reine and others along with the support of the Haitian Refugee Center led to the founding of the Haitian Educator's Association in Miami. This association eventually joined the emerging statewide coalition as plaintiff in the case.

During this time, we also learned from Dade County Haitian sources of the work of the Ft. Lauderdale NAACP branch who had taken on as its own the needs and concerns of the growing numbers of Haitian and other Caribbean Islander students in Broward County. The support of the Ft. Lauderdale and the Miami branches led to the State Conference of Branches' decision to join the case as plaintiff as well. This was the first time that a NAACP branch anywhere in the country had joined as plaintiff in a suit focusing on the needs of linguistic minority students. (It may well have been the first time that an NAACP branch had been asked to do so.)

The importance of the state NAACP's participation in the case must be understood against the background of language politics in Florida. English-only and other anti-immigrant advocates have long sought to tap and exploit working-class Black resentment of the preceived employment threat posed by cheap, nonunion Latino immigrant labor. These efforts have taken an especially vicious turn in Miami, feeding, in part, off the racism of many Cubans and other Latinos. Such tensions were further exacerbated by the trial and acquital of Colombian Miami police officer William Lozano for the murder of an unarmed Black man. They also build on the generalized perception that Cuban economic success is in significant part due to favored treatment by the federal government, contrasting sharply with federal mistreatment of Haitians and of Black Mariel Cuban refugees. Similar tensions in varying forms mar African American and Latino relations and hamper potential alliances throughout the country (see e.g., Rohter, 1993).

Certainly, Florida has known its share of group tensions: (a) among Latino groups (primarily Puerto Ricans, Mexicans, and Cubans), (b) between Haitians and Latinos and between Haitians and African Americans, and (c) between Latinos and African Americans. All of these tensions, we learned, would have been much worse if any of these groups had gone unrepresented in the coalition and the Network. It is, moreover, the combined leadership, participation, and presence of each of these groups that provided the basis for the coalition's legal and political achievements, thereby enabling the founding of the Network.

An additional challenge has been the rift between groups and communities based in Miami and those from elsewhere in the state. From the beginning, we resolved that the case would not be Miami-centered, in part because of these tension and in part because Dade County programs for Spanish-speaking limited English proficient (LEP) students tended to be much more sophisticated than those elsewhere, even though still plagued by serious flaws. At the same time, no case could have been viable without the support of representative Miami-based organizations. The three key Latino participants in the plaintiff coalition from Miami were the SALAD, AHEAD, and Aspira.[4]

POLITICAL DEFEAT PAVES WAY FOR LEGAL VICTORY

In 1988, a statewide English-only referendum was introduced at the ballot box. U.S. English, a national organization committed to making English the "official"

---

[4]SALAD was led by Osvaldo Soto, a Cuban civil rights attorney and activist, who played a key role in the political and legal battle against English-only. Soto also helped initiate nationally the concept of "English Plus"—a linguistically and culturally inclusive response to the exclusionary orientation of English-only.

AHEAD represented both a powerful interest group, primarily Cuban teachers and administrators, likely to be affected (both positively and negatively) by the outcome of the case. Similar educators' groups have played important roles in bilingual education litigation in cases in Colorado, Texas, California, and Massachusetts.

language of the United States, targeted Colorado, Arizona, and Florida for such initiatives in the wake of its 1986 success in California. In each instance, the vehicle was a bid to amend the state's constitution to declare English as the only official language with additional restrictive wording varying from state to state (see Crawford, 1992a, 1992b). The Florida effort ultimately became its biggest, although transitory, victory.

SALAD, LULAC, the Farmworkers' Association, and others who were part of the natural constituency of an educational rights case were committed to mounting a successful effort to defeat the English-only referendum. A statewide gathering of these groups convened by LULAC in May 1988 in Orlando ended up passing a motion in support of statewide educational rights litigation; agreement was that the filing of the case should be postponed until after the November referendum vote in order to avoid making bilingual education an electoral issue. This postponement was politically important because bilingual education programs, along with bilingual ballots, have always been a central target of English-only advocates.

The triumph of the English-only referendum had a somewhat contradictory impact on the prospects of statewide litigation. Many of those involved in the nascent plaintiff coalition were demoralized by the results but at the same time felt more determined than ever about the need to obtain legal protections for the state's linguistic minority children. While no enabling state legislation was passed to give legal effect to the 1988 vote, the 1990 Federal Court order that we won in the LULAC case effectively nullified the referendum as far as Florida educational policy is concerned.

THE DYNAMICS OF THE LITIGATION

After the 1988 vote, our clients felt that Florida had hit rock bottom as far as linguistic minority rights were concerned. As such, they felt that even if the potential gains from litigation were speculative, there was nothing to lose. Our best hope was to put together a case that could stir the kind of political pressure and momentum that would force the then State Education Commisioner Betty Castor to respond in the least adversarial way. Castor, a former Democratic state senator from Tampa who was familiar with Latino issues there including a once active LULAC branch, was known to be committed to educational reform and equity issues overall. She was also interested in higher office.

On our side were the objective strength of our claims in legal terms given clear precedents for state obligations to set and monitor adequate LEP standards in cases in Texas, Idaho, and Illinois, and the political strengths of our plaintiff coalition. Both were essential; the theoretical legal strengths would have had little consequence if it had not been for the political strength of the coalition.

One of our most important advantages as things developed was the decision to sue only the state board and state deparment of education and not any local school boards. In this way, the focus was kept on state educational policy rather than on the complexities of 67 different large county school districts with widely varying conditions.

Castor's immediate response to our demand letter notifying her of our intention to sue was to contact SALAD and the Haitian Refugee Center in Miami and suggest that we talk. In the first test of comparative legal and political momentum, we insisted that her representatives fly out to META's office in San Francisco instead of us flying to Talahassee. Castor agreed.

Negotiations continued intensively throughout the next 11 months, culminating finally in the joint submission of a consent decree to Judge James L. King for his signature, rendering it an enforceable Federal Court order, on August 14, 1990. A new state law and comprehensive set of detailed regulations were adopted by the state legislature and state board of education, fleshing out the terms of the decree.

The negotiation process was immeasurably enhanced to our benefit by the participation of Stefan Rosenzweig as co-counsel for the plaintiffs. Stefan had not been involved in putting the case together but had just moved to Florida from California in time to participate as director of the Legal Services Office in the Florida Keys. He had litigated a similar statewide case in California in state court with our META counsel, Peter Roos. The two of them had had extensive experience in negotiating parallel issues of state standard-setting and monitoring in the California case, *Comite v. Honig*. Roos had also negotiated a landmark bilingual education remedy in the *Keyes* case in Denver in 1984. I had negotiated a detailed out of court settlement to a complex bilingual education case in Lowell, Massachusetts together with META East Coast counsel Roger Rice during 1988,[5] and a comprehensive *Lau* remedial plan in Cleveland, Ohio for the Hispanic Parents Union in 1986. Florida's state deparment of education counsel had never been involved in a case of this type. Although we were outnumbered by state department of education personnel, our greater experience with language minority educational concerns certainly played a role in the dynamics and outcomes of negotation.

The combined effect of the consent decree and new state legal requirements put linguistic minority children and their communities at the center of state educational policy for the first time, if only for a brief period. Each school district was compelled to draft a comprehensive plan to serve LEP students according to the new standards and to establish "Parent Leadership Councils" representative of linguistic minority groups in the school system and charged with monitoring compliance with the new standards.

Districts were required to implement "home language" programs ("bilingual education" was considered terminology too explosive for Florida) or to show

---

[5]For a discussion of this case, see Kiang (chapter 6, this volume).

that programs teaching English as a second language through content instruction were equally effective at insuring equal educational opportunities and promoting the self-esteem of participating LEP students.

Widespread confusion and recalcitrance in the wake of the new standards demonstrated, once again, the limits of formal legal reform absent constant vigilance and mobilization by those affected. The only guarantee of attaining compliance with the court order's minimum requirements remained the active and aware participation of the constituencies most concerned with its effects.

THE NETWORK TAKES HOLD

Unlike in other situations where legal victories mark the end of a story, the victory achieved by the Multicultural Network signaled an expanding role for grassroots groups that sought educational equity in Florida. The key community players who first joined to bring attention to the question of services for LEP students resolved to take responsibility to see that their achievement became a reality. In practice, this has meant that parent trainers and organizers, members of the Network, have traveled throughout Florida to inform other parents, teachers, and community organizations of the content of the Consent Decree and, in turn, to help monitor actual progress in the schools.

At the same time, Network members, and especially the Network's African American leaders, have pointed to a range of issues beyond the strict LEP concerns of the Consent Decree that they wished to address on a multicultural basis. For example, the Network had taken on the issue of standards for admission into gifted and talented programs. Traditionally, those programs have ultilized standards that work to exclude African American, Latino, and other students of color. The Network has advocated in a variety of forums for a broadening of standards to extend gifted-and-talented opportunities to all students.

Similarly, the Network had identified the issue of resource disparities as a crucial problem for schools attended by African American and Latino students. Florida school districts are organized on a countywide basis. Often, however, there is a vast disparity in the wealth and political clout of people living in different areas of the same county, with most of the economic and political power, and a disproportionate share of the educational resources being directed toward the more affluent areas of the county. Network members are currently investigating and documenting these disparities with the intention of achieving more equitable distribution of resources and opportunities.

Indeed, while the Network, which came together around LEP elementary and secondary issues remains committed to seeing the decree become a reality, the current agenda now includes a whole array of educational reform questions all with an overlay of concern that Florida schools truly reflect their multicultural constituency and its own self identified needs.

Crenshaw and Peller (1993) wrote of the Rodney King verdict that it is necessary to explore the relationships between law, power, and ideology in order to understand that the acquittal in that case was typical, not extraordinary. The result in Florida, by contrast was extraordinary, not typical—which is both its triumph and its greatest weakness.

The result here turned heavily on the political mobilization of the communities most affected by it. Lawyers and legal standards come and go, but it is only the people themselves who can insure that this legal victory becomes a living victory that endures.

REFERENCES

Brice-Heath, S. (1985). Language policies: Patterns of retention and maintenance. In W. Connor (Ed.). *Mexican Americans in comparative perspective* (pp. 257–282). Washington, DC: Urban Institute Press.

Crawford, J. (1992a). *Hold your tongue: Bilingualism and the politics of English only.* Reading, MA: Addison Wesley.

Crawford, J. (Ed.). (1992b). *Language loyalities: A sourcebook on the official English controversy.* Chicago: University of Chicago Press.

Crenshaw, K., & Peller, G. (1993). Reel time/real justice. In R. Gooding-Williams (Ed.), *Reading Rodney King/reading urban uprising* (pp. 56–70). New York: Routledge.

Fishman, J. (1985). The ethnic revival in the United States: Implications for the Mexican-American community. In W. Connor (Ed.), *Mexican Americans in comparative perspective* (pp. 309–354). Washington, DC: Urban Institute Press.

Macias, R. (1985). National language profile of the Mexican-origin population in the United States. In W. Connor (Ed.), *Mexican Americans in comparative perspective* (pp. 285–308). Washington, DC: Urban Institute Press.

Rohter, L. (1993, June 20). As Hispanic presence grows so does Black anger. *New York Times*, p. 1.

Starr, J., & Collier, J. F. (1989). Introduction. In J. Starr & J. F. Collier (Eds.), *History and power in the study of law: New dimensions in legal anthropology* (pp. 1–15). Ithaca, NY: Cornell University Press.

Tushnet, M. (1987). *The NAACP's legal strategy against segregated education, 1925–1950.* Chapel Hill: University of North Carolina Press.

Villaneuva, T. (1984). *Shaking off the dark.* Houston, TX: Arte Publico Press.

8

Grassroots Multiracial Organizing for Parent Empowerment in Education

Suzanne Lee
Douglas Brugge

In June 1993, Massachusetts Governor William Weld signed into law an educational reform package. The development, content, and focus of this legislation was part of a 2-year debate among various constituencies and factions. This chapter explores a grassroots effort in Boston during this time to build a multiracial coalition capable of having a positive impact on education reform at the local and state levels. It provides some background on the Boston schools and offers an overview of the problems of city and state mainstream reform efforts, including the lack of attention to the needs, realities, and perspectives of urban students and parents of color.

The core of the chapter is an interview with some Boston Chinese American and African American parents who have been active in the grassroots effort. Finally, it examines the significance of this effort for parent organizing, multiracial coalition building, and translating grassroots knowledge and ideas into policy.

BACKGROUND

The Boston Schools

Race is never far from the center of Boston city politics and by extension is integral to any discussion of education reform. The seminal point in recent history was the crisis over forced busing to end segregation in the public schools

83

in the 1970s. The issues from that time still resonate through the politics of education in and around the city. At the time that busing began, people of color made up less than 20% of the city and about 40% of the children in the schools. In the 1990s, Boston is 25% African American, 11% Latino, and 5% Asian American (more than 40% people of color), the schools are more than 80% students of color, whereas the teachers remain mostly White. Approximately one third of the students speak English as a second language (ESL).

Despite the diversity of the city and the schools, Boston continues to be run by White elected officials. In the early 1990s, the mayor, who was White, succeeded in his campaign to replace the elected school committee with a committee that he appointed. There is currently only one minority official elected to a citywide seat in Boston.

No longer able to blame the elected committee for the state of the schools, the mayor lashed out at the superintendent who was African American. Disunity between racial groups became heightened by the fact that the newly appointed school committee had an Asian American and a Latino member.

Unlike some other large urban centers where people of color are a clear majority and hold significant positions of power, there is limited experience in Boston with multiracial coalitions and none that have held actual power. The unsuccessful Rainbow Coalition campaign of Mel King for mayor in the 1980s was the most notable example. Indeed, so narrow is the range of people in power that the city has had only "Yankee" and Irish mayors.

The city is characterized by neighborhoods that are separated along racial as well as White ethnic lines. Where cooperation between different sectors of the political and business leadership has happened, it has tended not to include the grassroots. Whatever lessons or examples can be drawn from building a grass-roots, multiracial coalition should be of interest in moving toward a future in which people of color will be the majority of the city.

Proposals for Education Reform

The national debate about public education has engendered a similar debate in Massachusetts and in Boston. Amidst a fading commitment of public funds, there are regular stories in the local media of how the schools are failing young people. Several proposals were put forth at both the state and local levels that purported to address these problems.

One set of proposals came from Democratic state legislators. These plans consisted of providing added funds to the hardest pressed school systems in the state, mastery tests ("tough measurable standards") that would be necessary for graduation and teacher tenure challenges. These legislators were often openly hostile to issues of multiculturalism, parent input into the schools, and concerns about tracking. Public hearings on these proposals were held across the state.

The Boston hearings were the very last; the legislators arrived with a predetermined agenda and little interest in the public's concerns or comments.

A second set of proposals came from the Massachusetts Business Alliance for Education Reform; they concentrated on inserting competition into the public schools. In these plans, the principal was seen as a chief executive officer, the students as commodities to meet labor needs. They supported early childhood education, parent outreach, and professional development for teachers.

Republican Governor Weld's agenda added its own so-called "choice" proposal to that of legislators and business. It differed with the Democrats over how much money to spend on public education—Weld offering less. On top of all this, the Catholic Church and the president of the state senate advocated for public money vouchers for private schools.

That they ignored people of color and excluded parents from the discussion made the proposals useless, from our perspective, for achieving real and effective reform. All of the proposals avoided addressing the pressing issues of the growing immigrant community and of the African American community.

Building a Grassroots, Multiracial Coalition and Addressing Parent Empowerment

In the Winter of 1991–1992, Unity Boston,[1] sponsored a monthly discussion series on education reform through which we developed our views about education and began to actively look for a way to participate in the educational reform debate that would be multiracial and grassroots in nature. The agenda that emerged included increased funding and fair distribution of funds, community control over the schools, parent empowerment, staff that reflects the diversity of the students, multicultural and relevent curriculum, staff development, support for bilingual education, fair testing, and afterschool programs.

In April 1992, we attended a broad-based meeting in the African American community, and helped put together an "action group." With the backing of a group of parents, educators, legislators, and community activists, the action group launched an effort to have an impact on the course of the education reform debate in Massachusetts. A good cross-section of community groups and agencies from around Boston were represented, in what became known as the Community Education Reform Coalition, including Freedom House, Latino Parents Association, Chinese Progressive Association, Hispanic Office of Planning and Evaluation, Urban League of Eastern Massachusetts, Massachusetts

---

[1] Unity Boston is a chapter of the Unity Organizing Committee (UOC), a nationwide, progressive, grassroots organization of people committed to working for a just and genuinely democratic society. The UOC stands for restructuring social, political, and economic relationships in order to ensure the equitable distribution of wealth and power; and for a United States in which people of color can achieve full equality and self-determination, where women have equal rights, and children are nourished and protected.

Asian American Educators Association, St. Stephens Episcopal Church, Lesley College, Massachusetts Advocacy Center, and William Monroe Trotter Institute.

The action group proceeded to organize forums to inform and to gather input from the African American, Latino, and Asian American communities in Boston. In contrast to the other reform "efforts," this group was trying to make a real difference by going to the people themselves for ideas. The discussions we held were open, conducted in the native language and/or bilingually and the ideas of many parents were aired. In each community, parents identified parental and community participation as crucial to educational reform.

Parents' specific critique of the reform proposals (which by this time had been submitted as legislation) focused on five points. The first was tracking in the form of a test called a "certificate of initial mastery" which, at the 10th grade level proposed dividing students into college preparatory and vocational programs. Second was the absence of any mention of cultural diversity in the core curriculum. The third was the absence of a meaningful plan for parent input into the schools. The fourth was the absence of language ensuring fair representation of racial groups on proposed school governing bodies. Fifth, there was concern over the fact that the proposals were developed by politicians and business executives without input from grassroots communities.

It quickly became apparent that the task of writing a comprehensive reform bill that could serve as an alternative on all of these points, while remaining connected to and in participation with the grassroots base would be formidable. However, there was one point that was clearly held with the highest conviction across all of the parent groups: parent empowerment.

Our primary interest was to bring together a multiracial coalition, thus working on a concern that each community shared seemed the best way to start. We therefore decided to focus our efforts on writing a "parent empowerment" piece and submit it as an amendment or independent addition to other state education reform proposals.

The issue of how legislation could address parent participation in education was broken down into governance on school councils and ways of opening up broader parent rights of access to information and the schools. Parents felt that broad access was more important than governance because councils involve only a handful of parents and can often be manipulated by the administration.

In order to put the ideas of the parents in the coalition into legal language, we engaged in a discussion with the Education Law Task Force, a group of lawyers concerned with progressive models of education reform. These lawyers were willing to research existing examples from around the country and present them to us as well as assist us in putting the parent's ideas into a "Parent Participation Bill," which was submitted to the State Legislature in 1993. What follows are parents' and community activists' perspectives on the development of this bill and on the significance of the multiracial, Community Education Reform Coalition.

The Perspective of Parent and Community Activists

The interviews detailed here involved Har Yee Ann Wong (AW), a Chinese immigrant, with two children in the Boston Public School (BPS) system; LaJaugh Chaplin (LC), an African American, single mother of five children, four of whom are in the BPS; and Suzanne Lee (SL), a community activist and educator, with one child in the Brookline Public School system. All were active members of the Community Education Reform Coalition. Suzanne Lee lead the interview.

Q. *Tell me why you got involved in the state education reform process?*

LC: Initially we got together to fight the education reform bill proposed by the governor and the legislature. When we saw the bill, it did not address what we thought needed changing, didn't include our agenda, our point of view, at least not for the schools that we are using—that's why I got involved.

SL: When I saw the draft bill from the governor and the legislature, there were many things in it that talked about accountability, curriculum, and a whole lot of stuff that we need to reform public education. But as you understand it more, you see it really doesn't address the fundamental question—how are our kids going to learn in school. Particularly those in the inner city where the majority of the students are immigrants and students of color. I felt that the bill did not address any of their needs. As an educator and a community activist, I feel every child deserves to have an equal opportunity and access to good public education. That's why I got involved. Unless parents and a lot of community people get involved and put out what we think and put our agenda in it, this education reform effort is just a lot of hoopla.

LC: There's never any problem with financing when the issue only addresses the whites. Once things involve more minorities money gets scarce, accountability is compromised.

SL: One of the issues I was really concerned about was testing. Even though they talked about testing as an accountability issue, we all know that how it works a lot of the time for our students is that it forces a lot of them to drop out. So we asked, "How does the testing they are proposing benefit our students? And how are students and parents rights protected?"

There are important issues to address, but unless we can get a lot of people concerned and voice our opinion and get something in the bill, we will not have any impact on it.

Q: *How did you get involved?*

LC: I went to a big meeting at Roxbury Community College that was called for community folks and educators to talk about how the Black community should respond to the education reform bill. Should we fight it or find some way to be part of it? I was the only parent there. We divided into two groups, the action and a vision group. I wanted to be in a committee that I knew could do something, so I signed up for the action committee. We met to talk about how to get as many opinions as possible and how to do outreach. People were very honest, not afraid to say what they thought, and, most important, not afraid to listen to other opinions.

AW: I get involved through Suzanne. She told me about the reform bill. We had discussions with Chinese speaking parents to let them know what was going on and asked for their opinions. Then I helped with a meeting we had in Chinatown at the Quincy School and later went to some hearings.

SL: I was always very concerned about how reforms happen. I feel strongly that the process of how we get changes is a big part of the reform. We have got to involve the people who are using our schools to be a part of the reform. In order to have an impact on the reform we need to have people from all different communities working together and listening to each other about what needs to be changed. All through this process, the business community, the teachers union, the politicians all have had their say and input into the bill—everyone except the children and their parents.

Q: *Why did you all decide to push for a Parent Participation Bill?*

LC: I got involved in the schools about five years ago. I never spoke up in parents meetings until I heard a parent speak at my child's high school. After that I began to feel parents can do something about their children's education. I had never felt the schools listened to me or other parents.

It is a shame that we have to write legislation to have something in the books to make schools do what they should have done all along. Parents should be able to give input and be valued at their children's school, so that they know they have a hand in helping schools to meet the needs of their children. If parents are not involved in the process, I feel the reform is not going to happen the way it ought to or needs to happen.

I thought a lot of what people were saying was missing the point, which is educating our children. That needs to be in the forefront of any education reform. Parents are their children's first teacher, but we are always being overlooked.

AW: Even if the law is passed, nothing will happen unless we make it happen. But with a law in writing, parents will have a chance to make the schools listen to them—not the way it is now. Parents have no say. I want to be able to say to the schools what is not right and make them listen. With the parent participation bill we have a better chance to do that. If not, I feel our children have no future.

SL: The significance of the parents' participation bill is that it is a good organizing tool. Even if the whole bill is passed, they are not going to implement it in the right way unless people push to have it done. The parents' bill is aimed at breaking down barriers that schools put up to make it difficult for parents to participate. It requires that schools provide basic information to parents so they can participate. What's being taught, how their children are being taught, how they are being assigned, that kind of basic information. It is amazing that many parents don't have the kind of information necessary to make informed decisions. To me, this bill gives the community the tool to organize parents to have input. It is not going to completely change the education process but it opens the door for parents to have a say. If you have that, changes will come that benefit the students.

LC: I see a lot of schools where teachers and administrators listen to parents but do not respond to what they hear. I don't see any implementation of parents' ideas. With this bill, at least we can hope to have some response to parents' input. If the principals know they have to do something then they will make sure that teachers do it. It doesn't matter if you are Asian, Latino, African American, Haitian, we all want the same things—good education for our children. We have been led to believe that Special Ed and Bilingual Ed cost a lot of money. So what if they cost a lot? If the end result is that you get an educated child, the end result is the most important.

AW: I agree with what LaJaugh says about responding to parents and children's needs. At least with a bill we have a better chance of making the schools open their doors to parents.

LC: It is not parents who are already active that we are concerned about. It is the vast majority who are not involved now that this bill is aimed at. Parents know better how to get other parents involved. That's what happened to me, it was seeing another parent having an impact in the schools that encouraged me to be involved. I could really identify with her. This is what this bill aims to do, for parents to empower other parents so we can have more people involved in the schools. I see the same parents going to a lot of the same meetings, but what we need is to empower those who are not involved yet. They have got to have information to do that. Once the door is open for parents to be involved, those parents can decide what they want in that school. I don't think veto power is the key thing for parents' empowerment. If the majority of the parents know what is going on in that school and you get many parents to come out to make the decisions, that is already power. Every school is different. Parents in that school ought to be able to decide with the principal and the teachers what is best for the students of that particular school. It is not the legislature's place to decide for them.

SL: I remember that many parents talked about the way parent councils function, where the principals hand-pick a few people and the rest of the school doesn't know what's going on.

It is important to remember that not all parents can go to meetings, but they all want to know about their children's education. It is the school's responsibility to provide the information to parents and allow them access to have input into their children's schooling. The key here is more and more information for more people.

LC: I don't see this bill being able to solve all the problems of education, but what it can do is important: opening up the door of schools to parents. I can't say it enough, there is no education without participation. Everyone who is involved in the child's education ought to be involved in making decisions, and having input. Teachers, principals, and parents all need to have a say. The sooner teachers understand and believe in that the better.

Q: *What is the significance of this coalition? How is it different from other groups that you participated in before?*

AW: In other meetings I've been to before, I was not listened to by other people. My opinions did not matter to them. In this coalition people really respect each other. We listen to each other. The other thing I like is that there are different sectors of people in the group: parents, community people, advocates, lawyers, educators. And people are from different communities.

LC: In this coalition, everyone's opinion was listened to. Even when there were disagreements, people were not pushed out of the group. You really feel respected and wanted and valued, which is very important. So often when parents speak out we are not so articulate, so educated, or so financially well off. But we all have family, all have kids, we all have the same emotions and needs. We are all human beings and deserve to have the same respect regardless of where we come from.

SL: I really agree that the significance of this coalition is the multiracial coming together of people from different sectors working together and agreeing on the central piece: that parents have rights and must have a key say in the education of their children. All these people came together to support this idea, not in words but in action, to fight for legislation that would open the door for parents participation.

While everyone knows that building multiracial unity is so important, how do you actually do that? It is something that a lot of people are trying to figure out. I feel that this process of working together has done much in breaking down the barriers between people. Its only when we came together to work on similar things that we began to break down some of those barriers.

Q: *What have you learned through this work?*

AW: I learned that there are many people who truly care about the education of our children, and that immigrant parents are not alone. Through our meetings, I learned that other parents have similar views. I also learned that we can't give up, and that we have to go on to work together to fight for what we think is right.

LC: As an African American parent, I never knew that Asian parents feel the same way that I do going through the system. We actually think quite similarly. Another thing that I learned is that your economic status is not a big barrier. We might be poor and small in number right now, but we are big in spirit. When we come together and want to fight for the same thing, it is quite powerful. You know the old saying that "you can't fight city hall"? I realize that you can, when you have people from all different backgrounds coming together for the same thing.

Going to the State House was really an eye-opening experience for me. We always thought that when you voted somebody in to represent you, you had the right to meet them and be able to talk to them. That was not what happened. It took so long to get to see somebody—you get to talk to everybody but the legislator. When we finally did get to meet somebody, it was already at the end of the process. I personally did not feel we benefited, other than the fact that they heard us. But it was important for them to hear how far their reality is from ours.

Those committee hearings were something else. There were seven or eight of them at a time. Someone is always getting up to walk around and get a phone call or something. Even when they were there, they weren't really listening and paying attention. I don't care who's up there, they should have to listen. The only time I saw them listening was when another legislator came to talk. When we common people, who they are supposed to represent got up to speak, no one was listening!

Q: Would you feel disappointed if you can not get the legislation passed? How would you define success?

AW: As far as I am concerned, we are already successful. The reform bill is a big topic in the news, and many people are talking about it. Our work helped parents to be aware of it, and there are more discussions in the community.

LC: What we have done so far has surpassed my wildest dreams. When I first came on board, I didn't know what to expect or what we could do. Now we actually have a bill that's written with our ideas and opinions. That is already a success to me. I made a lot of friends in the process and the whole thing was such a learning experience for me. I am really happy and proud of the process and how we have worked together. It will be great if we can get the bill passed but, as I said, I already feel that we have accomplished a lot.

SL: Regardless of whether the bill is passed or not, we have developed a tool to rally other parents together to push for what they want in their school districts. We don't need it to become law to actually to begin in each local area to go to the school committees and use the draft bill as a basis to raise the ideas. To see parents respond to our bill in such a positive way as we show the bill to them has been testimony that we are on the right track. That in itself is already a success. The fact that we have people from different backgrounds, different races, and different communities working together is another success.

LC: Another success is that we are putting out there publicly the idea that we all need to work together to get good results for the education of our children. So many who run and work in our schools are not from the community. They don't know what happens to the child before they show up in school in the morning. They don't really understand the whole child. All they know about the child is his test score. I am not anti-teacher or anti-administrator. But teachers can't do it all, they need our help as parents and as people in the community. Unless people in the schools see that and welcome everybody's participation we are not going to be able to change our children's education that much.

LESSONS FOR OTHERS

What have we learned from our grassroots multiracial organizing for parent empowerment in education? There are three primary facets to the work of our coalition that we have learned from and that hold lessons for others. They are impacting education reform, building multiracial coalitions, and figuring out ways that grassroots knowledge and ideas can be translated into policy.

Education Reform

Our coalition has achieved the first mission that it set for itself, that of writing and submitting education reform legislation. Passage of the legislation will require a campaign that builds broad support and it is unlikely that it will be passed its first time through the legislature. In the meantime it may be possible to have the bill enacted at the municipal level. The bill will provide a core of ideas around which to organize parents. We have consistently viewed the writing of legislation not as a primary goal, but as a way to organize parents. Legislation is unlikely to solve issues of parent empowerment. What it can do is provide openings that give successful parent organizing more impact.

In the course of formulating the parent empowerment legislation we found that just by being a part of the debate we could have an impact. We attended community hearings, met with and were covered by the local media, had private meetings with legislators, and attended education reform hearings at the state house. It seemed that with each passing month we made a little more progress, which encouraged us to keep trying. More importantly, those involved were learning more and more about what passes for education reform and a political process in this state. In turn, we were educating a broader sector of people around us. Coalition members were becoming more convinced that there had to be something better and that the coalition had something to offer.

Multiracial Coalitions

We found that using the basic issues that people have in common as the starting place for uniting a grassroots, multiracial coalition is a useful strategy. The grassroots parents in our group, once they started working together discovered that despite prevalent myths, they had a lot in common. For instance, a couple of the myths we discussed were that Asian American immigrants have it made in terms of education, and that African Americans have greater knowledge about and access to elected political power.

It was necessary to use meetings and newsletters in Chinese to involve the Asian parents. Working with people who do not speak the same language requires attention to detail so that communication is maintained and everyone can play a part in the work. Having parents and activists involved who had strong and deep ties to their communities was critical to keeping ties to the grassroots alive.

By building unity among the different communities we had a greater impact on the education reform debate than we had expected. Even a relatively small and young multiracial coalition can have considerable impact, especially in a city like Boston where multiracial politics are rare.

The struggle for democracy in both the coalition and the struggle itself was an important aspect of building multiracial unity. The struggle was about expanding democracy for parents in the arena of education reform. Within the coalition, there was an atmosphere of mutual respect. That the parents were able to make their voices heard within the coalition helped them break down stereotypes and work together.

Finally, the relatively small core of the coalition made it easier for members to build trust and get to know each other on a personal level. For people who have been continually locked out of being able to have an impact, feeling comfortable was very important. Larger scale multiracial organizing may have to be built slowly in the absence of a broad scale social movement such as the civil rights movement. Such larger efforts may require very close attention to organization and structure, rather than the more informal, personal approach that was taken here.

Grassroots Impact

Despite considerable skepticism at the grassroots about elected officials, business leaders, and professional groups, the experience of the coalition has helped people deal with the issue of working in a united front and the need to make compromises in order to win victories.

Maintaining and building the coalition requires that the grassroots folks involved see that they have actually been listened to. They need to see that the input that they provide results in something happening and that they get reported back. Furthermore, the grassroots ideas that were the basis for our campaign seem to reflect the interests and agendas of other parents that we meet. Even suburban parents who already have a lot of access to their schools offered support in solidarity.

We see that there are original, important, and valuable ideas and knowledge held by parents who, although not education experts, are intimately aware of and deeply concerned about the education system. Furthermore, these ideas are amenable to being written into legislation, provided lawyers and activists are willing to provide the necessary support and assistance.

More importantly, it is doubtful that meaningful education reform can take place without parents taking a strong stand. Parents are the primary constituency for quality education, but the percent of households nationally with children has fallen from 46% in 1950 to 35% in 1990. At the same time, if the fairly new and relatively small coalition described here can have an appreciable impact then, a larger, broader parent's movement might be just what is needed to save public education in this country.

9

Ways of Looking, Teaching, and Learning: A Tapestry of Latino Collaborative Projects

La Colectiva Intercambio[1]

The unsuccessful attempts of reforms in dealing with the educational failure experienced by many Puerto Rican children prompted Puerto Rican researchers and practitioners to begin to address the issues in nontraditional ways. Through informal contacts and networks, a group of researchers from Puerto Rico and the United States started sharing their work. They came to realize that the populations they were concerned about formed communities that shared historical ties, cultural and linguistic backgrounds, and social conditions. A formal exchange was initiated by faculty members from the University of Puerto Rico, Rio Piedras (UPR) campus and staff of the Centro de Estudios Puertorriqueños, Hunter College (CUNY) in 1987. Almost simultaneously, a parallel exchange began to occur among Puerto Rican scholars in the United States. These efforts have led to the *Intercambio* Research Project, five collaborative projects in Puerto

[1]Members of *La Colectiva Intercambio* belong to one of the five collaboratives. As our projects have evolved, the individual members have changed. The members who participated in writing this document are presented in alphabetical order by institution. From Hunter College: Carmen I. Mercado, Pedro Pedraza, and Jorge Ayala; from the New York City Board of Education: Marceline Torres and Miriam Pérez; from Teachers College, Columbia University: Maria E. Torres-Guzmán; from the University of Arizona: Luis Moll; and from the University of Puerto Rico: Ana Helvia Quintero and Diana Rivera Viera. This effort would not have been possible without the financial support provided by the Intercambio City University of New York–University of Puerto Rico Academic Exchange Program and its director, Antonio Lauria Perricelli. We would also like to acknowledge the support that each of us has received through our respective institutions.

95

Rico and the United States that not only share in their concerns for the education of Puerto Rican/Latino groups, but also in research methodology.

We, the members of the Intercambio, decided to explore more in depth our commonalities and differences through collective writing. This chapter is the result. The descriptions of the individual projects serve to illustrate the common threads that create our tapestry of diversity. All five collaboratives involved Latino students, practitioners, and researchers in Arizona (Moll), New York City (Mercado, Pedraza, & Torres-Guzmán) and San Juan, Puerto Rico (Quintero & Rivera Viera). Initiated in different settings and under very different conditions and levels of funding, each collaborative created responses that grew out of and reflected the particularities of their settings; the collaboration had many theoretical and methodological assumptions in common. This was no coincidence. In addition to our common concerns and ethnicity, we employed ethnographic procedures to document, explore, and learn from what happened when we worked cooperatively with teachers and students to improve the conditions for learning in schools and other educational sites.

The collaboration that occurred among us, in spite of the geographical distances, has permitted us to share and reflect on our individual projects. During this process of discussion, and now in writing, we have tried to critically analyze our educational and research practices. As a result, we have further developed our ideas about educational practices, research, and teaching and learning. Our collective experiences support the importance of this approach in educational research, practice, and educational reform.

We believe that problems in education are not resulting solely from a lack of resources. Many of our projects have been developed with very small budgets; all of our collaboratives were developed by combining and redefining our task and our resources. Conceptions of what teaching and learning are and what needs to be done to promote student development also need redefinition. We believe that one of our main tasks for improving education is to promote conceptual shifts concerning ways of teaching and learning.

The researchers, practitioners, and students in the projects collaborated to create a text that, in effect, presented their teaching and learning practice. But, additionally, we collaborated in creating a parallel text, an interpretation of the first. In other words, our reflections and evaluations of the process were at multiple levels and were constituted by multiple voices, not just those of the university researchers who came into the process of research with their particular baggage of concepts, theories, and motivations. Students and teachers became involved in the process as well, and new, unheard voices emerged as a result. In transforming the research context, practice, and investigations in this manner, and in sharing our perspectives with others, it is our hope that the definition and activity of research will also begin to change.

In the next section, we describe the individual projects. In the spirit of presenting our multiple perspectives, we have decided not to impose uniformity of style. We want our voices and their written expressions to show our diversity. In the section that follows the descriptions of the projects, however, we focus on the methodological and theoretical commonalities and differences as we see them collectively.

DESCRIPTIONS OF THE COLLABORATIVES IN THE INTERCAMBIO RESEARCH PROJECT

Each of the collaboratives is complex in its own right, but we decided to present them in a specific order: from the teacher–student–researcher collaborative to the community school district–university collaborative. We felt that concepts such as change, collaboration, and so forth, could be better understood if elaborated in this fashion.

The Bronx Middle School Collaborative

Purpose of the Project. This collaborative partnership between Marceline Torres, a classroom teacher and Carmen Mercado, a university professor, began in the Spring of 1989 as a result of the graduate course on reading and language arts that Carmen was teaching at Hunter College. The initial focus of the collaboration was the application of research to practice for the purposes of improving "reading comprehension." The relationship we started has now evolved into a significant personal and professional one in which we work together with our research colleagues, the students of an intermediate school.

What we have been doing is as simple and as complex as initiating multiethnic students, two thirds of whom are Latino and who come from homes with low or subsidized incomes in the northwest "South" Bronx, into the world of research as practiced by educational ethnographers. Students in a Chapter I school, whose ethnicity, family income, and academic histories make them prime candidates for the type of low-level curriculum that characterizes instruction in "inner-city schools," are learning about the work of educational ethnographers and conducting original research that goes beyond the type of library work they are typically assigned.

The project draws from Brice-Heath's (1985) pioneer work in this area, endeavoring to "put ethnography into the hands of those, who would use it to improve their knowledge of what was happening to them in their learning and their skills in oral and written language" (p. 18).

By sharing her world as a teacher-educator and educational ethnographer, Carmen wanted students to understand and to value the work of researchers, and she expected that these experiences would open up unimagined worlds and opportunities to young adolescents who are at a critical juncture in their development. In addition, the expectation was that students would develop

school-related literacy through direct involvement in research activities requiring a great deal of reading and writing, rather than through more traditional
direct-comprehension instruction.

Creating a Student-Centered Curriculum. Our collaborative efforts have
sought to give students increased responsibility in the teaching–learning process
in a number of ways. First, students study or research topics of personal interest
and significance. It is instructive, but not surprising that students favor topics
such as drugs, teen pregnancy, AIDS, the homeless, and children's illnesses.
When given a choice of what to research, students tend to focus on trying to
understand their lived experiences. For example, they ask some of the following
questions: How does it feel to be a teen parent? Why does this happen? and
What can I do about this?" Explanations and insights of complex social
phenomena, particularly from the perspectives of those who are most affected by
them, are not typically forthcoming in school, and neither are the means for
addressing them. In different ways, we – the teacher, the students, and the
researcher – are driven by a commitment to understand and assume responsibility for doing something about situations or conditions that affect the education of our youth and the quality of life in our community. It is this common
mission that binds us and gives us strength to persevere despite the occasional
tensions, conflicts, and contradictions that are inherent in the collaborative
process.

Second, students are encouraged to learn with the assistance of more capable
others, and to understand that they can learn from their peers, parents, and
other authorities. This year, Angel, a student in last year's group, has willingly
given up his lunch period and seizes any other opportunity that presents itself,
to work with us as a research assistant. He shares his knowledge of research
through formal presentations as well as through group and individual consul-
tations. He has also had a major role as organizer and moderator of our research
presentations, a role he has truly mastered.

As their adult collaborators, we have played a key role in helping students
remain focused, explore, and take advantage of the many opportunities that
present themselves naturally to create sources of data, and reflect on what they
have done and what they are learning from their research activities. Recently, a
train ride to Boston where we were invited to make a presentation at a literacy
conference became a 5-hour adventure during which we experienced how
students were beginning to make the research process their own. The students
took opportunities that presented themselves naturally, interviewing and engaging in conversations with a soldier and a school teacher, passengers who
provoked one student's curiosity or whose curiosity was provoked by the way
they saw us relating to one another. We have also made students aware of the
especially rich, but usually unrecognized, sources of information that exist
everywhere, beginning in their homes.

These collaborative activities have been an essential means of accomplishing tasks students initially characterized as challenging ("hard") and beyond their individual capabilities. Students have become aware that they are capable of doing "college work" that is also more interesting ("fun") than the "boring board work" usually assigned. As some students have expressed, we have let them "discover on their own" real life, "the life of a teenager." We have not lectured to them or told them what to do. We also did not anticipate that ethnography would be the powerful instructional tool that it has proven to be with these young adolescent learners.

Learning From Ethnographic Research on Social Issues.   First year data, derived from field notes of observations and conversations with classroom participants, and written products developed by the students, yield rich insights about the power of ethnography as a process for inquiry, a process for teaching and learning, and as a mechanism for instituting change.

Students are learning a great deal about learning through their research activities. That is, they are learning to take notes for different purposes, to elicit information orally, to organize and synthesize information in different formats, and to make oral presentations.

By engaging in the literate practices of researchers, students have produced an impressive variety of written documents. For example, students have produced notes of our sessions together (scribe notes), of their group meetings, and of their research plans. They have transcribed interviews, written abstracts of their projects, and developed speeches for conference presentations. Throughout, a great deal of reading, discussion, and thought have accompanied the presentation of these documents. Wells (1986) referred to this as "literate thinking" preferring to emphasize the practices of literacy, particularly the primacy of writing and its relationships to reading, talking, and thinking, aspects not captured by the more popular term *reading comprehension.*

Through these activities, students have also learned a great deal about the power of writing as a tool for learning. This year, we have begun to develop portfolios of students' written work as a means of documenting more carefully this progress. We are beginning to see that not only is the quality of their written expression becoming increasingly detailed and clear, but that students express enjoyment of writing. As Peilian, one of the students, said recently, "I can't stop writing!"

A distinctive aspect of the research activities is that the students have organized and conducted our conference presentations. The students have gained confidence in their own abilities as they share their work in academic settings where adults usually do the speaking for them.

Some students have also movingly described how the research activities are bringing them closer to their families. For instance, they have told of conversations with relatives and friends about the realities of being a teenage parent, as

Rebecca did last year. Conversations and interviews with a variety of authorities have also been an important means of gaining insights on issues that concern these young adolescent students.

However, ethnographic documentation is not the only form of documentation that we have relied on. Analysis of scores on the Degrees of Reading Power (DRP) test administered last spring revealed dramatic gains in reading, in some cases by as much as 16 points (a 4-point increment is considered significant).

Perhaps the most surprising finding to date is that students are learning to be caring, compassionate individuals through their research activities, a finding that Angel and John first called to our attention last year. That is, these and other students have voiced the need to care about the homeless, to care about their communities "even if at times you want to get away from it all."

It is difficult to reduce an organic, dynamic process to a few simple words. This description is but a pale representation of the "real thing." However, it is an important means for reflecting on past accomplishments and for planning for what lies ahead. At this time, one of our most pressing challenges is to create a narrative that captures more fully our individual voices, a difficult though not impossible endeavor. We need to continue telling our story to ourselves and to others.

The Alternative High School/Teachers College Collaborative Project

Purpose of the Project. The initial intention of the university–community collaborative was to document the development of a bilingual/bicultural, empowerment-oriented alternative high school. The specific focus proposed was on parental involvement in curriculum development and the cultural underpinnings of such curriculum. The collaborative began in the Fall of 1987 and within a period of 3 months experienced a change in focus. For the remaining school year, the data collection period, the collaborative focused on documenting and examining how empowerment was manifested in a variety of domains—instruction, curriculum, and organization.

The collaborative was composed of researchers, graduate students, teachers, high school students, and staff of the community-based organization (two of whom are the authors here: María E. Torres-Guzmán and Miriam Pérez). One of the researchers, one of the graduate students, one of the teachers, and the majority of the students and the staff of the agency grew up in, or were members of the Williamsburg, Brooklyn community. Although the data gathering and analysis of the project findings for the final report occurred from July 1987 through February 1989, the principal investigator and the teachers at the time of this writing, were still engaged in analysis and reflection of classroom processes.

The research was ethnographic in nature. Members of the research team observed classrooms and "hung out" at the agency once or twice a week and on special occasions. Students, teachers, staff, and parents of the youth were interviewed formally and informally, in groups and individually. School site, agency, and community documents were also gathered. An explicit agreement of the collaborative, from the very beginning of the project, was that the data gathered was "property" of its producers – the teachers, students, parents, and staff. The interpretations, however, were mutual undertakings.

The relationships initially established in the collaborative unintentionally followed fairly traditional roles; there were clear distinctions between teachers and researchers. Breaking with these distinctions was a goal of the type of research collaborative proposed. The differences in interpretation about what was observed among the researchers led to establishing mechanisms for eliciting the teachers' perspectives. As such, the dialogue established between researchers and teachers came to take a "collaborative" and "reflective" nature; together we began to explore various interpretations of what was going on in classrooms and in the school, including interpretations of empowerment.

By asking teachers to define their concept of empowerment and by examining how they went about integrating their conceptions with what they did, we came to understand that empowerment had as many definitions as there were teachers – one definition was centered on enabling students as learners and another on developing community leadership. Even the students of the school, through the organizing of a school strike, made known what empowerment meant to them – participation in organizational decisions affecting their lives. The school events illustrating how the participants in the school negotiated the concept of empowerment in the classroom, in the organization, and in the community were numerous: the integration of students' lived experiences and language and culture, the lived curriculum developed around environmental science, and the students' organizing around governance. These events became vehicles for examining the relationships between language, culture, instruction, power, and social change. The following are but "key incidents" (Erickson, 1977, p. 61) that highlight our findings.

The "Student Experience Approach." Our discovery of the student experience approach occurred early in the Fall of 1987. The university research team observed that the way one of the teachers organized instruction altered the relationship between the learner and the text. The suggested order of instruction provided by the text had been changed. Instead of reading the selection, followed by the identification of the vocabulary and follow-up activities, the teacher did the reverse. She began by introducing the vocabulary, relating the vocabulary to the students' lived experiences, and then proceeded to read the text.

Understanding that they were already knowledgeable to a certain extent about the concepts discussed positioned the students in a lateral relation to the text. The unit was about civil rights and the vocabulary included concepts such as racism, discrimination, segregation, emancipation, ghetto, freedom, among others. Elaboration of concepts was first embedded with students' known experiences. The teacher elicited an affective and cognitive response to the topic by using the examples provided by the students. Validating the voices of students through the retelling of their experiences in the form of examples, the teacher was altering the relationship between text and reader. Traditionally the text is viewed as the authority; here the student was also an authority. The interaction of the student with the text could be transformed into a critical one; the reading of the text could be seen as the process of negotiating truths established by the collective discussion between the teacher and the students and in contrast to, or complemented by, what was presented in the text.

Close examination of the classroom practices of this teacher repeatedly demonstrated how she used the students' language, lived experiences, and culture as pedagogical tools to legitimize new social relationships of power (Torres-Guzmán, 1989, 1990).

Leadership for Community Development as Empowerment. The environmental science curriculum was developed by a teacher who focused on developing a pedagogical approach incorporating, in his words, "a process of action-reflection-action." It is an example of an integrated curriculum aimed at building leadership for community development and empowerment.

Early in the Fall, the class had a series of field experiences: a walk through the neighborhood, a visit to a tristate storage facility for toxic and radioactive waste, and a nearby park preserved as a "natural environment." Students with photographic skills found a role as visual recorders. The class, soon to be known as the Toxic Avengers, observed, analyzed, read, and wrote about what they saw and experienced. Contrasting environments within the discussion of individual and community rights to healthy environments set the stage for future action.

A lot four blocks away from the school, which was used by an adhesive factory to store barrels of residue, became the target of their investigation. Daily visits permitted the students to count the barrels and determine the traffic flow in and out of the lot. Getting close enough was creatively approached by staging the accidental throwing of a football onto the premise. Establishing a faintly disguised excuse to trespass on private property and their continued presence in front of the lot had its effect. The number of barrels stored began to decrease (from 200 barrels to 30), the liquid of some of the drums was spilled into the gutter, one of the students and the teacher were "bullied" by one of the adhesive plant employees, and a high sheet metal fence crowned with barbed wire was erected. The counting came to an end. But the students had taken some samples of the spillage from which a chemical lab confirmed the presence of hazardous and toxic waste.

Meanwhile, in the classroom, the students learned about cell structures, chromosomes, mutants, chemicals, toxicity, and so forth. They distinguished between the different categories of hazardous material and the specific effects these could have on an individual's health and on the environment. Their experience with the lot also helped them frame their social studies learning. They studied about government structures and lines of authority. In trying to determine which authorities would be helpful with their cause for a better, healthier environment, the students learned about zoning laws, the Environmental Protection Agency, and the role of the fire chief, mayor, and governor. Although they never found a need to send the letter they collectively wrote to the fire chief, they experienced the writing process—determining audience, purpose, message, and editing—as part of their learning.

The environmental science curriculum embodied many principles of a pedagogy that promotes transformation. Students were not passive recipients of knowledge, but active creators. The students and the teacher assumed the posture of active coparticipants in the process of learning/teaching. The task was sufficiently complex so as to require that they rely on each other's strengths and engage in collective action. The experiential and abstract learning were facilitated by the integration of classroom learning and community action. The learner had to apply what was learned in the classroom to what happened in the community, and their community action informed and gave meaning to the classroom learning. The students' actions were embedded in the passion, morality, and caring they felt for what happened to their family and friends in the community. Reflecting on the significance of what occurred permitted the students to distance themselves sufficiently so as to gain understanding of the political, social, and scientific complexity of their work. They entertained multiple perspectives on what occurred as well. For example, although they felt victorious, they understood why they were to, in their presentation of the events, cautiously refrain from claiming a causal relationship between their daily presence at the chemical lot and the eventual clean-up.

Reflections. The teachers and students were involved in change in various domains. Teachers were reflecting on their conception of teaching as they examined what empowerment looked like in their classroom and in the school. They were involved in establishing alternative relationships with the students and positioning student learning so that the students themselves were creating change within the school and in the community. Although there were many occasions in which the interactions described here were far from being the norm, the school was a positive experience for many of the students as it provided the support, love, and safety of a *familia or un segundo hogar* (Carrasco, 1984). What the teachers did to create this positive environment for students had much to do with understanding that the language and culture of the students, their parents, their community were valuable tools for organizing instruction (be it through the use of cultural images, lived experiences, or through the use of the neighborhood as a learning site).

Incorporating students' experiences, cultural background, lived experiences, and language as a way of validating student voices changed the relationship of power and collaboration in the classroom. Students became active participants in molding their own lives. The content became accessible and the learning process became meaningful and purposeful. Furthermore, the learning environment created in this alternative school provided spaces for the students to explore their own relationships as individuals in the broader societal context.

The stories also say something about research and the relationship of theory and practice. Research on teachers' conception of learning and teaching practices can be incredibly powerful in bridging the gap between theory and practice that so often makes the activity of research and research findings so alienating for the practitioners. The students, teachers, and researchers became partners in molding the direction of the research and the interpretation of the findings. Matin-Baro (1989) summed up how we came to see our work—research that is centered on what is important to and at the service of those it proposes to serve. We know that research that aims at change can be transformative.

Afterschool Research Project

Purpose of the Project. The Centro de Estudios Puertorriqueños at Hunter College has over the last 2 years conducted an intervention research program at a community-based site in East Harlem. Pedro Redraza and Jorge Ayala are the two authors here engaged with this project.[2] The program works with an afterschool elementary grade level student population that is comprised of African American and Puerto Rican children who reside in the surrounding low income housing projects and range between 7 and 12 years of age.

The purpose of this intervention program is to improve the literacy, math, and science skills of the children in a learning environment that emphasizes participation in schools and society in general.

Experts in mathematics and science education acknowledge that children's negative attitudes and low motivation for learning could be major hurdles in these fields. They also propose that teaching elementary school children the process of scientific investigation and introducing the principles of mathematical and scientific reasoning is more important than having the students memorize scientific facts and/or acquire mechanical skills.

Our approach to curriculum development has been guided by a sociohistorical, cultural perspective. This approach to cognitive development has been promising particularly with school children who have often been treated as subjects of remediation. The perspective we take views cognitive development as emerging from the nature of social interactions, from educational activities that

---

[2]Marianne Hedegaard and Seth Chaiklin were involved in earlier drafts.

are motivated by goals derived both from the content domain and from the culture and interests of the communities to which the learner belongs.

A feature of this approach is that the content around which the curriculum is organized is primary. The development of intellectual skills depends on working with the relationships and contradictions in the subject matter. Second, the content must be carefully selected. The objective is to focus on questions that are fundamental to the children and their position in society. Third, the effective use of content in educational activities requires careful planning. And, fourth, the approach is activity based. Intellectual development comes from working directly with the relationships in the subject matter.

In addition, we want to develop a critical consciousness in our children. We define this critical consciousness as containing an historical and socioeconomic understanding and knowledge of the community. The development of such consciousness gives students a sense of their potential human agency, and potential for action, by providing them with a perspective of continuity and possibility not afforded by explanations that ascribe the cause for poor community conditions on cultural, racial, linguistic, or personal factors. We believe that being knowledgeable about the past helps students understand the present in ways that could connect to future solutions of social problems.

Two aspects of such a learning process that we have not explicitly developed but are intrinsically important to our approach is the role of positive self-esteem and strong cultural identity. They are important to our theoretical approach for two basic reasons. One is related to the issue of self-determination and the right of people to maintain their identity and culture. (In the case of Puerto Ricans in the United States this has a particularly legal constitutional basis as well since we are born U.S. citizens.) The second reason is related to our implicit analysis of society and the strategies for social change that derive from this analysis. Essentially, unlike the schools, we believe that the strategies for change should be community or socially based (the schools focus on individual achievement and upward social mobility, usually as the way out of the community, as the answer). If collective response and action are needed to change social reality then we must begin preparing children at an early age. Good and effective citizenship needs to be nurtured rather than expected to magically arrive with the coming of voting age.

Our general approach is to help children build an identity as a Puerto Rican minority group so that they become integrated, as opposed to assimilated, to the city where they live. The belief is that through a knowledge of the history and background of the Puerto Rican culture, the children can develop self-respect and reflect on cultural practices; that is, they can gain an understanding of the factors that affect the origin or maintenance of particular practices. In short, we would like to help the children develop a theoretical approach to understanding their identity.

A theoretical approach is important for the following reasons. Done properly, the children will have a deeper, richer understanding of cultural practices. They will be able to understand these practices as reflecting solutions and adaptations to particular material conditions in which their ancestors lived. By understanding their culture in this historical way, they will start to appreciate the processes that generate cultural practices. Consequently, in their own lives, they can help to adapt and extend their culture, examining what practices can and should be maintained in an urban environment, and maintaining the spirit of other practices, even if the forms are changed to accommodate present conditions.

Characteristics of Our Methodological Approach. We conceived our approach as intervention research in settings of daily life. We have worked within various educational institutions such as schools and afterschool settings. We have experimented with institutional activities by planning and outlining new ways of interacting with the content to be taught and learned.

The aim of the intervention research is to change educational and social institutions in general. Through our approach to experimental teaching in an afterschool program we exemplify how teaching/learning activities can be organized in alternative ways. This way of teaching can bring understanding of how to better motivate children for learning and how to develop specific areas of knowledge. The social intervention and experimental teaching is planned based on the theory of Vygotsky. At the same time, the theory is also constantly evolving.

Our concern with the content of teaching and learning and with the process of the activity calls for our research methods to be primarily qualitative in order to describe the content and follow the process. Defining research as research in daily life activities also means that the researchers are part of these activities. The researchers cannot be seen or perceived as outsiders as if in a vacuum untouched by the daily life of the participants in the research. The researchers are in constant interaction with teachers and children and it is through these interactions that the research can be viewed as intervention in daily life activities. The basic characteristic of our theoretical approach to teaching and learning activities are:

1. teaching is based on a conceptual model of the basic relations inherent to the subject matter being taught;
2. teaching is planned as guided research;
3. that children are learning through problem solving and exploration; and
4. children are actively researching and exploring problems genuine for both the teacher and the children.

Conclusions. There have been difficulties in our project. First, and foremost, is the strategy of working in a community-based organization (CBO) setting. In brief, after an attempt at working in an in-school site, we decided that the CBO would allow more freedom to experiment and to create a model that could be duplicated by others. These centers of afterschool child care we believe, are untapped resources for educational development that can complement or supplement what occurs in schools. However, these centers themselves have internal dynamics that have affected the development of the project.

Another difficulty we have faced is that of developing activities that are nontypical of school, yet that are instructional. Although this is an ideal, in our practice we have found this hard to accomplish because of the pervasive ideology of schooling. Also, basic to our theoretical approach is the premise that a thorough understanding of content is needed to develop curricular activities. However, there are gaps in our knowledge of the community and the teachers lack the time needed to learn and absorb all of the content they may need to develop the curriculum and to take advantage of spontaneous developments in the classroom.

Finally, a logistical problem of planning, evaluating, and coordinating the project in terms of time has been difficult to resolve. We have recently taken the drastic step of cutting one of our three weekly sessions with the children to see if this will help resolve this logistical problem. We have found it difficult to schedule enough time to go over the content profoundly, develop learning activities accordingly, and then evaluate the results in a manner that can be useful for future planning. This we will have to work on in the near future.

The Arizona Community Project

Purpose of the Project.   The design of this project, described here by Luis Moll, consisted mainly of three main, interrelated activities. First, it included an analysis of the use and communication of knowledge and skills within and among households in a Mexican community in Tucson, Arizona. Second, the researchers and teachers examined classroom practices and used local resources to experiment with literacy instruction in an afterschool site. And, finally, classroom observations were conducted to examine methods of instruction and to explore how to apply what was learned at the afterschool site. During the first year, a study was undertaken in 28 households in which data on literacy practices in Spanish and English and on the structure and functions of social networks within the community were collected. Self-report questionnaires, literacy checklists, and ethnographic field notes were used to gather information during prearranged visits to these homes by the members of the research team. The instructional component occurred in two distinct settings: an afterschool lab and in school-based classrooms in two districts.

Households are Repositories of Knowledge.   Particularly important in our work has been our analysis of households, how they function as part of a wider, changing economy, and how they obtain and distribute their material and intellectual resources through strategic social ties or networks (Velez-Ibañez, 1988). In contrast to many classrooms, households never function alone or in isolation; they are always connected to other households and institutions through diverse social networks. In our sample of primarily Mexican working-class families, these social networks facilitate different forms of economic assistance and labor cooperation that help families avoid the expenses involved in using secondary institutions, such as plumbing companies or automobile repair shops. For families with limited incomes, these networks are a matter of survival. They also serve important emotional and service functions (e.g., in finding jobs and in assisting with child care and rearing so that mothers may enter the labor market). In brief, these networks form social contexts for the transmission of knowledge, skills, information, and assistance, as well as cultural values and norms (Greenberg, 1989; Velez-Ibañez, 1988).

The knowledge exchanged through these types of social ties or networks we refer to as *funds of knowledge*. Greenberg (1989) defined funds of knowledge as an "operations manual of essential information and strategies households need to maintain their well being" (p. 2). Our analysis shows that funds of knowledge are related to the social and labor history of the household members and the participants in the networks. With our sample, much of the knowledge is related to the households' rural origins and, of course, current employment or occupation, such as soils, cultivation of plants, seeding, and water distribution and management. Others know about animal husbandry, veterinary medicine, ranch economy, and mechanics. Many of the families know about carpentry, masonry, electrical wiring, fencing, and building codes; to maintain health, often in the absence of doctors, some families employ folk remedies, herbal cures, midwifery, and first aid procedures. And the list goes on. Needless to say, not every household in our sample possesses knowledge about all of these matters. But that is precisely the point. It is unnecessary for individual persons, households, or classrooms to possess all this knowledge. When needed, such knowledge is available and accessible through social networks of exchange.

Clearly, the idea that these families are somehow devoid of abilities and skills is simply erroneous. The common view that their children suffer from a deficit of "funds of background experience" is seriously challenged by our work. From our perspective, these families represent a major social and intellectual resource for the schools. The extent of their funds of knowledge justifies our position that the community needs to be perceived by others, especially educators, and probably by the community itself, as having strength or power, as having resources that schools cannot ignore.

In an important sense, the schools are in an analogous situation to the households we are studying. All schools consider that they need more resources in addressing the needs of students, especially if these students are minority children and from poor neighborhoods. It is common for teachers to bemoan the scarcity of resources. Dealing with scarcity of resources, however, is an everyday issue in the households. The exchange of funds of knowledge, as we have explained, is a major strategy to deal with the lack of resources, a strategy developed to harness, control, and manipulate resources. The idea is to do the most with what you have.

Accessing Funds of Knowledge for Academic Learning. Ina, the sixth-grade bilingual teacher, had a classroom that contained all of the elements necessary to experiment with literacy instruction. Although she followed the assigned curriculum, she deviated often to implement supplementary activities. For example, she supplemented the basal reader with novels, newspaper, and magazine stories, and poems. She also had the class write often, including poems, short stories, narratives, and descriptions. Ina joined the afterschool setting already sharing the group's belief that the use of outside, community resources could give more meaning to the learning experiences of the students.

Ina introduced the theme of construction, which had been discussed in the teacher study group, to her class. Although she discussed with the students possibilities for research on this topic, she believed that the work required conducting a unit would be more in depth and extensive than anything they had done before.

Ina started by asking the students to visit the library to look for information on building or construction. The students obtained materials in both English and Spanish on the history of dwellings and on different ways of constructing structures. Through her own research in a community library and in the school district's media center, the teacher identified a series of books on construction and on different professions, including volumes on architects and carpenters, and decided to use them as part of the module. The students built a model house or other structures as homework and wrote brief essays describing their research or explaining their construction.

In short, the teacher was able to get the students to write about their experiences and in the process, she improved the activities she had learned about at the afterschool site. The teacher, however, did not stop there. She proposed that the class invite parents as experts to provide information on specific aspects of construction. The teacher reported that the children were surprised by the thought of inviting their parents as experts, especially given some of the parents' lack of formal schooling, and were intrigued by the idea. She invited one father, a mason, to describe his work. She was particularly interested in the father describing his use of construction instruments and tools, and how he estimated or measured the area or perimeter of the location in which he works.

The teacher also invited other people in the community to contribute to this unit. The teacher invited parents and others in the community to contribute substantively to the development of lessons; to access their funds of knowledge for academic purposes. Theirs was an intellectual contribution to the content and process of classroom learning. The parents came to share their knowledge, expertise, and experiences with students. This knowledge, in turn, became part of the students' work or a focus of analysis. These visits helped create a new instructional routine in this classroom that helped the teacher and students exceed the curriculum, stretch the limits of their writing, and expand the knowledge that formed lessons. In total, about 20 persons visited the class during the module implementation and the teacher used different sources of funds of knowledge: the students' own knowledge, that of the students' parents and relatives, the parents and relatives of other students, the teacher's own network, the school staff and other teachers, the community members who did not have school-age children, and university faculty and graduate students.

Establishing social networks to access funds of knowledge for academic learning generated many important secondary activities that went far beyond the initial module and the activities around the theme of construction became more central to the classroom activities. The teacher started to generalize the module by incorporating the "core" curriculum within the module's activities. This generalization illustrates the extent to which the teacher and her class had appropriated the initial model's activities and created something new to address the needs of this specific classroom.

Concluding Vision. We started the project convinced that there were ample resources in the students' community that could be used to help improve literacy instruction. We set out to document these resources in terms of the funds of knowledge found in the households and were struck by the breadth of the knowledge and by the importance of social ties in making this knowledge available to others.

We soon realized that the insights gained from studying households held special relevance for the study of education. But we also realized that household funds of knowledge could not simply be imported into classrooms, especially as currently organized. We needed to work closely with teachers to figure out how to create circumstances where these funds of knowledge would become legitimate resources for teaching and learning. We formed an afterschool setting where we could develop innovations and soon learned that any initiative for change, and the bulk of the work to make it happen, had to come from teachers. The afterschool site became a teachers' study group, where teachers could share their funds of knowledge about teaching and create a social network among themselves.

Meanwhile, we observed in classrooms, and realized that under the best conditions, those classrooms where the children were eagerly using literacy to explore and understand issues of interest to them and the teacher served as good analogues to the households: very different settings but both using social processes and cultural resources of all kinds to get ahead. It is here, in the strategic combination of resources to help students learn and develop, that we see the greatest potential for change.

University of Puerto Rico's Partnership with the Schools

The University of Puerto Rico's Partnership Project with Schools was initiated in February 1987, with the participation of school personnel at different levels— teachers, school directors, supervisors, the district superintendent, representatives from the Puerto Rican Department of Education Central Office—as well as university professors from different disciplines, including sociology, psychology, planning, public administration, mathematics, science, language, history, and education. Ana Helvia Quintero and Diana Rivera Viera are two of the professors involved in the project. The project's main objective was to identify alternatives for dealing with major educational problems in the San Juan II School District, which with 97% of its families below poverty level, has one of the lowest income levels in the island. The project was initially organized around a seminar where participants from the district and the university met on a monthly basis to identify the multiple variables that are interwoven in the district's educational problems.

During the initial months of the project, the 40 project participants met to develop a socioeconomic and educational profile of the district. In this process, we found that educational passivity and disengagement among students in the upper elementary grades and high school were frequently cited as symptomatic of the educational problems. In order to deal with this situation, a smaller group of seminar participants met during the Summer of 1987 to develop specific projects that would make schoolwork more relevant to the students' needs and potentials and transform teaching into a more active process. One of these projects is described here.

The Resource Center Project. The Resource Center Project at the Manuel Elzaburu Middle School was initiated in October 1987. The focus of our work was to improve students' writing and reading skills using their interests, potentials, and community resources as the basis for learning. Four general tenets guided the project's orientation and development. First, the improvement of student performance should be based on an enrichment program that focuses on their strengths and utilizes community resources as an important basis for themes and activities. Second, student learning will be enhanced when activities are student centered and teachers are willing to view themselves as social scientists whom observe how students develop, identify their strengths, and use these as the basis for their teaching. Third, the students' community must be viewed as an important source of knowledge and not as problematic. Fourth, teachers need to reflect continuously on the relationship between educational theory and practice in order to make teaching a more relevant and dynamic experience.

It involved a group of 20 seventh graders receiving service through the Chapter I program. Although this program proposed to help students get out of Chapter I, our experience was that students never left the program because their work remained below the expected performance level.

The project was viewed as a demonstration using an innovative interdisciplinary approach and involving professors from the University of Puerto Rico, mainly from the Laboratory High School of the School of Education who worked together integrating theater, visual arts, and language arts through an enrichment program.[3] The university professors met weekly with the seventh graders (*El grupo de los 20*) using the amount of time usually allotted to the regular Chapter I services. Traditional teaching had not been successful with these students, so new avenues were needed.

The Barrio Obrero Community surrounding the school is overridden with socioeconomic problems, but it is also very rich in its popular culture. Some of the most well-known singers of popular music in Puerto Rico were born and raised in Barrio Obrero. Thus, we decided to build around the history of the popular music and performers of Barrio Obrero. Students became involved in diagnostic reading and writing activities by reading and discussing a newspaper article about Ismael Rivera, a famous "salsa" musician who had died several months before. Ismael Rivera was born and raised in the neighborhood and had been buried in the local cemetery just a few blocks away from the school. The students were able to share bits of information regarding the musician, his music, his involvement with drugs, details of the burial, and so forth. As a result of these discussions, we thought about what other things we wanted to know about his life and what sources of information we could use. Among them were interviews. The group developed questions to include in several interviews to community members who could provide some answers to their concerns. Students read different portions of the newspaper article and took turns answering questions about the article. The reading samples were taped. Afterward they wrote brief paragraphs summarizing what they had read. These initial activities provided valuable reading and writing samples to be examined as our work progressed. While some of the professors worked with the students, others observed them and took notes of their reading and general classroom behavior.

We were aware that these students did not find academic activities interesting and that they experienced low achievement and frustration in school. Several were very uncomfortable reading aloud and made fun of one another's poor reading ability. We were committed to working with their reading and writing

[3]The participants were William Padín (theater); Carmen Rodriguez (art); Jorge Cruz, María del C. Curras, and Diana Rivera Viera (language arts) from the University of Puerto Rico; and Ileana Quintero from the Universidad del Sagrado Corazón.

skills in an environment that made them feel secure in their abilities, using the strengths they brought into school and recognizing their community as a source of knowledge useful to their school learning. We needed to modify their view of teachers as authority figures who corrected their mistakes continuously and viewed their community as problematic. This was not an easy task. We began by deciding that reading and writing mistakes would not be corrected by the professors. Students were asked to use self-corrections whenever their reading didn't "sound right" or "make sense." A great deal of collective writing production occurred, thus requiring small efforts from each participant. At the very beginning, students were either very loud, exhibiting unacceptable classroom behaviors such as disrupting activities, or were extremely passive, unable or unwilling to judge their own work. A great deal of time was spent discussing what behaviors the group thought necessary to observe in order to work productively.

We also used semantic mapping activities to encourage the expression of their thoughts about a particular idea or word. Several significant activities occurred around a single word, for example "ambiente." We found that the group initially expressed very few positive views about the "ambiente" in their neighborhood. As time progressed and with some prodding, the students began to view positively, among other things, their music, their sense of family, and their concern for community.

Group writing activity evolved around experiences they had as group participants, and through theater exercises they began to explore the use of their bodies, voices, and facial expressions as creative outlets for their ideas, feelings, and stories. An experimental theater group known as the *Teatreros Ambulantes* worked with the students during several sessions. Photostatic theater was particularly exciting as a means to express the stories they were writing. A trip to a well-known *mascaras* (masks) artisan in the city of Ponce helped the group see how crafts can be made from materials such as newspapers. Consequently, art activities involved the use of materials available in their environment. Each student selected the artistic means he or she wished to explore in order to represent different milestones in Ismael Rivera's life that resulted from the research. The students became involved in art or theater activities according to their own interests and strengths.

The professors met weekly to assess what was occurring, the students' interest and development of their language art skills, and changes in student behavior. They planned accordingly. These meetings became a means for reflecting on pedagogical theory and practices. It helped develop a sense of cohesiveness among the professors who in the school setting were deeply involved in examining what teaching strategies were useful and successful in working with students who had almost given up on school. For this group of professors, these weekly activities and the work with the students also affected their own teaching at the School of Education.

The Process of Change.   When we began the project and asked students to talk about the community and themselves, they expressed very negative feelings about their community and were unable to point out any positive aspects. In school, they were passive and quite confused by the environment created in the classroom. Self-expression had obviously not been part of their schooling experience. They were amazed at the topics brought up for discussion. Crime, drugs, and dissatisfaction with schooling were the subjects they wanted to talk about. The perception held by the students not involved in the group about the group members was negative because these students were known for their poor school performance. They were initially confused with our expectation that they assume the role of active learners when we offered them the possibilities of determining class materials and activities.

A dramatic change began to occur around the third month of the project, when students suggested changes in the programmed activities and opted for collective story writing. They became involved in self-correction of their work and made positive remarks to others in the group concerning ways to improve their writing. A trip to a drama class at the Laboratory High School of the University of Puerto Rico was another milestone because the students at that school dramatized the skits that they had written. Thus, their creative writing became significant outside of their community and came alive. It broadened their perspective of writing as a means of communication. By the end of the first year, other students in the school wanted to join the group. *El Grupo de los 20's* image had changed and a sense of cohesiveness had developed. They decided to keep the group as it was and change the theme of our work to center around their own experience as a collective.

From the participant teachers' perspective, change occurred in their teaching as a result of the intensive weekly meetings. By discussing student behavior and performance, the teachers had to reflect continuously on their own expectations and teaching. Students' active learning, in turn, although an expressed objective from the beginning, produced conflicts in how teachers viewed themselves. It required a great deal of discussion and resolution of conflicting views concerning how student suggestions affected our proposed objectives. It demonstrated that although we thought our classroom was centered on student learning and their interests, we frequently imposed our interests as their own. Our experiences challenged our notions of productivity in the classroom and how other school personnel viewed our teaching.

Throughout the project, collaboration was a key issue. Collaboration among teachers, among students, and between teachers and students was stressed. Collaboration promoted genuine collective work and created a very strong bond among all participants strengthening their individual self-esteem. Looking back on this project we find that change in student and teachers' perceptions of learning, schooling, and the power of collaboration were among the most significant gains of the project. Our commitment to empowering students with the knowledge that they are part of a resourceful and rich community that needs and should be present in their schooling proved to be a powerful tool in bringing about change in students attitudes and behaviors in school as well as in ourselves.

COMMONALITIES AND DIFFERENCES

In this section, we move from the descriptions of the collaboratives to a discussion of the commonalities and differences in our methodological approaches and the theoretical underpinnings guiding our work.

Methodological Issues

Ethnographic research, we found, can be a powerful means for improving instruction. The five collaborative projects described in this chapter illustrate how an ethnographic approach can be powerful as a process for inquiry, a process for teaching and learning, and as a mechanism for institutional change. The projects also illustrate how the traditional distinctions between and among research, practice, and staff development can be broken down. The following is a discussion on the particularities of the methodological approach and the issues that emerged in our discussions.

In the Alternative High School Collaborative, Torres-Guzmán initially assumed a more classic role of ethnographer, documenting what occurred by gathering data from a variety of sources, recording and analyzing activities, and creating opportunities for participants to reflect on and interpret observed occurrences and events from their perspectives. The latter aspect of her work is particularly significant in that participant perspectives are typically omitted from traditional research approaches. The use of ethnography in this setting was linked to the school's concern in "identifying those aspects of this alternative educational model that were successful in meeting the needs of at-risk Latino students." In other words, it was tied to understanding practice. Through this collaborative partnership, school personnel gained greater understanding of what was being accomplished and reports and presentations resulting from these efforts enabled others to understand as well. Similarly, the ethnographer was transformed by the experience, leading her to question the appropriateness of the concern for model building. In effect, the researcher and the research context had been changed in the process, a change that was made possible by the methodology that had been employed. Quintero and Rivera-Viera used ethnographic procedures to study and document the process of changing school practices in settings that are more resistant to change. Unlike the Alternative High School, change in the San Juan II School District was prompted by a shift in educational policy instituted from the top, by the Department of Education in Puerto Rico. Guided by the principle that policy and implementation must go hand in hand, Quintero and Rivera Viera collaborated with two schools in the San Juan II School District to explore ways of making learning more relevant to students, while at the same time being consistent with the goals of the new policy. From the initial stages, members of the team from the University of Puerto Rico worked with school personnel and directly with students with a variety of instructional approaches. Although all had something to contribute, "none of the collaborators had all the answers" (Quintero, 1989). In effect, all were both learners and researchers in their explorations. Together they grappled with the factors that constrained change and with the limitations of the existing theories and research models on change in order to find new solutions.

Mercado used ethnographic research similar to what Brice-Heath (1985) had done. The research process went as far as involving students as legitimate members of the research community through presentations made at authentic research forums. Thus, ethnographic procedures were utilized to monitor an "ethnographic experiment" as it evolved in this particular setting, but also as a teaching tool. Through this process, the teacher has become more conscious of her role as a researcher and the researcher has learned a great deal about the conditions in the community and the lives of students.

Similarly, university researchers in the El Barrio collaborative, guided by a sociohistorical, cultural perspective, worked in consultation with an elementary school teacher to design and implement an innovative curricular approach. Specifically, they were concerned with giving in-depth attention to the history and character of "El Barrio," contrasting it to life in Puerto Rico before migration. With this as a focal point, ethnographic procedures were used to document the process and to guide students as they became engaged in gathering data on their community. The fact that this project exists in a community-based afterschool center freed it from the constraints of those working within traditional classroom settings, as occurs in the Arizona, Bronx, and San Juan projects. However, through the documentation process, the research team has become aware of other types of constraints that affect what they are doing. Ethnographic data derived from the documentation of this process are thus yielding important insights for others working in similar settings.

Of all the projects, the Arizona project is the most far reaching in demonstrating that Hispanic homes and communities have important cognitive resources for instruction that schools typically ignore or underestimate, and in documenting how this knowledge can be used for academic learning purposes. Instructional planning occurred both within the setting of an afterschool lab as well as within traditional classroom arrangements. During the first year of the project, an ethnography of Spanish-speaking households in the Tucson area was conducted for the purpose of identifying the content and manner of the transmission of knowledge presently going on in these homes. Preliminary analyses revealed at least nine domains of knowledge contained in these households and how social networks were established and negotiated. At the same time, researchers and teachers utilized an ethnographic approach to create literacy modules developed around themes that reflected understandings gained from the household study and from practical concerns that surfaced in different classrooms. Later, the teacher study groups developed and became another vehicle for bringing about change in instruction and incorporating community funds of knowledge.

The five collaborative projects used ethnographic approaches to research, create, and demonstrate innovative instructional approaches. All of them have been successful in adding to the existing knowledge about creating alternatives for children who have traditionally failed in schools. Much of this has occurred because they have established sustaining partnerships between university personnel and teachers and because the methods used have been flexible enough to include previously unheard voices with new solutions to many unsolved educational problems.

Theoretical Issues

Five issues were common to the theoretical approaches of all the projects: educational and social change, collaboration, communities as intellectual and cultural resources, pedagogy, and the relationship between theory and practice. These issues were critical to all our projects, but how we dealt with them revealed our diversity.

Educational and Social Change. Change is a common theme to the projects both because the societal and educational systems are failing to adequately deal with the needs of many Puerto Rican and other Latino youth and because education is a dynamic, interactive process. All of the projects conceptually view change as on-going, occurring at multiple organizational domains, spheres of action, and levels. However, the emphasis we place on any given level in which change occurs differs among the projects.

One of the themes embraced by all the projects, for example, is the relationship between educational and societal change. In addition to assisting children to become educationally and socially competent individuals, the projects aim to promote changes in community and group relationships by creating educational alternatives. For example, through the lived curriculum of environmental science in the alternative high school in Brooklyn, the Toxic Avengers forced the clean-up of a chemical lot in their neighborhood; the middle school student in the Bronx proposed to challenge the "one grade-one teacher" organizational structure of their school by petitioning to see the principal about their future class assignment with the teacher who had introduced the innovations in their classroom; the San Juan II students, upon assuming greater responsibility for what was going on in school, moved the curriculum toward the study of their community; and the East Harlem afterschool students assumed a posture of social action by writing a letter to former Mayor Koch of New York City about the homeless when they began to see connections between everyday life and city policies. In other words, all of the projects aim at self-affirmation and human agency through collective action.

The San Juan II and the Arizona projects are most complex in their strategies for organizational change in schools. The San Juan II aims at changes in educational conceptions held by groups of students (e.g., the Chapter I, *Grupo de los 20*), and individual teachers (e.g., seminar and school personnel of different levels). The Arizona Project is explicitly organized as a system whereby home/community, school, and an afterschool educational lab are combined. The community study is explicitly based on the belief that communities can be intellectual resources for schools, and their objective is to discover these community funds of knowledge. This knowledge, in turn, is brought into the afterschool lab for educational experimentation in a setting that is less constrained than a school classroom. The afterschool lab and the teacher study groups were proposed as spaces where staff development could occur simultaneously. Teachers could not only come to observe, they could try out some of their ideas in this context before implementing them in the classroom. The other three Intercambio Research Projects are smaller in scale and their emphasis on strategies for change are, thus, more focused in scope to community settings. The Alternative High School project focused on the teachers conceptual and practical changes in the classroom. The middle school project produced changes in the methodology and content of instruction, at the same time strengthening the relationship between students, researcher, and teacher. The East Harlem Afterschool Project is focused on the cognitive development of the children in relation to the curriculum and organization of instructional activities.

As we dialogued about our differences, we saw relatively few contradictions in underlying assumptions about change. The differences were more at a practical level and resulted in a very enriching exchange. Our conclusions were that not all problems can be dealt with at the same time nor can all opportunities be seized at any given point without the overall project losing its effectiveness. The independent goals and lives of the institutions represented (the schools, the CBOs, the boards of education, and the universities) pose different and context-specific requirements for change. Thus, we see that although we work with different aspects of the educational system, we have all come to see our projects as focused on developing new ways of thinking about educational processes and organizational structures.

Collaboration.   Any attempt to study education in connection to the complex social relationships and cultural practices of human beings, be it in classrooms or in community settings, requires the participation of different colleagues. This emphasis on collaborative activity implies the need to create new arrangements for research of learning, and of how to develop and sustain change in educational practice.

Our projects are collaboratives within schools and outside. The levels of collaboration differ. The UPR–San Juan II Project brings together the most varied groups of people and the greatest numbers of institutions, including professors, administrators, school administrators, support personnel, teachers, community agencies, and students and their families. Both the Arizona Project and the Alternative High School actively bring together three distinct groups: the school (including administrators and bilingual teachers), the community (parents and/or entire networks of exchange), and the university researchers and graduate students in an attempt "to combine basic research and educational intervention in a single project that arranges for a two-way flow of information between the school and other social institutions" (Cole & Griffin, 1987, p. 90). The East Harlem Afterschool Project was housed in a CBO, like the Alternative High School, but does not deal directly with schools. The collaborative in the middle school was initially more focused on the collaboration between the teacher, her students, and the researcher, but the research interest of the students that grew out of their concerns and connectedness with the life and soul of their community, have brought the parents and other staff into the project.

Three elements proposed by Tharp and Gallimore (1988) are central to our work. The first is how we have established joint projects. In most cases university personnel have initiated joint projects; some of the projects were encouraged by individual teachers (as in the middle school) or by members of the community (as in the alternative high school). A second element is the interdisciplinary research posture that all our projects have taken. This interdisciplinary nature of our work promotes a more holistic interpretation of what is occurring and takes into account the complexity and interrelationships of the issues involved. The third element is how each of the projects has connected what happens in schools and in communities to other contexts (e.g., the students' concern with homelessness in the East Harlem Afterschool Project with city policies, the chemical lot with the Environmental Protection Agency, and so forth).

Community as Resources.   Human thinking and development always occurs in sociocultural context. They are inseparable from human social and cultural activities. As Lave (1988) said, "the point is not so much that arrangements of knowledge in the head correspond in a complicated way to the social world outside the head, but that they are socially organized in such a fashion as to be indivisible" (p. 1).

The projects find their homes in Latino communities in New York, Arizona, and Puerto Rico. Low educational attainment in schools and low achievement are part of the educational legacy many of the Latino youth we work with face.

Whether in East Harlem, Brooklyn, or Cantera, educational failure (dropping out, low levels of literacy, etc.) is the main accomplishment of the educational system. But, educational failure is not the only reality the youth we work with face; the students and their communities are also victimized by inadequate health service delivery, low wages, prices of basic necessities beyond their means, substandard housing, violence, and drug-infested environments. Furthermore, they face a historical, sociocultural, and political relationship of subordination in relation to the structures and cultures of power. Thus, the social realities of everyday life for many of the youth is one of struggle and survival.

Yet, these students, and their families have ample social and intellectual resources that are generally not acknowledged nor used as a bases for organizing instruction. We start from the premise that the students' lived experiences, their cultural backgrounds, and their symbolic cultural referents are intellectual resources that can be powerful and transformative when connected to the learning experience. We believe that the culture and the experiences students bring to the act of learning should be the basis for developing the curriculum and the foundation for future growth. Their experiences as children living with economical constraints and their experiences as Puerto Ricans or other Latinos (i.e., language, beliefs, values, customs, and traditions), are the basis for determining what the context of the curriculum should entail. For example, the transformation of the initial curriculum on Ismael Rivera in San Juan II to a study of the community, the selection of topics such as teen pregnancy, AIDS, and homelessness in the Bronx middle school classroom, the study of Puerto Rican and barrio history in the East Harlem Afterschool, and the salience of the issues of civil rights and environmental health in the alternative high school in Brooklyn were ways in which the students' experiences became part of the curriculum.

The experiences and cultural background of students can also be the basis for determining how the instruction will be organized. One of the characteristics we had in common was the integration of curriculum across subjects. For example, in San Juan II history, language arts, and art were integrated; in Arizona writing and social action came together; integration also occurred in science, social studies, and language arts in the environmental science curriculum in the alternative high school; literacy and research were integrated in the Bronx project; and finally, computers and science were combined with knowledge about the history of the community in the East Harlem Afterschool Project.

The Nature of Teaching.   There is nothing natural (or neutral) about schools or other educational settings, they are culturally (historically and politically) created settings, characterized by certain discourse practices, socialization patterns, and differential expectations of success. The "nature of instruction" within these settings usually differs according to the social class standing of the students. Working-class and poor children, for example, generally receive a different type of instruction than students from wealthier classes. The former receive instruction that is rote, highly structured and redundant, and that contains a low intellectual content. Within these classrooms, the teacher is always in control, the students are assumed to possess little knowledge, and are allowed very little decision making or choice in their education (as was evident in the resistance of *El grupo de los 20* when asked to assume more responsibility for their schooling). This form of instruction is so common that it is easy to assume that this is how schooling must be for these children; these schools and classrooms are assumed to be a necessary part of the status quo, and they start even seeming "natural." However, when children are shown to succeed under modified instructional arrangements (as depicted in the projects presented herein), it becomes clear that the problems our children face in school must be viewed in great part, as a consequence of institutional arrangements that constrain children and teachers by not capitalizing on their talents, resources, and skills.

Not only are certain types of knowledge used to reinforce and mask unjust relationships of power, there are also certain ways of knowing and generating knowledge that serve the same function. Thus, the organization of knowledge within our projects aims at interconnectedness versus isolation and what drives them is the need for authentic and meaningful rather than contrived and decontextualized situations. Teaching is organized so that the cognitive and affective dimensions are tapped, whereby students and teachers jointly discover and generate new knowledge that will help them face problems or undertake projects in a collective way.

The social environment of teaching is created by people's actions and interactions. How teachers and students accomplish the instructional tasks is only partially conditioned by where and when they are interacting. The interpersonal aspects of teaching and learning are constructed by the people present and what they are doing. In other words, they serve as social contexts for each other.

The emphasis of our work is on studying persons-in-activity, rather than studying persons (especially students) as if divorced from contexts. Given that culture is not a "storehouse of artifacts" and that knowledge is not imparted to students in measured doses, the relationship between the learners and the teacher and among the learners change. They are now coparticipants involved in the act of learning and teaching. Students become sources of knowledge and authorities, they participate in determining the direction of the curriculum and they become reflective of their own individual and collective learning process. In other words, the students are also collaborators in building community.

Theory and Practice. We propose that educational research must not only analyze the different contexts of education, but must focus on creating fundamentally new and challenging instructional activities and environments. This transformation of practice, in effect, results in the transformation of the contexts of research, thereby addressing some of the limitations of research. Traditional formulations of research can be misleading because the shortcomings of theories of teaching and learning, in terms of their potential for changing practice, have been largely left unexamined.

Changes in educational practices, and theories about changing practice, must legitimately emerge from the collaborative attempts with teachers and others to modify and improve practice within specific social and historical circumstances. Just as there are no quick fixes in education, there are no grand theories that helped accomplish or circumvent the painstaking work that are represented in the joint efforts described in the preceding pages. Why and how students succeed or fail, we would argue, are inseparable questions whose answers must be found in social attempts to produce educational change.

REFERENCES

Brice-Heath, S. (1985). Literacy or literate skills? Consideration for ESL/EFL learners. In P. Larson, E.L. Judd, & S. Hesserschmidt (Eds.), *On Tesol 114: A brave new world for TESOL* (pp. 15–25). Washington, DC: TESOL.

Carrasco, R. L. (1984). *Collective engagement in the "segundo hogar": A microethnography of engagement in a bilingual first grade classroom.* Unpublished doctoral dissertation, Harvard University, Cambridge, MA.

Cole, M., & Griffin, P. (Eds.). (1987). *Contextual factors in education. Improving mathematics and science instruction for minorities and women.* Madison: Wisconsin Center for Educational Research, School of Education, University of Wisconsin.

Erickson, F. (1977). Some approaches to inquiry in school-community ethnography. *Anthropology and Education Quarterly, 8,* 58–69.

Greenberg, J. B. (1989). *Funds of knowledge: Historical constitution, social distribution and transmission.* Paper presented at the annual meeting of the Society for Applied Anthropology, Santa Fe, New Mexico.

Lave, J. (1988). *Cognition in practice.* Cambridge: Cambridge University Press.

Matin-Baro, I. (1989). La investigación y el cambio social. *Cuadernos de investigación* (Vol. 1). Puerto Rico: Centro de Investigaciones Educativas, Facultad de Educación, Rio Piedras, Universidad de Puerto Rico.

Quintero, A. H. (1989). The University of Puerto Rico's partnership project with schools: A case study for the analysis of school improvement. *Harvard Educational Review, 59,* 347–361.

Tharp, R., & Gallimore, R. (1988). *Rousing minds to life: Teaching, learning, and schooling in social contexts.* Cambridge: Cambridge University Press.

Torres-Guzmán, M. E. (1989). *El Puente/Teachers College research collaborative* (Final Report). Washington, DC: Hispanic Policy Development Project.

Torres-Guzmán, M. E. (1990). *Bringing it closer to home.* Paper presented at the Ethnography Forum at the University of Pennsylvania, Philadelphia, PA.

Velez-Ibañez, C. G. (1988). Network of exchange among Mexicans in the U.S. and Mexico: Local level mediating responses to national and international transformations. *Urban Anthropology, 17,* 27–51.

Wells, G. (1986). *The meaning makers.* Portsmouth, NH: Heinemann.

III

TRANSFORMING PEDAGOGY

Part III gives attention to that which goes on in the classroom, that is to learning, teaching, and the social relations and realities that frame them. High school students, a former public school teacher, and university-based educators are all the authors here; their perspectives, research, and experiences challenge the notions that students of color, particularly those who speak a language other than English at home, are disinterested, unmotivated, or disadvantaged learners. They also defy traditional assumptions about teaching and learning, curriculum, and student–student, student–teacher, and teacher–teacher relations.

The educational reform discourse and literature have given little attention to classroom pedagogy and even less to specific pedagogical concerns related to culturally and linguistically different students. National, state, and local reform efforts talk about standards, core values, assessment benchmarks, and teacher competencies but generally devote little or no attention to addressing the fact that the teaching and learning practices in place in most schools work to enable some and disable others. Of course those that are disabled are typically not the children of those involved in making the reforms – they are the students of color, bilingual students, and poor students, those outside of the White, middle-class norm that continues to structure and shape much of curriculum and instruction in urban, suburban, and rural school systems throughout the nation.

This section offers insight into some of the pedagogical issues and concerns that should be critically considered for culturally and linguistically different students and for all students living and studying in today's social world. Its focus is not on instructional recipes nor on programmatic placement or organization (e.g., bilingual education, ESL, mainstream education). Rather, it is to offer you, the reader, the opportunity to consider pedagogical problems and possibilities in ways you may have not before, to look through the lenses of the varied authors here—all of whom are engaged in work toward pedagogical and educational transformation.

The section begins with the reflections of Teresa Barrientos, a U.S.-born Puerto Rican and bilingual teacher who, about 1 year after this reflective piece was written, left the profession out of frustration. I chose to begin with her words because they help reveal the difficult, complex, and problematic realities of not just students but also teachers of color in White, hegemonic educational institutions. As Barrientos speaks about the school-based struggles that she faced as a Puerto Rican and bilingual teacher, you can begin to get a feel for the isolation, marginalization, and racism, for her anger and her strength. Recognition of such realities and emotions are absent in much of the discussion and literature on educational reform and on pedagogical change. Yet, authentic pedagogical change necessitates attention to the people—to the teachers and students—who are the participants and actors in the teaching and learning process, and to the social realities that structure and shape in-school and out-of-school living.

Barrientos' words should encourage thought about your own racial/ethnic background and how it positions you in your educational work, as well as thought about how school environment and support shapes personal and collective possibilities. Most importantly, they should serve as a reminder that pedagogical transformation requires a recognition of and a willingness to deal with societal ills, with the human elements that frame teachers' lives as well as the lives of students.

The chapter that follows (chapter 10) is collectively written by a group of present and former high school students—Mexican, Chicano/a, and Vietnamese—from Channel Islands High School in Oxnard, California who are actively working in their schools and community for educational and social change. The writing of the piece is demonstrative not only of their shared commitment to educate others and to promote a different kind of educational reform but is also demonstrative of their own pedagogical talents in terms of dialogue, problem posing, and collective learning. Inclusion of the authentic words and thoughts (not the adult interpretations) of students is rare in the educational literature but even rarer yet is an article written for educators by students.

In their chapter, the Students for Cultural and Linguistic Democracy (SCaLD), as they call themselves, discuss the problems with education and the possibilities critical pedagogy offers for transforming the curriculum, student–student, and student–teacher relationships and student voices. Drawing from the belief that curriculum and instruction must be grounded in social reality and that schools must make explicit the connections between teaching, learning, and students' everyday lives, they discuss how one critical teacher and his classroom at Channel Islands High School served as an initial motivation, challenge, and support for new understanding, thinking, and interaction. They then go on to chronicle how they, as students who because of their racial/ethnic and social backgrounds have been oppressed by the system, have come to look differently at their collective experiences and to struggle and take action to make change in the school, their communities, and in their own lives. Whether you are an activist, advocate, administrator, present or future teacher, or just an interested citizen, these students collectively written words offer powerful lessons for thinking about youth and for rethinking education.

In chapter 11, "I Like Making My Mind Work," Sonia Nieto counters the typical notion that there is something wrong with language minority students by focusing on what is right, including the ways their experiences, cultures, and languages can be used in more productive and beneficial ways in the classroom. Nieto discusses the research on effective curriculum for language minority students; to show how curriculum is operationalized in schools with language minority students and how schools might improve, she discusses findings from her own research with academically successful middle school and high school students from a variety of language and cultural backgrounds. The lessons that emerge from her research – raising academic expectations about students and using students' languages, cultures and family and community experiences in the classroom – are ones that all present and future teachers should particularly take heed of.

Chapter 12 takes a visionary look at a native language arts classroom for Latino children. Alma Flor Ada, an internationally recognized children's author and teacher educator, takes us beyond the overwhelmingly traditional and skills-based orientation that is typical of many language arts classrooms, particularly for poor and minority students and in bilingual education programs. Her constructed vision, one that can be applied to all racial/ethnic and language groups, is where children's realities are made central, where creativity, aesthetics, joy, and critical discussion abound. In so doing, Ada employs us to think beyond current pedagogical approaches and environments, to envision classrooms in which students can come to better understand themselves, their parents and communities, and come to be creative readers and writers – the authors of their own lives and their own realities. She offers us the opportunity to dream, to conjure up our own visions of pedagogical transformation, and then to work toward making this dream a reality.

The last chapter in this section (chapter 13) is written by a Boston-area high school student, Sandra Marcelino, who is immersed in the struggles, difficulties, and realities of adolescence, school, and urban living. In her chapter "OYE (Listen)!! Do You Understand. . . ," Sandra reflects on what it means to be a Latina in school and out and how teachers, schools, and society tend to ignore, exclude, and not understand the complexities that she and others carry. In a strong, direct voice, Sandra speaks directly to teachers, recounting her own experience, challenging stereotypes and limits, illuminating emotions, and presenting the issues and student needs that must underlie and shape classroom reform and pedagogical transformation.

Each of the chapters in this section present different understandings and possibilities for how classroom pedagogy might change. In the different voices, however, there are common threads, common pleas for more radical transformation. As you read the chapters in this section, it may be helpful to consider the following questions:

- How do the authors similarly or differently understand pedagogical transformation? Does their position—student, teacher, university-based educator/researcher—appear to influence their understanding? How does their own sociocultural background and lived experience seem to shape their perspectives of and their approaches to transformation?
- What kinds of pedagogical transformations are they suggesting? Who are the players that can make these transformations possible? What role do teachers, students, parents, and community play (individually, collectively, in interaction) in these transformations?
- How do the chapters support or challenge your own pedagogical experiences, practices, and beliefs? How do they support or challenge your experiences as a student?
- What lessons can you take from the chapters for your present or future educational work?

A Window:
Testimony of a
"Minority" Teacher

Teresa Barrientos

Another day to defend my language, culture, and history. Another day to defend my parents and students. When will it all end? Will I burn-out, give up, resign, or do I continue to defend the rights of my parents and students? If I stop, who will suffer? I cannot give up! I still have some fight left in me! As long as I know who I am, as long as I have love and pride in my cultural heritage; I will continue to defend my rights as a Puerto Rican and the rights of my Puerto Rican students and parents.

The above dialogue is one that is constantly in the back of my mind. It changes depending on the events of the day. It is difficult to come home and feel positive about your job as a minority teacher if you are constantly confronting faculty or staff members of your school on your fundamental right to speak your language of birth, and the fundamental rights of your parents and students. After years of being on the defensive you begin to feel as if each day is just one more day of struggling for survival in a school system that just doesn't care.

The negative racial attitudes are sometimes down right obvious but most of the time they are subtle; such as sitting in the teachers lounge and noting the obvious segregation among bilingual and mainstream staff. Watching a mainstream teacher observe in silence a group of bilingual teachers and aides communicating in their native language. The facial expression showing no signs of feelings, but from experience and past confrontations, you know what she is thinking.

Being in a workshop discussing multicultural education, and actively participating; saying, "The curriculum should reflect the culture of the students." Once again seeing the expressionless faces, knowing what they are thinking. "Send them back to Puerto Rico on the banana boat they came on!"

Having your rice and beans for lunch, and having a teacher say, "What is that smell?" A look of disgust on her face and you respond, "It's my lunch."

Having to explain to the secretary of your school that a hispanic parent is not going to walk 2 or 3 miles to attend a parent meeting in the evening; and the response, "Well, I remember walking 10 miles in the snow so I could attend a parent meeting."

These are only a few examples of the daily battles a minority person has to endure. It becomes a matter of survival that begins to take the form of a daily dialogue between yourself, family, and friends. It is sad that the fate of the minority teacher in the end is to survive. We begin with commitment and enthusiasm and end-up struggling to maintain that commitment and enthusiasm as a result of constant devaluing of our identity. Then we wonder why there is a scarcity of bilingual people.

10

Reclaiming
Our Voices

Students for Cultural
and Linguistic Democracy (SCaLD)

In April 1992, at a staff bilingual/bicultural development meeting regarding changing area demographics and the high dropout rate of district "Mexicans," a group of multiethnic teachers and students decided it was time to take a risk. Challenging the educational system itself, these individuals identified the leading causes of failing student–teacher relationships and the high push-out rate on campus as racism along with curriculum that was completely unrelated to students' realities.

The main presentation was an unprecedented display of voicing. Students formed a panel in front of the entire faculty and shared their personal experiences with discrimination from faculty members. For their voicing, the group was chastised and ridiculed by the faculty, and peers, but their struggle, although painful, is proving to be worthwhile. From the original panel, seven students and one determined English as a second language (ESL) educator continue on.

Today, that panel is known throughout the state of California as the Students for Cultural and Linguistic Democracy (SCaLD). We represent a wide spectrum of ethnicities, from Latino/Latina to Vietnamese, and from recently migrated ESL students to the number one honors student in our high school. Collectively, our main goal is to rediscover education for cultural and linguistic democracy and transform educational pedagogy to include emanicipating curriculum from a critical real-world perspective. The reason for our coming together can be summed up best by this quote: "Never again will we walk away and let the voices of our people stay forgotten."

We as SCaLD have written this chapter collaboratively. Our collective experience is a result of what we have shared and discovered through our co-learning. This chapter is about our perspectives on the problems we have seen and encountered in education as multiethnic students and teachers today, and the possibilities that a more critical pedagogy can offer. Members and their ages at the time of writing include Adriana Jasso (age 18), Jose Luis Serrano (age 18), Marcela Sustaita (age 18), Minh Trinh (age 17), Pedro May (age 20), Rocio Soto (age 20), Nick Crisosto (age 17), and Bill Terrazas, Jr. (educator).

THE PROBLEM: EDUCATION

This morning around 9 a.m., Joey got expelled from high school because of behavioral problems. Funny because, well, it was right about this time of year, a year ago, that I had a strange encounter with Joey.

It happens that a small group of friends and I were returning from a Bon Jovi concert and were on our way to drop off a couple of guys. As we accidentally detoured into a dirty rundown trailer park, I saw a young, slender guy wearing dark pants, three sizes bigger than his own, and a white, JC Penny X-large T-shirt (all homeboys wear JC Penny T-shirts). He was sitting to the side of the road, beside a fallen porch rubbing his arms and legs desperately because well, it was about 4 o'clock in the morning and it was cold! I recognized him as Joey (high school freshman at the time and in Mr. Stone's Math 9 Basic class where I was a paraeducator).

Joey said, "What's up?"

"Joey!" I said, "What the hell are you doing out here at this hour? You forgot you have a test tomorrow or actually today in a little while?" The truth of the matter was that Joey couldn't have cared less about the exam.

Joey went on and gave me a sad story about not being able to sleep because his mother's boyfriend had been drinking with a bunch of friends and had been cranking some oldies at full volume all night long. Joey had an aunt across the street but he felt he shouldn't bother her because she had just lost her youngest son in a drive-by shooting and he didn't want to give her any more problems. I told him I understood everything but that he had to hang in there when the going got rough. But to be honest, Joey's behavior in class and his attitude toward teachers and his studies showed that he never liked school; that was the real problem.

Well, Joey is now out of the school system and out of peoples' hair. This means one less bad attitude for the teachers, one less headache for the administrators, but unfortunately, one more homeboy walking the streets and defacing private property by spray painting on walls and breaking windows.

At a recent Faculty Meeting/Staff Development Workshop, some teacher who for some reason liked Joey made an accusation to the faculty that teachers were not being sensitive to Joey, and others like him. But as the other teachers pointed out they didn't have anything to do with him screwing up. It wasn't their fault he didn't understand numbers. It wasn't their fault he didn't dig Shakespeare, and it definitely wasn't their fault he had to light up the school's trash cans to get some attention. It was his, his parents', and his friends' fault.

The school system knew that Joey needed guidance. This is why Joey was labeled "at risk" upon his arrival in high school, for his own good. He was always a trouble maker. He was hostile and rude toward everyone. It seemed like he was always angry and that he just didn't want to learn. What is a teacher supposed to do with a kid like that? Joey was expected to dropout or get kicked out before the end of his sophomore year, and he did. Everyone knew it would happen from the day he arrived. The school system has been dealing with the "Joeys" and their problems since Day 1. Getting rid of the kid and his problems is for his own good. This way he can get a job, and the kids who want to work hard and really deserve a good education can get one without all of Joey's interruptions.

Joey's story illustrates the problems, tensions, and conflicts in today's schools. As present and former high school students who are Chicano/Chicana, Mexicano/Mexicana, and Vietnamese, we know from experience that there is little or no connection between our real lives and education. The struggles to stay in school and to cope with life are, for us, daily struggles.

The ideal goal of the system of education in California, if not in the entire country, is to see all students reach their full potential, isn't it? Sadly to say, statistics show that California has one of the highest dropout rates in the nation. More than 14% of 16- to 19-year-olds dropout; for Latinos/Latinas the push-out rate is more than 52%. Higher and higher percentages of teenagers in California alone are reportedly involved in sexual activity resulting in pregnancy, involved in drugs and alcohol, involved in gangs, not to mention the increasing percentages of teenagers who choose suicide as an escape from life. The ideal is far from being real.

The realities of the situation of a large percentage of students continue to go unrecognized. Several more real-life stories serve as examples:

Sixteen-year-old Benito Garcia found it easier and less frustrating to go to work in the celery fields with his father and help out with the bills, than to stay in school. By doing so, he could also save up for a car. Benito seems to be doing okay, although he sometimes finds it hard to sleep at night because of the pains in his lower back.

Fourteen-year-old Amelia Castro has just gotten out of the hospital after a cocaine overdose. Amelia is now on probation and has a police record because of substance abuse.

Eighteen-year-old David Morales, an "A" student in high school, had been going on burglary missions with his older uncles for several months. At first it was nerve wrenching but after a while he figured that since all he had to do was drive the get-away car, he really wasn't causing that much harm. He thought he would never have to hurt anyone. Plus the easy money was breathtaking. It wasn't till not long ago, David saw one of his uncles get shot while trying to flee from the scene of the crime. David, in a moment of panic, responded with gunfire and killed a man with a shot in the chest. David had never served time in jail. Now he is ranked "red band" in prison and has a good chance of making death row.

Three years ago, Ruth Pinela left school as a sophomore and ran off with her boyfriend. She now has three kids to take care of so she holds two jobs. Ruth gets beaten by her husband quite often.

Straight percentages never mean anything when talking about people, and their lives. However, Benito, Amelia, David, Ruth, and Joey are the people behind the percentages, and they have real problems. There is nothing simple, and nothing that deserves a clinical definition about any of these students; so how do they receive help? How do they become a part of the ideal hope of education, and overcome their circumstances, and become caring, knowledge-able individuals?

Dropout rates, teenage pregnancy, sex, drugs, gangs, and a whole slew of other problems face society everyday, and our teachers are the ones in contact with these problems the most. It is not enough to try and solve these problems separately. There are questions that have to be asked before attempting a solution. Why are students so bored sick of school? Why do students dropout? Why do students get married so abruptly? Why do students turn to drugs and alcohol? Why do students, only 15 years old, kill themselves? It is because teenagers are so entirely reckless and destructive, or is it something else, something deeper, something not easily seen or shared?

Benito Garcia (fieldworker) knew he would accomplish several things when he went to work in the fields. Not only was he helping his family and himself economically, but he was also escaping an ineffective, half-done bilingual program; one that was run by unqualified teachers who really weren't there for the right reasons; a program that was so watered down that it made him feel incompetent and even stupid; a program that was completely unaware of the frustrations and struggles of entering a new culture; a program ignorant of the difficulties of learning a new language; a program that completely turned Benito off from school.

Amelia Castro (drug user) wasn't just seeking a cool high when she overdosed on cocaine. She was seeking acceptance, appreciation, approval, and respect from her peers; something she had never felt before from anyone, especially from her teachers who blamed her for not trying hard enough to be polite and a good person.

David Morales (jock, school boy, murderer) never though he would hurt anyone, but David had no will power. His self-esteem was low. The only way he knew to get attention and feel good about himself was to do what others told him was right, including his parents, teachers, and peers. His weak character allowed him to be manipulated and pressured by his uncles. It also allowed him to become blinded by easy money.

Young mother and wife, Ruth Pinela, wasn't really eager to have kids and get married. Actually she really didn't know her boyfriend all that well when she left with him. All she knew was that the guy promised her a better life than the one she had at home, and so, thinking she would be better off, she left with him.

As students, the real stories of our lives are denied, ignored, and neglected. The deeper questions that get at the "whys" are seldom, if ever, asked. Yet, when you look at the problems in the classroom and the problems that show up in so many students' lives, you find connections.

A lot of these "visible problems" (the problems that everyone sees all the time, like gangs, teenage pregnancy, and graffiti) aren't actually the real problems. These problems, however disquieting, are only the consequences of deeper issues. Students are blowing off steam, running away from abuse, trying to find a place where they are accepted, and in a desperate sort of way, trying to solve the real problems that are hurting them (and us) so much. It is difficult to understand how joining a gang and beating up other teenagers is a solution, for example, to the fact that parents don't have time for their children. Similarly it is difficult to understand how getting high on "pot" and snorting cocaine solves a student's frustrations about how to deal with sexual harassment or molestation by a teacher.

It is not that the activity is a solution to the problems. It is that the "action" provides an opportunity to ignore, and hide from having to face up to the problems, even though that oasis of action is another problem, but now it is a problem for someone else, and a temporary solution for students, like us.

To most of society, and teachers, this sounds logical, and is something that can be accepted. Sure, a kid has problems at home with his dad so he starts not being able to concentrate on his homework, and so he drops out of school, leaves home (but eventually) gets a job, gets married, and lives happily ever after, right? The lack of confidence, self-esteem, and parental support appear to be solid grounds on which one can justify students wanting to quit school. It is not the teachers fault. Does that mean that teacher's can cross their arms and give up? Is the situation useless, or is there something else, an even more severe problem, that is rectified would irradicate all these other problems?

Teachers are the ones who are with students 8 hours a day, so how can the educational system not be contributing to all these problems? Has our educational system really taken assertive steps to try and reach these students who have had extremely difficult experiences? Has our educational system tried to reach the parents in a sincere and affective manner? Has our system really tried to team up with these students and parents, and does our educational system want to? Or, does the idealistic goal of "education" only apply to an elite, minority of the population?

The truth is that our educational system is often insensitive toward its students. Many teachers and administrators are not looking for ways to help students with the "source of the problems" in their lives. Instead, they are looking for ways to cover up or eliminate the "visible problems," but that's not a solution. In order for society to find the real problems, the "hidden problems," it is absolutely critical that we examine our educational system itself.

We believe that the problem lies with teachers and their relationships with students, teacher training, with classroom pedagogy, and with the orientation and focus of the educational system. In their preparation, teachers specialize in a certain area, whether it is algebra, earth science, or composition. This training places value on the academic alone; it never actually gets into the realms of building up a student's self-esteem through student empowerment, affective dialogue, active listening, problem solving, and cross-cultural awareness. Why aren't we training our teachers on these topics? Is "students coming into class with problems" a 1990s phenomenon? Hasn't it always been this way and won't it always be this way? Isn't it problematic that many teachers see social realities and the curriculum as separate? That they continue to ask: "Why should I load myself with more stressful work and concern myself with the students' lives?"

Part of the problem lies with the fact that what is being offered to preparing teachers and to high school students isn't reality. Education should not be preparing to live in an abstract, distant, world, it must be living, today. Students have backgrounds, history, and most importantly, students are human beings. The human aspect of teaching and learning is one that is most often neglected. Teachers need to know that the passion for their subject and the desire for students to succeed in the context of the content of their lesson plans must never take precedence over the desire to see the students grow as humans. This means that even before the love of learning, a teacher's attitude must be "I am here because I love my students, and I want them to love themselves."

If teachers were encouraged to enter the profession with the mentality that the love they felt for their subject is great, but second to the love they feel for their students, then the question "Why should I put up with the extra burden of dealing with the student's lives?" wouldn't even come up. A teacher that loves his or her students realizes that students are human beings with strengths, weaknesses, and of course, struggles. A teacher who loves his or her students realizes that such human characteristics and feelings are part of each unique and special student and those feelings and emotions can't be turned on and off like a light switch.

A teacher who loves his or her students refuses to become part of the "hidden problem." In other words, such a teacher would treat someone like Joey (the boy who was expelled from high school) with respect and would focus his or her efforts on the "source of the problem," referring the student to some tutoring, counseling, or simply by lending an ear when needed, instead of attacking the "visible problem" (Joey breaking school regulations) by simply expelling him from class or labeling him at risk, thus letting him know that he is already viewed as less capable and won't have to work at being a slacker, it's just expected of him. A teacher who loves his or her students looks for solutions to the high failure rates in the classroom instead of looking for excuses to justify the class' low achievements.

In actuality, teachers themselves are not the real problems; it's their training, and it's the system. The idea of loving and getting close to students frightens many teachers. To cope with this, too many teachers adopt a "Rubik's Cube" view of what students are ideally supposed to be like. A Rubik's Cube is a toy made up of little cubes that can be manipulated and all put together to form a larger cube. When everything is in its proper place the cube has a different color on each side. Often, teachers see students as if like the cubes, they were made of many separate parts, each with little or no connection to the another. For example, if the red side of the human cube represents the artistic side, then it would be said that the red side should only emerge in the art class. If at all seen anywhere else, it would be said that the student was disruptive and lacked concentration. If the black side represents the personal problem side, then its proper place to show up would be in the "hall of personal problems," where ever that might be, "but not in my class." And if the baby blue side of the human cube represents the academic side, then that's the side that belongs in class. A speck of black within the blue will automatically label the cube dysfunctional and therefore less capable. In other words, during "baby blue" time, the other components of the cube, because they are unrelated should be nicely tucked away and asleep, because they are "irrelevant" during academic time, and are not considered part of the lesson plans.

Is this so? Are we actually tiny independent particles put into one baggy? Don't these particles ever intermingle with each other? Of course they do; they do so all the time. Why does it seem easier to teachers to try to ignore the fact that we as humans carry a load of frustrations? To act as if these frustrations, issues, problems have no impact on the learning and teaching process?

Teachers need to realize that students are humans. We have experiences, bad and good, and we each have our own family, culture, and traditions. In the traditional educational system, a student never gets validated for being who he or she is, only for answering the questions out of the back of the book correctly. For students of color, especially for "new arrivals" or first or second generation students of color, there is nothing in the educational system that they can identify with. Our culture, language, life history is severed, there is nothing in the content or the relations that is recognizable to our lives. If the education that is being offered to students has nothing to do with our lives, why should we consider education anything important?

The real problem society faces is that the educational system is set up in a way that neglects the fact that students are very much individuals. It starts with the way the system has trained our teachers to feel that it is better to stay away from touchy issues, like family, sex, and life, since they have enough problems with their students already, if they don't want to be overwhelmed. To those teachers who do fear they'll be overwhelmed, a question: Aren't you being overwhelmed already? Look closely at your present situation. Are your students bored? Do they sleep in class? Do they disrupt the class, curse at you, or simply ignore you and your curriculum. Surprise! All of these are different ways in which students express their personal problems in your class; by ignoring these problems you are pushing students to act out and resist more. As a result you end up having to deal with your students and their frustrations on more and more difficult terms.

Schools point the blame for social problems like gangs and drugs at our "out-of-control" youth or decaying families. Parents who work too many hours to support their families, who in turn are forced to neglect their children, may be a source of many students needing to search for the validation they find in gangs and drugs. But the deepest and most serious problem in society isn't parents, students, or even negligent teachers. The real problem is that the educational system is not designed to create individual, free-thinking students. The system is dehumanizing. It forces us as students to forget our family, cultural truths, history, and how good it feels to be loved; it teaches us that validation and success is an "A."

The educational system needs to be transformed. As students, we are the future. We deserve the opportunity to learn to speak and be listened to and to act in the world to make ourselves strong; we deserve the best education possible.

> Fifteen-year-old Roberto Chaires is mentally disabled and requires special one-on-one assistance. Despite this, Beto has been put in ESL classes with students who are moving much too fast for him. The reason he has been put in these classes is because Beto speaks only Spanish and despite the 75% Latino/Latina population in the school, and despite the fact that this percentage has been increasing for the past 9 years, the teachers in the Special Education program only speak English. Recently, Beto was asked by one of his teachers if he liked school. He answered that he didn't. The teacher, with a puzzled look on his face asked him, "Why not? Do you have problems at home?"

Everyone involved in the educational process needs to begin searching critically for answers and stop blaming the victims.

THE NEED FOR CRITICAL PEDAGOGY: THE NEED FOR VOICES

The history of the world, the history of this country, is that the dominant culture attempts to conquer all other cultures and assimilate the people. The biggest qualm of the government of the United States is that if the people don't like who's in office or what the legislature is, then why don't they get up and vote for the changes they desire? The answer to that question is very simple; the dominant culture in control of the government realizes the power of voices and does not want the masses to make change; the masses are forced to remain silent. From Day 1 in education, students of color are programmed into silence. This silence carries on into their adult lives in their work, church, and advanced education and takes away their spirit and energy to stand up to oppression and make change.

To make change, to keep this country strong, to bring peace to the world, the voices of the masses must not remain silent. Decisions cannot continue to be made by the dominant culture for the good of the people. We believe that the only way to achieve a true, free, fair, democracy (and a democratic education) is to stop training the majority of people on this earth into silence, and a minority of the elite into power. Education should be learning to voice and not allowing yourself to be oppressed.

All throughout this country, everyday, students are being hurt by the authoritarian, oppressive, traditional educational system. The destructive impact of the system is most severe in the lives of multiethnic students; the implanting of servility and silence is coupled with discrimination and institutionalized racism. Rather than an enabling, empowering education, the 13 million students of color, as well as all other students, receive a disabling education of silence.

At Channel Islands High School in Oxnard, California (87.2% multiethnic students), we have worked collaboratively with one teacher to implement a very different kind of education. This radical teaching methodology known as Critical Pedagogy is far from traditional. It is based on students' lives, families, and everyday social realities and is designed to empower oppressed students of color and bring voices to the silent masses. With knowledge and the discovered power in their voices, Critical Pedagogy challenges and empowers al students to stand up for their rights, to take risks and to act to transform their community and rid society of ignorance and injustices through understanding and communication.

Critical Pedagogy is an educational theory first introduced to us by Paulo Freire. Its focus is to create critically conscientious and thinking individuals through dialogue, collective experience, and collective action, who with their newly found voices and knowledge will transform their community and challenge the oppressive educational institutions. Students learn about themselves and their cultures but most importantly see themselves in relation to the world and all its people. Students' strengths are the focus of the curriculum, a curriculum that is developed collaboratively by both teacher and students. Emphasis is placed on validation rather than reproaches for failures.

The most radical aspect of Critical Pedagogy is how freedom from the oppressive authoritarian power structure in the classroom and the opportunity to voice opinions and share personal experience, transforms students and teachers, alike. Everyone is a co-learner, and a co-teacher; no one is taught; everyone is empowered; everyone becomes a protagonist of his or her own life; no one is silent.

We believe there is a need for Critical Pedagogy in this country, in the world. Critical Pedagogy helps us to rethink education's focus and possibilities. Education can be a key to peace, when it is not discriminatory and disabling. It can bring about emancipation through understanding and can allow students to explore their realities, to question society, and to take collective action to transform oppressive conditions, including the educational system itself.

OUR CRITICAL CLASSROOM

In Room 18, at Channel Islands High School, Bill Terrazas, Jr. (T, as we affectionately refer to him) has been teaching for 20 years. Over the past 3 years each of us has had the chance to either be in one of his ESL classes or English 12 classes for seniors, or has had the chance to be a guest speaker for one of his classes. The only way our student panel, SCaLD, could have ever formed is a credit to T's unique, empowering educational attitude. T's class is much more than an English class. His dedication to using Critical Pedagogy techniques has transformed Room 18 into a breeding ground for socially conscious student activists. We all understand how vital education is to freeing multiethnic groups from oppression. Room 18 is a critical classroom filled with problem-posing minds.

When you walk into our critical classroom, the first thing you are most likely to see is a poster on the door that says, "Learning is Living, Not Preparing to Live. Enter at your own Risk and Dialogue."

The next thing most likely to strike you are the brightly colored posters of our collective writings on themes relating to our real, every day lives. These posters are plastered on the walls, ceiling, and in every corner of the room, all showcases for any one who enters the room to see. Our writings include our autobiographies, cultural books, morals and values booklets, and stories of our real-life struggles.

There are motivating posters such as "No Guts, No Glory!" "No Pain, No Gain!" "Take a Risk!" "To make workers you must make humans first!" and "Success is the far side of Failure." You also find the flags of various countries, pictures of Martin Luther King, Jr., Malcolm X, and the United Farmworker's flag or other civil and human rights materials.

When you walk into our critical classroom it will be very obvious to you that you are not dealing with a teaching attitude or a learning attitude that conforms in any way to the authoritarian, traditional educational ways. This critical classroom is designed to allow active learning to take place, not directive teaching.

Traditional classrooms have students lined up in desks in several rows. When the bell rings, students know to be in their seats, attentive, waiting for the teacher's instructions. The teacher stands up in front of the class, looming over the students, and teachers. The teacher has all the power, controls everything that happens (or tries to), and is the absolute authority in the classroom.

In our critical classroom our teacher is no longer a demi-god; our teacher is someone there to learn, just like everyone else. Everyone sits in circles or at round tables and there is no longer the physical reminder that "I am the teacher. I am right. Don't even think about telling me I am wrong."

Our critical classroom is facilitated by a motivating teacher who truly loves and cares for his students. T is a student and we as students are teachers. We all work together to learn collaboratively. The teacher is no longer the problem solver with all the answers. He is a problem poser who stands by the side of his students and struggles to find the answers by looking at the world and thinking critically about everything that is going on in the world. Every one has a voice and knows the power that voice carries. In this classroom, education starts with dialogue and collective sharing, growing into a collective experience that leads to our collective action outside the classroom; learning is no longer restricted to the confines of the classroom walls. As students, we are able to get a sense that what we are learning is something that is relevant to our lives, to understanding who we are in the world.

THE CURRICULUM: OUR VOICES

The curriculum in a critical classroom does not come from a textbook written by someone on the other side of the continent. The curriculum forms out of discussions that are vital to the learning process; it is a problem-posing curriculum, geared so that students become problem solvers in their lives. The curriculum allows us to learn to voice, dialogue about the world, share and synthesize our social realities into one collective experience, and then take collective action to improve social reality by transforming educational policy; the curriculum empowers students so they can transform themselves.

During these discussions, it is not merely academic experiences that are our topics. In our classroom, for example, the themes range from our experiences with divorce, discrimination, gang violence, abuse, sex, and drugs, to whatever other topics might be relevant to our everyday real lives. Other themes form from present day history, like the U.S. interventions in Somalia and even local events like the restructuring of the school's schedule and classes and what impact that would have on the student body.

Critical Pedagogy begins with our voices as students. Because the curriculum has so much to do with us, our discussions take on a very dynamic form. Gradually, all the students begin to see how we are affected by the topic, and eventually we find in ourselves the desire to express these connections. At first, because being listened to is so foreign to most students, it can be difficult to voice. As time goes on, and the students begin to see how important speaking up for yourself is, they begin to voice. The problems that we are being faced with every day are the topics and to find the solutions to these problems we know we must share our experiences and voice to the entire class. When students reclaim their voices, they find the power to radically change their reality.

A brown "little Mexicana" went to Room 18 two years ago. Like many students, all she wanted was to learn English so she could get out of ESL classes and into the college preparatory courses. This "little Mexicana" learned lots of English, and something else, something that no one had ever tried to teach her before. She learned that she had a "voice." She learned that she was someone other than just a "Hispanic girl." She learned that she didn't want to be "Hispanic" or anything else people decided to label her. She wanted everyone to know that she was "Mexicana" and that she was proud of her "cultura."

She voiced to the whole class and learned to listen and dialogue and respect the whole class. Her voicing let her see in herself that she had love and something more to offer the world than just a fieldworker. Her voicing also let the class see into her and accept her for who she was. This "little Mexicana" found her soul, like so many of us when we have the chance to express our true feelings and see who we are. Voicing helps us find out that we are capable of loving those people who are different than us.

This voicing does more than just let the students' opinions be heard, it lets us feel the power, and the abilities we have. The voicing of struggles breaks the silence, which for so many students of color was the only thing we knew, and the transformation within us as humans begins, and empowers others to share and add to the discussion. Voicing is the first step students take as they discover the power they have within themselves and begin to transform their lives.

What is unique about our collective discussions is that they are not dominated by the teacher or the seemingly most intelligent person in the class. All the discussions are dialogues, with everyone voicing what they feel, as well as actively listening to the opinions and feelings of others. For instance, when we talk about relationships between guys and girls, we do it on two separate days. On the first day, the girls might have the chance to get asked questions and share their ideas first, then the guys would get to respond and share some of their ideas. On the second day, the guys would get asked questions and they would get the first chance to share their ideas, then the girls would get to respond and share their ideas. In this way, both sides of an issue would have a chance to voice and both sides would have a chance to listen. Our dialogue would give us the chance to come to a consensus about relationships or at least learn about how our feelings as guys or girls can differ.

DIALOGUE/COLLECTIVE SHARING

When the teacher in a traditional classroom speaks, everyone is expected to listen. When a student in a traditional classroom speaks, usually it is in response to a question posed by the teacher. The only listening that takes place is by the teacher who listens for the right response, and if the response isn't there, then the teacher explains what the correct answer is; the class is expected to learn.

Voicing lets students express themselves, but dialogue lets students learn. Dialogue helps teachers and students become learning partners; now learning is a give and take relationship. Dialogue is a discussion where everything anyone has to say is viewed by the entire class as a valid opinion. We learn to risk by sharing personal experiences with everyone in the class, building trust, tolerance, and solidarity. Students are validated, nurtured, and encouraged to participate, especially when they see others participating. There is no fear of being told your answers or opinions are wrong nor is there fear of being scorned by anyone for our opinions; we know that no one will laugh at us. Everyone learns that there can be many right opinions on one subject and to live in a multicultural society you need to learn to respect every individual's point of view. Students become open-minded and learn to respect others for their differences as well as to be proud of themselves, their histories, cultural truths, and experiences.

Once students learn how strong their voices are in our classroom, they don't want to stop using them, but voicing isn't enough. Students must learn to listen and dialogue. Dialoguing about problems we face in the world helps us to not only release some of their own frustrations, but it also shows us that we are not alone in any of our situations, problems, and experiences. Collective dialoguing, or collective sharing of personal experiences is the unified investigation students participate in when discussing a problem; it is a way to research our own lives and provide ourselves with validation. There is an explosion of knowledge during the sharing exchange that is nothing like knowledge in the traditional educational system; it is knowledge that comes from exploring issues that are completely relevant to our social and cultural realities, communities, and the world around us. In our class, we have seen that dialogue and collective sharing create a radical transformation in students' awareness of themselves and their social realities. Slowly, students begin to understand that they are not alone in their struggles and can begin to search for answers collectively.

THE COLLECTIVE EXPERIENCE

When students have the opportunity to share collectively with one another their thoughts, feelings, and struggles, they have the opportunity to see that they are not alone. The solidarity that the students feel gives them a sense of strength. Voicing and dialogue create a unique phenomenon in the classroom. Students don't just learn facts, they create knowledge and a collective experience about the society they live in and what problems there are within that society. The power of the authoritarian teacher is gone, and the students new, deeper awareness of their realities unifies them.

The collective experience is more than just listening to others' ideas, it is taking everyones' ideas and synthesizing the ideas into the idea. The collective experience is the understanding that students have after they voice and dialogue and share collectively. Not only do we begin to see new points of views, we begin to see relationships between ideas and opinions. Most importantly, we are not just exposed to opinions that may be different than our own, we are exposed to the reasons for these other ideas. Such a process offers an opportunity to know and understand why someone would choose to think differently, and this understanding promotes an open-mindedness and respect for one another. This is a radical education process that helps destroy the walls of ignorance, fear, and prejudice.

Through the collective experience, each student has access to a broad background of knowledge about the world as a whole. New traditions, morals, and values help the students examine their own set of ideas and decide if there is anything new that they themselves agree with and would like to adopt as their own. The collective experience helps students realize and appreciate the beauty, complexity, diversity, and mystery of their existence. The understanding gained in the collective experience knocks down walls that may have made the students feel confined and helps the students conquer their inability to communicate with others.

The collective experience is growth. The students are actively engaged in thinking about their own struggles, as well as struggles of past and present day historical personalities, and are able to learn about how those struggles have the potential to shape their own ideals. Collective experience lets the students be involved in learning tasks that stimulate the growth of their abilities to think, feel, and question. Students then will learn to find ways to sort out their deepest longings, thoughts, and feelings. The collective experience allows students to feel the connections they have with others in the struggles in their lives and the solidarity they create gives them the strength to question their social reality and seek change where it is necessary and justice where there is injustice.

COLLECTIVE ACTION

Critical Pedagogy is an educational methodology geared for more than just acquiring knowledge. Without the authoritarian system of education students explore a foreign curriculum, a curriculum made up of their life histories and cultural truths. Voicing, dialogue, and collective sharing help students create a collective experience that gives them the strength to question their social situation. The knowledge of the collective experience coupled with the power and willingness to risk from the students voicing and dialoguing transforms the students individually and frees them from oppression and silence.

The students' personal transformations leave them with the need to transform their communities as well as the oppressive, authoritarian, educational system, and fight for justice and equity. The students know the power of their individual voices, and with their collective experience and understanding, they understand the power of their unified voices. The students can now take collective action and challenge oppression.

"The whole is greater than the sum of all its parts," is the power of Critical Pedagogy. The collective education in the classroom spreads out into the community and what happens in the classroom, happens outside as well. Working together, students, parents, teachers, and the community can take action to create a political base and not only challenge, but transform the authoritarian, oppressive educational system. When the masses that were once silent speak out, the government must listen; the academians who have failed, the policymakers who have failed, the university teaching methods that have failed all must change.

Collective action occurs when students and community realize that injustice prevails, not freedom, and that the power to transform society is theirs. Students are able to go out into the community and motivate their parents and teachers to persuade oppressive administration that change is desired. Critical Pedagogy does more than provide students with an education. Critical Pedagogy provides students with the opportunity to empower themselves, take action to empower their community, and use the political power of the masses to create radical change and overthrow the authoritarian power of the oppressive educational system.

CRITICAL PEDAGOGY IN ACTION

In Room 18 at Channel Islands High School, the largest and most ethnically diverse campus in the Oxnard Union High School District with 87.2% students of color, Critical Pedagogy has been put into practice every day. As present and former students from the ESL class and senior English class, we have not only been voicing and dialoguing, we have been challenging the educational system and taking collective action to bring about change.

Every day, the students in Room 18, all students of color, had the opportunity to voice and dialogue, and even though at first everyone didn't feel comfortable about voicing and sharing of their personal experiences, eventually we we're all actively participating in the class discussions. During the Friday Cultural Awareness series we not only explored our different ethnicities and cultures, we talked about common problems that all people of color face. We began to ask questions like, "Why is the student government mostly non-Mexicano/ Mexicana when there is 60% Mexicano/Mexicana population?" "Why aren't there any real bilingual teachers for Vietnamese, and Philippino/Philippina students?" "Why are all the bilingual classes considered remedial and are used as a dumping ground for multiethnic students?" and most importantly, "Do we think it's fair?"

By voicing and dialoguing about what we had experienced in school we were able to see that even though the "minorities" were the majority, the people of color had no real representation and no real power. All the activities were run in English; it also seemed as if the representatives of the student body in the student government weren't listening to any students of color. We began to look more closely at the school curriculum, discovering that to graduate every student was required to take a world civilizations class that only touched upon European civilizations, as well as an American government class. What little view students were given of Latin America in any class was limited to the "Christopher Columbus syndrome," where our ancestors have been portrayed as unorganized savages waiting for the imperialistic European to bring technology and civilization to their worlds. There were no ethnic studies classes or any real multicultural classes with a true cross-cultural curriculum that genuinely tried to validate every culture for its own accomplishments and worth.

We also noticed that a lot of the bilingual students didn't like to speak in their mother tongue at school and that a lot of immigrant students didn't like to talk about their culture at school either. We began to question why students didn't want to express pride for their heritage, and what the school had done to promote this. Finally, we decided that there was a need for change, and for collective action to create the changes.

On October 29, 1992 students organized and celebrated the multicultural open house, which took place immediately after the school administration's open house (while parents and students were encouraged to leave the gym and visit the classrooms). The program, which was translated into both Spanish and English, attracted close to 1,500 parents of color and packed the bleachers. The multicultural open house is the only event where every culture at the high school is represented by its students from Brazil, Vietnam, Mexico, Africa, China, the Philippines, Korea, England, Saudi Arabia, Paraguay, and the Dominican Republic. Each culture brought to the program a presentation of song, dance, or a dramatic skit.

The highlight of the evening was the "Students Reclaiming their Voices" presentation. We and other students from the critical classroom called to our parents and shared with the audience the love for our people, family, and traditions, and our own pride in ourselves and our ethnicity. As many parents heard these passionate expressions of love for the first time from their children, they were amazed and many were moved to tears and cheers.

The purpose of the multicultural open house is to let different cultures and people come together. It lets the parents see the ethnic diversity of the community as well as at the school at which their children attend. More importantly, it allows each individual ethnic group to take pride in itself, as well as each other, which helps every one feel an even deeper sense of pride for the entire community as a whole. Student and parents get to see the strength of the "minorities" as the majority in the community and of the need for cross-cultural education and bilingual programs within the school, district, and throughout the entire county.

The multicultural open house, sponsored by the Critical Pedagogy classes in Room 18, brings the masses together. For the first time, the parents of the silent culture have the opportunity to express themselves and see themselves, not as fieldworkers and house cleaners, but as parents of a high school of students with their own struggles. They hear and witness the ways the school excludes their and their children's social and cultural realities. They face, for example, that there are no ethnic studies courses. They face the fact that the school and the community are a majority of people of color but only a handful of faculty members who are bilingual or of an ethnic minority group. The parents get to see their children taking pride in their heritage and traditions, and also get to see their children are learning nothing about multiculturalism in class, only about Euro-American history and traditions that have historically served to oppress all ethnic minorities.

The multicultural open house is more than just an entertaining program, it brings together the power of the masses and lets the authoritarian administration see the power of the numbers of the oppressed people of color. After the open house, parents became motivated enough to go out into the community along side a few caring teachers and motivate the entire community to support educational transformation. As a result of the multicultural open house, parents and students have created an Educational Task Force to challenge the injustices of institutionalized racism in the school district. With the Educational Task Force's help, the community was able to convince the district board of education to allocate $25,000 to add Chicano/Chicana and multicultural literature to the English Core Curriculum. The Educational Task Force also convinced the district board that a Bilingual/Bicultural and Migrant Education Department was needed at each and every high school in the district so that the education that students received would finally be something that would be relevant to our lives.

By collectively sharing our experiences, we were able to transform policy at Channel Islands high school. Critical Pedagogy gave us the opportunity to discover hidden voices to understand and to look more critically at what was going on around us. With these voices we began to challenge oppression and raise the awareness of the parents and the community so that educational transformation could be possible. With Critical Pedagogy, education is not limited to the classroom. What happens in the classroom is a model for what needs to happen in the outside world. Learning is living and as students we learn by changing the way we live.

11

"I Like Making My Mind Work": Language Minority Students and the Curriculum

Sonia Nieto

Language minority students have been invisible and silent in all too many classrooms across our nation, from underrepresentation in textbooks to the persistent policies and practices that consider the use of languages other than English to be a serious handicap or deficit. Results of this invisibility and silence are depressingly familiar: inordinately high dropout rates, diminished self-esteem, and disproportionately high rates of failure in general in our public schools.

Problems of low achievement among language minority students are not new to the educational scene, but have been with us for many decades. Responses from the educational establishment to academic failure have ranged from compensatory programs to somehow "fix" students so that they can achieve, to English immersion classes so that they can take advantage of the mainstream curriculum, to attempts to assimilate students and rid them of their native languages and cultures in an effort to give them a more equal chance at success. Although some of these policies have been well intentioned, they have missed the mark because most have been based on misguided thinking. That is, such policies and practices have often begun with the assumption that something is seriously wrong with students, their families, cultures, languages, communities, or with any combination of these.

The purpose of this chapter is to propose that this thinking be turned on its head: Rather than thinking about what might be wrong, we need to focus on what is right with linguistic minority students and to find ways to use their experiences, cultures, and languages in more productive and ultimately more

147

beneficial ways. Therefore, a rethinking of curriculum for language minority students is in order. This discussion considers some shortcomings of curriculum as it is currently defined, particularly how it fails to capitalize on strengths that language minority students bring to the educational process. In an attempt to understand experiences and educational environments that might help language minority students learn more effectively, lessons to be learned from a study with a small number of successful young people are explored. Lessons from these students serve as a basis for redefining the current educational reform efforts so that they include all students.

DEFINING CURRICULUM FOR LANGUAGE MINORITY STUDENTS

Curriculum has frequently been understood within limited and rigid parameters. Ask teachers or administrators about their curriculum and many will quickly cart out the textbooks used in particular classes. Although textbooks certainly play an important role in teaching and learning (some would say too large a role), they are not the entire curriculum because they fail to capture the tremendous complexity of the educational process. Alternatively, we can define *curriculum* as the total environment for learning provided by schools (Sinclair & Ghory, 1987). This perspective means that curriculum includes not only texts, but other instructional materials, the physical environment for learning, interactions among teachers and students, and all the intended and unintended messages about expectations, hopes, and dreams that students, the community, and the schools have about student learning.

Using this expanded meaning of curriculum significantly changes its role in the education of language minority students. If curriculum is the total environment for learning, then it is clear that students from language minority backgrounds bring with them a diversity of experiences, talents, and goals that can become an essential part of the total educational environment. Learning to tap into these experiences, talents, and goals becomes the responsibility of teachers and schools. This understanding of curriculum has specific and concrete implications for language minority students because their language and background have often been viewed in only negative terms. For example, in research with four Mexican American students in a bilingual program, Commins (1989) concluded that although their homes were rich environments for a variety of language uses in Spanish, the school was unwilling or unable to recognize their native language as an asset. In addition, she discovered that the content of the curriculum to which the students were exposed had little bearing on their everyday lives. The result was that a potentially productive source of learning was overlooked.

Viewing language diversity as a problem is not limited to students in elementary schools. Hurtado and Rodriguez (1989), in a qualitative analysis of students' open-ended responses to the question of how the schools they attended prior to college reacted to their use of Spanish, found that schools tend to view Spanish-speaking students as handicapped. This perspective of Spanish as a "problem" was based on the assumption that continuing to speak their native language was equivalent to persisting in being foreigners.

In contrast to this approach, Flores, Cousin, and Díaz (1991) reported on attempts of teachers in one inner-city elementary school in California to use students' experiences in more productive ways. The authors, critiquing the label *at risk* that is frequently used to describe students who are not from an English-speaking middle-class world, proposed four alternative views about language minority children that take into account their strengths rather than their supposed weaknesses. They reject "deficit myths" that too often doom students to failure before they even begin and, through anecdotal accounts, relate that a few months after reorganizing the teaching of language and literacy, teachers saw dramatic differences in the children's knowledge and use of written language.

In a related vein, much research has concluded that using students' native language as an essential part of the curriculum can actually benefit their general academic achievement. A significant longitudinal research study by Ramirez (1991) found that providing students of limited English proficiency with substantial amounts of native language instruction not only does not impede their acquisition of English, but also facilitates the learning of other content area skills. Even in a preschool program where Spanish-speaking children received a strong program in school readiness skills in their dominant language, the results confirmed higher cognitive achievement than among those children who attended a preschool that emphasized English acquisition (Campos & Keatinge, 1988).

Findings such as these are not limited to implications for practices in schools, but also for practices in the home. For example, Dolson (1985) found that students from homes that continued to use their native language rather than English tended to perform better in school than those from homes where older siblings or parents attempted to use only English. This finding is supported by the fact that Cuban students, although the most likely of all Latinos to speak Spanish at home, are also as a group the most academically successful of all Latinos (Valdivieso & Davis, 1988). Furthermore, in a large-scale study of Latino high school sophomores and seniors, those who were more proficient in Spanish performed better on achievement tests and had higher educational aspirations than those who were not (Nielson & Fernandez, 1981). Research of this kind underscores the conclusion that using Spanish, whether in the curriculum or in the home, is not the real problem. Rather, the issue of social class (Cubans, for example, are far more likely to be from the middle class than are other Latinos) as well as the way in which teachers and schools, and indeed the society at large, view the native language spoken by students and its place in the curriculum are probably more salient considerations. Cummins (1989), in placing bilingual education within its historical and political context, explained: "bilingual education, in itself, is not the major issue. The issue is the extent to which educators, individually and collectively, are prepared to use their creative energies to devise and implement programs that challenge the racist attitudes and institutions that historically have disempowered minority communities and students" (p. xi). Curriculum reform efforts are crucial in this challenge.

Moving beyond the curriculum provided in schools, Cortés (1981) suggested that we are all educated by what he called "the societal curriculum," or the informal curriculum of family, peers, neighborhoods, places of worship, organizations, mass media, and other equally crucial socializing forces. This suggests that societal norms and expectations play a role in what and to what extent students learn. However, although some aspects of the societal curriculum may be negative, it is necessary for schools to understand the complex dynamics that influence student learning, both inside and outside of school, and to use the societal curriculum in as productive a way as possible. In their attempt to provide an oasis far removed from what they perceive as unwholesome aspects of students' backgrounds and communities, schools may deny or overlook the positive aspects of their students' homes and communities. Ironically, the result may be that schools themselves become negative learning environments to the extent that they disregard and deny students' background knowledge. By reinforcing the perception that students' family and community contexts are inferior, schools often alienate students even further from learning.

RESEARCH WITH ACADEMICALLY SUCCESSFUL STUDENTS

In order to understand how curriculum is operationalized in schools with language minority students, I review research I have done with a small number of bilingual students that is part of a larger study with academically successful students (Nieto, 1996). For the purpose of this discussion, I focus only on the six students in the study who speak a language other than English, whether they learned it at birth or later, and who continue to speak it. All of the students, at the time of the study, were in mainstream programs, although two had been in bilingual programs for part of their schooling.

The purpose of this research was to explore how their experiences in school, at home, and in their communities had affected their achievement. The students participated in a number of in-depth interviews, usually over the course of several months, in which they talked about their schooling and hopes for the future.[1] At the time of the interviews, the students ranged in age from 13 to 19, and were enrolled in either middle or high school. All were considered to be academically successful based on the following:

- they were planning to complete high school and many had hopes of going to college;
- they had good grades, although they were not necessarily at or near the top of their class;
- they had thought about their future and had made some plans for it;
- they generally enjoyed school and felt engaged in it;
- in spite of this, they tended to be critical of their schooling and that of their peers; and
- they described themselves as successful.

A short description of each of the students follows.

Marisol Martinez

A 16-year-old Puerto Rican girl, Marisol was born and raised in the United States, living first in New York City and, at the time of the interviews, in Milltown, a small industrial city in the Northeast.[2] The fifth of eight children, Marisol lives with both her parents in a townhouse apartment in a city housing project. Her parents have made the apartment comfortable and warm, and have planted a small garden in the fenced-in patch of ground in the back. Older than most parents of children Marisol's age, Mr. and Mrs. Martinez are unable to work due to medical problems. They are a close-knit family and have clear expectations of success for their children. All of Marisol's older siblings have graduated from high school, a tremendous accomplishment considering the extraordinarily high dropout rate among Puerto Ricans in this city and in the country in general (ASPIRA Institute for Policy Research, 1993).

Marisol, a sophomore in the local high school, enjoys school a great deal. She is in an academic program, has very good grades, and likes all her classes, especially math and science. Although Marisol claims that she wants to go to college, she is undecided between becoming a nurse and a model. Fluent in both Spanish and English, she uses each in separate contexts. Marisol has never been in a bilingual program, a fact that she regrets only because she has not been

---

[1]I want to acknowledge the following colleagues who conducted the interviews on which I developed the case studies: Diane Sweet (James Karam and Avi Abramson); Dr. Mac Lee Morante (Yolanda Piedra); Carol Shea (Manual Gomes); and Haydée Font (Hoang Vinh).

[2]In the descriptions that follow, pseudonyms are used for the students' names and most of their cities or towns, except in the case of large cities.

encouraged to use Spanish in school. She is keenly aware of her academic success as compared to many of her peers, and it is a source of both pride and shame. Marisol is determined to "be someone," a constant them in her interviews.

James Karam

A junior in high school, James is Lebanese Christian (Maronite) and lives in Springfield, Massachusetts, a city with a historically cohesive Lebanese community, both Christian and Muslim. His mother and father are separated and, being the oldest of three children, he is expected to fulfill many responsibilities in the family. His mother, who was born in Lebanon, was brought here as a bride by her Lebanese American husband. They live in a quiet residential middle-class community in this ethnically and racially diverse city.

James is fluent in both English and Arabic. Although he has never studied it formally, Arabic is an essential part of his life and he wants to maintain it. One way of doing this is through his participation in the Maronite Church, an important haven for cultural pride and maintenance. This is in sharp contrast with his school which, although making some attempts to deal with the great diversity of its student body, has contributed to making James' culture an invisible one. James is a very good student, heavily involved in extracurricular activities, and eager to continue his education.

Avi Abramson

Avi lives in Talbot, a small and aging primarily working-class city in Eastern Massachusetts. In recent years, the number of young families has been declining, many moving on to more prosperous or promising places. This is evident in the dramatically declining enrollment at both the public and parochial schools in town. Avi attends the public high school, where he is among a handful of Jewish students. He attended public school until second grade, and then transferred to a Jewish day school until eighth grade. He is a good student, but this was not always the case, as he had a hard time adjusting when he first started public school.

With his mother and brother, Avi lives in a quiet neighborhood of single and multifamily homes. His father, who originally came from Israel, died when Avi was 10. His mother was formerly a teacher and is currently studying computers because there are now few jobs in Talbot for Hebrew teachers. Avi speaks Hebrew and is deeply involved in his culture and religion through the local synagogue.

Hoang Vinh

Having resided in the United States for 3 years, Vinh[3] is frustrated that his English is not better than it is. Nevertheless, he is a very good student and has just completed a rigorous academic program in his junior year in the highly regarded high school he attends. Eighteen years old, Vinh lives with his uncle, two sisters, and two brothers in a mostly middle-class academic town. The importance of maintaining their native language and culture are immediately apparent to any visitor: They listen to Vietnamese music, allow only their native language to be spoken at home, and cook Vietnamese food. In addition, the older members of the family assist the younger ones in writing weekly letters home to their parents.

Vinh's father was in the military before 1975 and worked for the U.S. government. Consequently, he was perceived to be a U.S. sympathizer and educational opportunities for his family were limited. Vinh and his brother and sisters were sent here for better educational opportunities and a more secure future. The emotional trauma that he has undergone is evident in a number of ways, from his feeling that he is no longer as smart as he used to be (because of the language barrier), to the depression he suffered shortly after arriving (what he describes as "I got mental"). Homework and studies take up many hours of Vinh's time and he places great emphasis on what he calls "becoming educated people," due in part to his family's rigorous academic demands and the high educational aspirations they have for him and his siblings.

Manuel Gomes

Nineteen years old, Manual can hardly conceal the happiness and pride he feels in his accomplishment of graduating from high school this year, the first in his family of 11 children to do so. The youngest child in this large family, Manuel came to Boston from the Cape Verde Islands when he was 11. His father cleans offices downtown at night and his mother is a housewife who has stayed home to take care of her children and perform the many attendant chores that an extended family demands. They live in a three-decker home with apartments that are used by other members of the family in this struggling urban community.

Manuel was in a bilingual program for several years after arriving in Boston. The language of instruction was *Crioulo*, the native language spoken in Cape Verde, a former Portuguese colony that won its independence in 1975. In 1977,

---

[3]The Vietnamese use family names first, given names second. The given name is used for identification. In this case, Vinh is the given name and Hoang is the family name (National Indochinese Clearinghouse, 1976).

the State Assembly of Massachusetts determined that students who spoke Crioulo be placed in separate programs from those who speak Portuguese. There is a strong sense of cohesion among the teachers, students, and parents in the program and the staff are well known and respected in the community. Because it allowed him to have a less traumatic transition to English and to U.S. culture, Manuel's participation in this program was decisive in his academic success. After graduation, Manuel would like to find a job in a bank and possibly continue his education.

Yolanda Piedra

Yolanda is a 13-year-old eighth grader who lives in a midsize, mostly low-income city in Southern California with her mother, brother, and sister. Her parents are separated and her father lives in Mexico. Struggling to survive in a difficult situation, Yolanda's mother, who works in a candy factory, is quite strict with her children and expects them all to take on appropriate family responsibilities. She is constantly reminding them of the importance of getting an education, a message that has gotten through to Yolanda.

Arriving in this country when she was 7, Yolanda considers herself to be Mexican. Her family speaks mostly Spanish at home, but she says that sometimes they speak English so that her mother can practice. Yolanda has had mostly positive experiences at school, first in a bilingual program and now in the mainstream program where she is a very successful student, having recently been selected "Student of the Month." Although one of the youngest students to be interviewed, Yolanda has thought about her future and thinks she might be interested in being either a computer programmer or a flight attendant. Her English is beautifully expressive and has traces of her native Spanish syntax and lexicon.

LEARNING FROM STUDENTS

Several of the themes that emerged through interviews with these language minority students have implications for classrooms, schools, and communities. In spite of the fact that they differed in language, social class, native language fluency, family structure, gender, and other ways, they were remarkably consistent in mentioning both positive and negative aspects of their schooling and that of their peers. They did not always agree on what schools were doing well or on how they could improve, but I focus on four areas of general consensus from which we can learn some important lessons: raising the demands schools have of students, providing creative and supportive learning environments, respecting students' language and culture, and developing curriculum related to community concerns.

Raising Demands on Students

The damaging role that low expectations may have on students has been documented for many years (Anyon, 1981; Ginsburg, 1986; Gouldner, 1978; Rosenthal, 1987; Rosenthal & Jacobson, 1968). Although the young people in these case studies were successful students, they often spoke about the effect of low expectations on both themselves and their peers. For example, some said that they and their classmates were often treated like babies and that they received undemanding work that was accepted no matter how poor the quality.

Teachers and schools, sometimes with the best of intentions, demand too little of students. They may do so to encourage students or because they know of the difficult circumstances in which they live. Unfortunately, the result often backfires because students learn that they need to do precious little work to get the approval of some teachers. Vinh talked about how the praise that teachers gave him was usually ineffective. This may have been due both to cultural differences and to his own exacting demands of himself. He expressed it eloquently when he said: "Sometimes, the English teachers, they don't understand about us. Because something we not do good, like my English is not good. And she say, 'Oh, your English is great!' But that's the way the American culture is. But my culture is not like that. . . . If my English is not good, she has to say, 'Your English is not good. So you have to go home and study' . . . So, sometimes, when I do something not good, and my teachers say, 'Oh, you did great!', I don't like it . . . I want the truth better." Yolanda also referred to low expectations when she said: "We are supposed to be doing higher things. And like, they take us too slow, see, step by step. And that's why everybody takes it as a joke."

Do the students in the case studies feel this way because they are more intelligent than most of their peers and thus naturally expect demanding work? Not necessarily, because from what they said, many of their classmates, even those who have not generally been successful, also felt this way. Other research on expectations of student achievement is enlightening here as well. In a particularly intriguing study, Spring (1985) investigated the effects of changing from a majority White to a majority Black student body on a small northern school system. He found that, although there was indeed a decline in academic standards, the primary cause was not due to the nature of the students but rather to the attitudes of White teachers and administrators toward these students. As the school population changed, teachers and administrators demanded less in homework assignments and shifted the emphasis from college preparation to vocational education.

The language minority students in the research reported here mentioned how their teachers' and schools' expectations differed from their own. Manuel, for instance, said, "I think [teachers] could help students, try to influence them, that they can do whatever they want to do, that they can be whatever they want to be, that they got opportunities out there. . . . Most schools don't encourage kids to be all they can be." For the most part, these students enjoyed challenging classes even if they received lower grades than in easier classes in which they got better grades. Marisol, expressing the views of many, said, "If I know I'm trying and my grades are down, the point is I tried." Vinh, although always pleased to get good grades, was more interested in learning in its broader sense. Grades, he said, "are not important to me. Important to me is education."

These students, although successful themselves, often criticized the school for not promoting success among their peers. They commented, for instance, on how hard other students worked. Avi said, "I think that anybody that goes to school tries, at least. Accomplishes something. . . ." Yolanda, when asked what she would like teachers to know about their Mexican American students, said, "they try real hard, that's one thing I know." She added, "I'd say, 'Get along more with the kids that are not really into themselves. . . . Have more communication with them."

Some of the students spoke about their own struggle to learn the language and culture of their new country. Vinh was particularly affected by this when he first arrived: "From the second language, it is very difficult for me and for other people." Although Vinh had felt that he was very smart in Vietnam, once he came to the United States, he no longer considered himself to be as intelligent. The effect was traumatic and Vinh said that he had become "a very sad person." Manuel too talked about the difficulty of learning English: "Some people are slow to learn the language and some just catch it up easy. It wasn't easy for me. Its kinda hard for me, like the pronunciation of the words and stuff like that." Yolanda talked about not liking school for the first 3 years until she had learned enough English.

In spite of the difficulties some of the students had experienced in learning their new language and culture, none of them expressed the view that standards should be relaxed. On the contrary, they wanted to work hard and they expected teachers to work even harder to teach them. Part of teachers' hard work, according to some of them, centered on learning something about their students' backgrounds. Vinh talked about teachers' responsibilities to learn about the culture of their new students. Yolanda spoke with great affection about demanding and caring teachers and in fact attributed her academic success to them: " 'cause I had some teachers, and they were always calling my mom, like I did a great job. Or they would start talking to me, or they kinda like pulled me up some grades, or moved me to other classes, or took me somewhere. And they were always congratulating me."

Many of the issues brought up by these students were highlighted by Moll (1988) in research on teachers of Latino students who were achieving at or above grade level on standardized measures of academic achievement. He found that these teachers were particularly effective at arranging, changing, improving, or modifying social situations to teach at the highest level possible. That is, they did not water down the curriculum, but rather made their classrooms highly literate environments where many language experiences took place. The major underlying assumption, according to Moll, was that the students were "as smart as allowed by the curriculum" (p. 467).

Combined with high expectations of their teachers, the students in my research had high expectations of themselves. Manuel, for example, in spite of the fact that he had to struggle to succeed in school, was uncompromisingly upbeat. "I know that I can do whatever I want to do in life," he said. "I believe that strongly." Yolanda was enthusiastic about learning: "I like working. I like making my mind work. . . . Actually, it's really fun around here if you really get into learning." She not only liked learning, but she loved the idea of education itself: "It's good for you. . . . It's like when you eat. It's like if you don't eat in a whole day, you feel weird. You have to eat. That's the same thing for me."

Providing Creative and Supportive Learning Environments

Although all of the students had caring and creative teachers, they also complained about boring and uncaring teachers. Along with a critique of stale methods, they made concrete suggestions about other approaches their teachers might use. Avi said: "There's some teachers that understand the kids better than other teachers. . . . They teach from the point of view of the kid. They don't just come out and say, 'All right, do this, blah, blah, blah. . . .' They're not so *one-tone voice*." He suggested they do other things besides "just walking in, writing on the board, erasing, and leaving." James said, "Some teachers are just . . . they don't really care. They just teach the stuff. 'Here,' write a couple of things on the board, 'see, that's how you do it. . . . Go ahead, page 25.' " He concluded by saying, "[Teachers should] make the classes more interesting. . . . Like not just sit there and say, 'Do this and do this and do this.' " Yolanda, who received an A in English, did not really like the class. She said that her English teacher "just does the things and sits down." Students placed a great deal of negative emphasis on teachers who were passive and unimaginative.

Specific suggestions about improving curriculum and instruction varied. Vinh particularly liked to work in groups because it gave him and his classmates who were learning English a chance to practice together: "And we discuss some projects. . . . And different people have different ideas, so after that we choose some best idea. I like work in groups. I like to discuss something. . . . Because when we learn another language, we learn to discuss, we learn to understand the word's *meaning*, not about how to *write* the word." Vinh's focus on group work is especially intriguing given the conventional wisdom that Asian and Pacific Islander students prefer to work on their own, confirming Suzuki's (1983) contention that such generalizations need to be viewed critically.

Other students suggested that teachers try to communicate more with students. Yolanda, for instance, said that she learned more from teachers when they talked to students about their own lives and suggested that teachers should do the same "cause you learn a lot from the students. That's what a lot of teachers tell me. They learn more from their students than from where they go study. . . ." Manuel had particularly enjoyed his theater group because it provided the students, many of whom were newcomers to the school and the country, with an outlet for their feelings. Other students suggested that their teachers make more time for their students, that they spend time after school to help them, that they use more challenging materials, and that they put more energy into their teaching.

Respecting Students' Language and Culture

One of the major lessons from these students was their steely determination to maintain their language and culture, in spite of the fact that none was currently in a bilingual program and that their culture was often invisible in the school setting. Although not directly asked, all volunteered that their language and culture were important to them. Typical of their comments were "I feel proud of myself. I feel proud of my culture" (Yolanda); "To me, it's important, you know, because I have to stand up for Puerto Ricans. . . ." (Marisol); and "You cannot forget about [your culture], you know. It's part of you. . . . You gotta know who you are" (Manuel). James made it clear that he identified as Lebanese: "My mother's really proud to be Lebanese, and so am I. . . . First thing I'd say is I'm Lebanese. . . ." And Avi, when asked how he celebrated Jewish holidays, enthusiastically answered, "With pride and tradition!"

The pride the students felt in their native languages and cultures was not without its conflicts. Both cultural pride and shame were evident in many of the students' statements. That is, although their culture and language were important to maintain, they were perceived as unimportant in their school environment. Marisol, for example, described a situation she had in junior high school related to her use of Spanish: "I used to have a lot of problems with one of my teachers 'cause she didn't want us to talk Spanish in class and I thought that was like an insult to us, you know? I could never stay quiet and talk only English, 'cause sometimes, you know, words slip in Spanish." Ironically, when asked if she would have liked to have a class in Puerto Rican history and culture, Marisol was quick to say, "I don't think it's important. . . . I'm proud of myself and my culture, but I think I know what I should know about the culture already, so I wouldn't take the course." Through the interviews, it was clear that Marisol had a very limited knowledge of Puerto Rican history, but she had accepted the hegemony of "American History" (primarily European American history) as the only authentic history that should be taught in schools.

James' experiences provide a particularly compelling example of the invisibility of his language and culture in school. Although his school was making a sincere attempt to incorporate multiculturalism in its curriculum, the results were often at a superficial level and left James' background and that of others out of the picture. He mentioned three specific activities: a "Foreign Language Month," a "Multicultural Festival," and an international cookbook. In all of these, both the Arabic language and his Lebanese culture were completely missing. He dismissed these events as "not really important," while wistfully adding that "It *is* important for me." In fact, the only mention of his culture throughout his schooling had been less than positive: he talked about a favorite elementary school teacher who used to call him "Gonzo" because he had a big nose and "Klinger," the character in M*A*S*H* who was Lebanese. The other reference to his culture was among his high school friends: "Some people call me, you know, 'cause I'm Lebanese, so people say, 'Look out for the terrorist! Don't mess with him or he'll blow up your house!' " Avi also talked movingly about experiences with anti-Semitism in his school, including one occasion when a student in a woodworking class carved a swashstika on a piece of wood. Although he had acted forcefully when these incidents happened, he concluded, "There's a few kids in school that I still know are anti-Semites. Basically Jew haters."

Because of the negative experiences they had in school and in the community related to their language and culture, most of the students felt that teachers should try to understand their students' cultures and the role of their language. Marisol explained, "I think [teachers] should get to know you, and whatever they don't like about Puerto Ricans, or they feel uncomfortable with, you know, just talk to you about it, and you can teach *them* things that probably they're confused about and they don't understand. That way we can communicate better." That teachers and others in her town had negative attitudes about Puerto Ricans was indicated by, for example, a proposal to limit the number coming into town and a brief but intense period in which municipal workers had been told that they could speak only English on the job. And in a particularly poignant statement, Vinh said, "[My teachers] understand something, just not all Vietnamese culture. Like they just understand something *outside*. . . . But they cannot understand something inside our hearts."

Developing Curriculum Related to Cultural and Community Concerns

The students in the case studies also talked about experiences at home and in the community that had encouraged their school success. For example, Avi, who was very active in his local synagogue in an aging and dwindling Jewish community, joked about being a "role model for 85-year-olds." This experience had helped him build up confidence in himself and develop other skills necessary for school success. One of these skills has to do with taking on other obligations. As Avi said, "I have different responsibilities than most people." James had similar experiences in his Maronite Church, and he still enjoyed going in spite of the fact that most of his age peers had stopped attending.

Developing leadership skills was another by-product of students' activities in the community. Manuel was often the cultural broker for his large family, having to interpret for them at all the agencies with which they interacted. For instance, because of a lack of Crioulo-speaking personnel at the local hospital, he had been responsible for having to tell his father several years earlier that he had cancer. A traumatic experience for Manuel, he was confronted with the agony of his father's illness and with the awesome responsibility of an adult role at an early age. As a result, he missed a great deal of school during that time and his grades had suffered. In spite of this, the experience helped him develop important communication and leadership skills. Unfortunately, such skills are sometimes not appreciated or taken advantage of by schools.

Other students in the case studies had equally important, although not as dramatic or negative, benefits of out-of-school activities. James' hobby, bicycling, has taught him many things: that practice is necessary in order to excel; how to not have a setback become a permanent loss; how to use a hobby to help relieve stress; and how to develop interpersonal skills that would be of great use in the future. Avi too understood that his work in the temple was helping him to develop important skills. "I enjoy being that kind of leader," he said. For Yolanda, participating in a Mexican folk-dancing group fulfilled the same role.

Within-school extracurricular activities were equally important in developing important skills for academic success. Marisol's involvement in the Teen Clinic at her high school supported and affirmed her resolve to be a good student and persist in getting an education. The rate of teenage pregnancy in her community is one of the highest in the state, and in explaining why she had been so concerned about this issue, Marisol seemed to imply that her work at the clinic was almost a vaccine against pregnancy: "There's a lot of girls out there getting pregnant and dropping out of school. I don't want one of those girls to be me, you know? I just want to stay away, you know? And I want to advise the ones that are not pregnant as to why they shouldn't get pregnant at an early age and how to prevent from doing that. . . . I would like the kids such as myself to realize what's happening out in the streets and not to put everything to waste." Her work at the Teen Clinic, although not directly related to academics, had a profound effect on her school work while also addressing an important community concern.

REDEFINING EDUCATIONAL REFORM

Research by Brice-Heath and McLaughlin (1993) sheds light on the positive role that the community can have on students' lives and what schools can learn from this role. These researchers studied the effect on adolescents of participating in nonschool community-based activities. Although most teenagers are not involved in such activities on a regular basis, their research suggests that schools can learn from those agencies that have been most successful in attracting and retaining children in their centers. They highlight six characteristics that make these agencies successful with children:

- they share a conception of young people as resources rather than as problems;
- they focus on developing activities that usually yield a recognizable product;
- they invest a significant amount of responsibility on the young people themselves;
- they have deep roots in the community;
- they are responsive to what the researchers call the "local ecology," that is, the untapped resources and unmet needs of those who become their members; and
- they are flexible and responsive to change (Brice-Heath & McLaughlin, 1993)

In their own words, the students in our case studies echoed these findings. They spoke with great feeling about their lives at home, in the community, and at school, but unfortunately, they could find little congruence in these settings. One implication is that schools need to learn to focus on what they can change, namely their own attitudes and instruction, rather than on their students' poverty or oppressive living conditions, which they can do little to change. Another implication is that schools need to undergo massive structural changes that effect school policies and practices at every level.

A great deal has been written about the need for educational reform in our schools. Most of the calls for reform have focused on such changes as longer school days and years, a mandated curriculum, and further testing, and thus fail to address the real issues of unequal access and equity that are the reasons for needed reform in the first place. Marisol, James, Manuel, Avi, Yolanda, Vinh, and many others like them pose a challenge to teachers and schools to rethink what it means to educate language minority students. We would do well to heed their lessons about raising academic expectations and using the languages, cultures, and family and community experiences in the curriculum in order to provide creative and supportive learning environments for all students. Yolanda's enthusiasm for learning should not be viewed as an individual idiosyncrasy, but rather as the collective material with which all students come to school no matter what language they speak. When schools can tap into that kind of motivation and energy, many students will, in Yolanda's words, "like making my mind work."

ACKNOWLEDGMENTS

This chapter is dedicated to Dora Gomez Fuentes (1942–1992), a good friend, cherished colleague, and inspired educator. Dora was committed to equal educational opportunities for all children and was an outspoken advocate for the rights of language minority students.

REFERENCES

Anyon, J. (1981). Social class and school knowledge. *Curriculum Inquiry, 11*(1), 3–41.

ASPIRA Institute for Policy Research (1993). *Facing the facts: The state of Hispanic education, 1993.* Washington, DC: Author.

Brice-Heath, S., & McLaughlin, M. W. (1993). Introduction. In S. Brice-Heath & M. W. McLaughlin (Eds.), *Identity and inner-city youth: Beyond ethnicity and gender* (pp. 1–12). New York: Teachers College Press.

Campos, S. J., & Keatinge, H. R. (1988). The Carpinteria language minority student experience: From theory, to practice, to success. In T. Skutnabb-Kangas & J. Cummins (Eds.), *Minority language: From shame to struggle* (pp. 299–307). Clevedon, England: Multilingual Matters.

Commins, N. L. (1989). Language and affect: Bilingual students at home and at school. *Language Arts, 66*(1), 29–43.

Cortés, C. E. (1981). The societal curriculum: Implications for multiethnic education. In J. A. Banks (Ed.), *Education in the 80's: Multiethnic education* (pp. 24–32). Washington, DC: 1981.

Cummins, J. (1989). *Empowering minority students.* Sacramento: California Association for Bilingual Education.

Dolson, D. P. (1985). The effects of Spanish home language use on the scholastic performance of Hispanic students. *Journal of Multilingual and Multicultural Development, 6,* 135–156.

Flores, B., Cousin, P. T., & Díaz, E. (1991). Transforming deficit myths about learning, language, and culture. *Language Arts, 68*(5), 369–379.

Ginsburg, H. (1986). The myth of the deprived child: New thoughts on poor children. In U. Neisser (Ed.), *The school achievement of minority children: New perspectives* (pp. 169–189). Hillsdale, NJ: Lawrence Erlbaum Associates.

Gouldner, H. (1978). *Teachers' pets, troublemakers, and nobodies: Black children in elementary schools.* Westport, CT: Greenwood Press.

Hurtado, A., & Rodriguez, R. (1989). Language as a social problem: The repression of Spanish in South Texas. *Journal of Multilingual and Multicultural Development, 10*(5), 401–419.

Moll, L. C. (1988). Some key issues in teaching Latino students. *Language Arts, 65*(5), 465–472.

National Indochinese Clearinghouse. (1976). *A manual for Indochinese refugee education, 1976–1977.* Arlington, VA: Center for Applied Linguistics.

Nielson, F., & Fernandez, R. M. (1981). *Hispanic students in American high schools: Background characteristics and achievement.* Washington, DC: National Opinion Research Center, National Center for Education Statistics.

Nieto, S. (1996). *Affirming diversity: The sociopolitical context of multicultural education* (2nd ed.). White Plains, NY: Longman.

Ramirez, J. D. (1991). *Final report: Longitudinal study of structured English immersion strategy, early-exit and late-exit transitional bilingual education programs for language minority children.* Washington, DC: Office of Bilingual Education.

Rosenthal, R. (1987). Pygmalion effects: Existence, magnitude, and social importance. *Educational Researcher, 16*(9), 37–44.

Rosenthal, R., & Jacobson, L. (1968). *Pygmalion in the classroom.* New York: Holt, Rinehart & Winston.

Sinclair, R. L., & Ghory, W. (1987). *Marginal students: A primary concern for school renewal.* Chicago, IL: McCutcheon.

Spring, J. (1985). *American education.* White Plains, NY: Longman.

Suzuki, B. H. (1983). The education of Asians and Pacific Americans: An introductory overview. In D. T. Nakanishi & M. Hirano-Nakanishi (Eds.), *The education of Asian and Pacific Americans: Historical perspectives and prescriptions for the future.* Phoenix, AZ: Oryx Press.

Valdivieso, R., & Davis, C. (1988, December). *U.S. Hispanics: Challenging issues for the 1990s.* Washington, DC: Population Trends and Public Policy.

12

A Visionary Look at Spanish Language Arts in the Bilingual Classroom

Alma Flor Ada

Latino children in U.S. schools continue to have the poorest academic achievement and the lowest rate of school completion as compared to any other racial/ethnic group. Instead of more critically examining what is wrong with the instruction that these students typically receive and the classroom and school environments, blame continues to be placed on the children, their families, and communities.

This chapter takes us out of the realm of "blaming the victim" and of remedial, skills-based, deficit-oriented education. Instead, it takes us for a dreamlike journey into a classroom where Spanish-speaking children are creative readers and writers, where their social, cultural, and linguistic realities are an integral part of teaching and learning, and where students are developing a more critical understanding of themselves, their families and communities, and the world around them. The context and space that are constructed here, while posed as imaginary, are very much grounded in the necessary and real. Although the children discussed here are Latino and their language Spanish, another movement of the brush on a parallel canvas could easily depict the racial/ethnic, cultural, and language-based reality of Asians, Haitians, African Americans or other children of color. Regardless of who the children are, this chapter should remind us that pedagogical transformation requires a hope and a vision.

—Editor

What would the ideal Spanish language classroom look like? To answer this frequently asked question I would like to share a vision. This vision is not born out of dreams, but rather it is a composite of actual practices.

Although I am aware of the difficulties and constraints encountered by teachers in general, and bilingual teachers in particular, I have also been privileged to witness exciting practices carried out in bilingual classes, despite limiting circumstances.

I trust that sharing this composite vision will be both a tribute to what teachers are already doing and an inspiration for renewed creativity.

Because I am describing an imaginary classroom with only one teacher, I was forced to make a gender choice. I have decided to speak of the teacher as "she," not excluding the possibility that it could also be, and in fact hoping that in many cases it would be, a "he." I wish to contribute to the awareness of how frequently the opposite choice is made, not in the spirit of confrontation, but rather with the hope that this form of inequality will eventually be eliminated.

My ideal classroom is one devoted to promoting transformative education. This education would facilitate the full development of the human being—physically, psychologically, cognitively, and spiritually—and would also encourage students to work toward transforming their society into one that is truly democratic, ecologically sound, and socially just.

Looking into my crystal ball, I see a classroom that could be of any grade (you can provide the setting—your own school or class), with no less than 1,000 children's books. The books, displayed in prominent places, are catalogued and cared for by the children themselves, who have access to them during periods designated for reading for pleasure. The children take books home each night to share with their parents and siblings, reading to one another in pairs and groups. They also read books to students of other classes, as well as to elderly members of the community, both those who visit the class as volunteers and those whom the children visit in their nursing homes.

These books reflect the best of children's literature and literature for young readers, both written originally in Spanish and translated into Spanish from many other languages. The books represent a variety of genres and also reflect the pluralistic composition of this nation. Significantly, many of them have been authored by the children themselves, by their parents, and by the teacher.

Many of the books are recorded on audiocassettes, so that students may have the added pleasure of listening to the words of the story. Although some cassettes have been recorded professionally, many have been recorded by the teacher, parents, and volunteers, and even by the students themselves—who have not only read the stories dramatically, but have also added musical backgrounds and sound effects.

A thematic educational unit is developed around a few exciting books, and each unit culminates in an activity outside of the classroom. The students' interest in the world of reading and communication has motivated the teacher to take them to local newspaper offices and radio stations. In fact, the students have become regular contributors both to the newspaper, for which they write a weekly column, and to the radio station, on which they air a weekly program. They have also visited local artists, designers, writers, print shops, and a publishing house. But the curiosity of the students has taken them even farther than places they can visit. One of their classroom computers is connected by modem to Project Orillas, which allows the students to share their ideas and writing with students in other states and countries.

Daily, one of the students retrieves mail for the class from the main office. Many envelopes have foreign stamps, but the letters from across town are received with the same enthusiasm. Some of the students' correspondents are children their own age from local as well as from distant schools. Others are adults: authors and illustrators of books read by the children, scientists, zoo keepers, circus performers, dog breeders, and community leaders. Many of the pen pals are retired senior citizens whose lives are brightened by the exchange. Some are hospitalized children and teenagers. Each one of them is a special friend to one of the students.

This classroom is an aesthetic environment, happy and lively, and not at all confining. It is rich in printed and written materials in addition to books, newspapers, magazines, and abundant displays of the students' own work fill the tables and bookcases, tastefully arranged. Comfortable rugs and pillows to lounge on while reading line the floor. A live tree stands in one corner, and an old claw-foot bathtub filled with cushions—a favorite place to nestle while reading—rests in the opposite corner. Plants and flowers bloom. Book covers and posters of books, which serve to motivate the students to read and to inform them of special titles, are treated like works of art. During the free reading period, classical music from throughout the world—Vivaldi, Mozart, Japanese flutes, and Andean rhythms—fills the air.

The school day starts with the sharing of a poem. Several times during the day, as the students move from task to task or as the teacher perceives the need to quiet them down or to wake them up, they join in singing or engage in brief moments of silent relaxation.

The teacher, in creating this aesthetic and peaceful environment, is aware that the classroom represents the geography in which a great part of the students' history unfolds. She has already questioned the soundness of keeping children locked up in a room for such an extended portion of the day. The resemblance of the typical classroom to a prison does not escape her. Therefore, she is eager to provide many opportunities for her students to physically leave the classroom, but she is equally committed to freeing the imagination of her students, so that they know no mental confinement.

Borrowing from a literary metaphor, the teacher has reflected on the fact that each person creates his or her own history. She sees that some people tend to act as protagonists. They confront problems and grow in the process; they are seen and heard; their feelings are recognized; all eyes focus on them; and they thrive. Others tend to remain in a secondary or background position. Now, the teacher is clearly aware that each person may indeed play different roles in different situations, but she is determined that each of her students experience the role of protagonist at some point – that they take responsibility for their own process of becoming.

Therefore, in her class, she constantly focuses on her students' lives and experiences. When discussing the books they read, students are encouraged to share any personal experiences that may resemble or contrast with those of the story's characters. They are invited to imagine what their feelings and actions would be were they in the position of a particular protagonist. Once a relationship has been established between themselves and the story, students are encouraged to reflect critically on the nature of the issues, to see the alternatives hidden in each situation, and to analyze the ethical consequences of following each one. Who benefits or suffers under the condition presented? Is it just? Democratic? Does everyone have the opportunity to be respected and heard? Are the solutions offered by the book acceptable to all people? How would people of different cultures, ages, and backgrounds react to them?

This critical discussion does not remain at an abstract level because the teacher invites the students to reflect on their own lives and on how they can be changed. The teacher does not expect her students to change the whole world. She remembers their youth, but she sincerely believes that all are capable of transforming their own reality. She has seen students improve their behavior toward each other, and affect their relationships with parents and relatives, once they have seen themselves as active and capable protagonists.

To build students' confidence, the teacher leads multiple activities. A very significant project is the interactive journal, in which the students write each day. She responds to their entries, without judging or pretending to give solutions, but rather emphasizing with their feelings. She sometimes shares anecdotes or feelings of her own, in order to communicate individually with each student.

Another significant activity is *Students' Own Books*. Every week, the teacher sits for a few minutes with each student, asking each to share significant thoughts and feelings. Although they can all write, she transcribes their words for them. She listens attentively, without questioning or prompting, so that their train of thought will neither be interrupted nor swayed. By doing the writing herself, she knows that the students will be able to concentrate more fully on intimately sharing their thoughts and feelings. Later, she gives them her transcription, and they illustrate it. If they choose to, they may copy it in their own handwriting. These papers are filed weekly in a folder. At the end of the year, they will form a full volume: a record of the student's life for that year. In addition, while the student speaks, the teacher records each one on an individual cassette. At the year's end, these cassettes will accompany the books as gifts for the students and their parents, by which to remember the year.

Every time she thinks of this activity, the teacher smiles. She knows how valuable and cherished these memories – words, drawings, voices – will be some day. She is pleased that her students will have much more than a report card and a class picture with which to remember their year with her.

In fact, the teacher takes pictures of her students often–candid shots of students reading, writing, working on science projects, doing math, on the carpets, at tables, in the playground, in the cafeteria, smiling, arguing, drawing, singing, storytelling. She tries to capture the characteristic attitude of each one. These pictures will illustrate a class book for that specific year. Because she puts so much of herself into her teaching she wants her own book by which to remember the class. She invites the students to write captions for each picture, and they participate eagerly in suggesting inclusions for the book: copies of programs, announcements of activities, samples of students' writings. The students know that the book will be kept in the classroom, so that they can come and view it in following years, just as they see former students do.

The teacher is very aware that in a highly literate society such as the one in which we live, the printed word has great power. She also realizes that many of her students come from homes in which literacy is rare. Many of the parents don't own any books, don't read as a daily practice, and seldom see their names in print–except on junk mail and bills. Before her students entered her class, none of their parents had ever written a book or been the protagonist of one.

She realizes that many of her students face contrasting environments: a home where literacy is not practiced versus a classroom where it is emphasized. She understands that if students were to accept the literate world and the richness of books, they would have to question the adequacy of their families. Because she knows that no amount of information imparted to them can substitute for the nurturance of their family in order to grow as healthy and whole human beings, the teacher works hard to make both her students and their parents protagonists, and thus validate the children's home life.

For this purpose, she has developed home–school interaction projects through which her students engage daily in reading and writing with their parents. These activities are multifaceted. Students take home books to read nightly with their parents, and lead their parents in activities similar to the ones they themselves do in class. After showing them the cover and the title and describing the characters, they ask their parents to predict what the book will be about. They read half the story, and ask parents to invent an ending; or after reading the entire story, they may ask them to tell what happens next.

Students also discuss with their parents themes mentioned in class. For example, after reading a book about friendship, students developed a series of questions to ask parents about the friends they had when they were young, how they interacted, and how they solved conflicts. They then reported in class about their parents' responses, and each student wrote a book on the subject. The enthusiasm of both students and parents was so great that now publishing books in which parents and family members are protagonists has become a regular practice. Parents and children now even co-author books at home.

The teacher feels that she is in true contact with both her students and their parents. She also feels extremely liberated. She is not aiming to be an all-knowing individual, in perfect control of her class, who decides exactly what her students are required to know. Rather, she is open to learning and discovery. She is constantly generating new knowledge with the assistance of her students, and thus her own intellect is stimulated.

The inspirational environment the teacher has created for her students benefits herself as well. During the daily "sacred" reading-for-pleasure time, she finds renewal in reading a poem or short story. By joining the children in singing and relaxation exercises, she herself has learned to unwind, and she now feels more energetic throughout the day. But above all, she believes that the high goals that she established when she entered the teaching profession are being fulfilled daily: to affect the lives of her students; to facilitate their discovery of the joys of reading and the magical worlds contained in books; to make them aware of the beauty of their own spirits; and to empower them to transform and improve their society.

The teacher does not ignore the difficulties that many of her students will encounter. On the contrary, she knows that many will face the danger of drugs and street crime, and the pain of prejudice and discrimination. Girls may face others, including low expectations and the possibility of early pregnancies. In addition, she knows how difficult it is for a child to be the first in his or her family to attend college, and she is not even certain that going to college is a solution in and of itself. She does not want her students to attend college as a way to distance themselves from their families and communities, but rather in order to bring knowledge and skills back to work for and with their own communities. But her understanding of the risks, difficulties, and complexity of her task does not deter our teacher from her goal of educating her students to the best of her ability.

There is a wonderful promise in education. And there is an especially significant promise in acquainting students with the world of books and in encouraging them to become creative readers, as well as authors of their own texts. Guided by teachers, as students become readers of words, they can also become readers of the world. They can understand themselves and others better. They can find new meaning in the life and reality around them. And as they find a space to reflect about their stories, and the stories of their parents and communities, they will discover that they have not only become authors of texts, but that they are becoming the authors of their own lives and their own realities.

13

OYE!!
Do You Understand . . .

Sandra Marcelino

In today's classrooms there are many times when we silently scream for someone to listen, many times we plead and fight *internally*. I ask this: What good will it do if no one can hear us? There are many times when we even try to communicate what we want to say and we are still not heard or, even worse, just ignored. Well, I'm fed up with trying to rationalize, to compromise, I'm fed up with trying to make everyone else comfortable when I myself am condemned to the floor. Yes, I understand that we all have a fear of the unknown and it is naturally human to err. That's *okay*, but if this fear turns into disgust because you can't understand something and teachers start to offend and belittle others because of your ignorance, that's when problems occur. No, I don't have any degrees or letters after my name. I haven't done extensive research. This won't be graphed out and you won't be reading a plethora of pages of literature trying to explain my philosophies, but I do have experience. I have experience, and I am going to share it with you because it's all I can truthfully offer you. This experience means very much to me. I think it can also suggest a lot for how teachers, schools, and society need to change.

Being Latina in school is hard. Why? First, being young is difficult enough in today's violent and frightening society. Being within a "minority" category makes it even more difficult. You see, I have gone to many different schools. I have attended public, parochial, and independent schools. I have had to adapt and learn to survive in each environment because they were all very different from each other. In the process, I have come to realize that being Latina adds a lot to my experiences. What does "being Latina" mean? It means I have learned

171

that it isn't I who is ignorant, It's the "American dream" mentality that brain-washes newcomers to this country that is a result of ignorance. When I use the term, "American dream," I am referring to one in which the father works 9 to 5 in an office building, and wears a Bill Blass original suit. The housewife/mother is cooking in their duplex watching over the two kids, who play with the dog in the yard while waiting for their dad to come home in his station wagon. Face it, this scenario is perfectly all right for some people, but for others it's not reality nor would they want it to be. It doesn't mean, however, that we should be treated differently because we don't try to live out that dream. Latinos, whether they live in Greenwich or in the South Bronx, have one thing in common: We all want to receive respect. Latino youth are going to play a major part in the future. We are not a lost generation, we are definitely struggling. Because of this struggle we have lost many of our peers only because I get the impression that many of the people (adults) declaring that we're lost, *actually want* to lose us. I know that our education is the basis of our survival, but if we don't feel wanted or cared about by our educators at school, what chance do we have? If it's truly in anyone's heart to help us, they should start by removing the labels and trying to look at the people behind the angry eyes and harsh faces: I can't count how many times I myself have felt anger and hurt because no one seems to care about the person I am, but cares more about what box I checked in the "Optional" section on standardized tests. No, we're not all the same. We don't all sell drugs and we don't all go around gang banging. Many of those who do, only do so because they have grown up being told that they can't do anything else. No, we don't all have children at 15 and if we do, it doesn't mean we're giving up and trying to get money through a system that doesn't know the meaning of respect. Who enjoys feeling like trash when the person on the opposite side of the desk tells them that they're lazy? Would you enjoy it? Would you feel motivated to do anything? Would you think you had a chance? I don't think you would appreciate being made to look inferior and of little worth. Being told this time after time you would start to question it yourself.

Do you understand the meaning of family? Have you ever lived with your grandmother and aunts and felt like you had three mothers? Do you understand what it means to have such close relationships within your family? That there never is a question whether the food that's cooking in your uncle's home is for you, too? Or that there really is no need for a special occasion to visit? Or that every time one of the younger family members has a birthday, no matter what, he or she is recognized and his or her existence is celebrated? Well, that's family to me. Along with that, comes so much intimacy and respect that the thought of a teacher frequently telling you that your family is second priority is unacceptable even though we are brought up to respect elders. Yes, I have had teachers preach to me that my attendance at school was more important than helping my mother. I don't believe that, therefore, how are we to determine who or what is priority? When you have influential forces constantly contradicting one another (in this case parents vs. teachers) it is difficult to find a balance that will appease everyone. There is no question about expectations that rules are to be followed faithfully and rigidly, no matter what the situation. Family is always first, we are expected to follow what our family sets down, it's part of growing up, yet there has to be an understanding that Latinos have a different culture and different values. (What is accepted here in the schools and school girl's life may not be in the island.)

One of the most difficult issues to understand for many Latino parents is the independence and liberty that North American children obtain. Many Latinas are living with parents who were brought up in their native countries. Being 18 here means personal independence from your home. Being 18 here and being Latina means conflicts, especially if your parents don't understand or agree with the North American ways. In Latin America when a girl turns 15 her family celebrates her transition from childhood to womanhood with a gala called a *Quinceñera*. This doesn't mean that she can do what she wants but there is an understanding that the girl is maturing. In the United States, this would be called "Sweet 16," but the birthday is not celebrated like *Quinceñera* in Latin America. When youth turn 18 in the United States, they are legally permitted to move away from their parents' home to live on their own. In a Latina household, many times, trying to move away is seen as trying to defy or rebel. Many girls are not allowed to have boyfriends until they are well into their late teens and if they have them at younger ages, it's a very conservative, strict, and traditional process (there are exceptions to the rule). Due to the fact that many aren't allowed this freedom, issues like sex, birth control, and sexually transmitted diseases are not discussed. I've known many girls who have boyfriends hidden from their parents. The girls often do not know how to protect themselves and end up becoming pregnant or infected with some type of illness. In school, we receive minimal education or misinformation concerning sexuality and health. Youth should have proficient resources concerning these issues. Unfortunately, we don't. We should have role models that understand our need for someone who is willing to talk and explain confusing issues. Many times this is not available at home or in our classrooms. Then what? As educators (if you are human and I know you are), you should try to make yourselves available and let your students know that you are available when they need someone who is willing to put aside their job for a minute and talk. I strongly recommend, however, that if you do this, you do it from your heart and not your paycheck.

Language is also another important issue. The Spanish language is part of being Latina and even though most people who don't understand it reject it, we will continue to fight for what is rightfully ours. The ability to speak Spanish is not acquired in order to talk about other people who don't speak English nor to intimidate people who speak a different language. It's our form of communication, our beautiful harmony of sounds that has been bashed, disrespected, and belittled, yet still survives. I myself struggle to maintain my Spanish, trying not to pay attention to teachers who have constantly forced me to cease speaking Spanish while in school even if I was speaking with my Latino friends on my own time. These teachers tried to make me believe that English was better. It also isn't fair for English speakers to assume that Latinos who don't speak English will surrender Spanish to learn. The language is part of our culture and always will be. There is nothing wrong with the assumption that Latinos want to learn English, but to believe that English is superior is pure fiction. Most people from other cultures understand that to survive in the United States you have to learn English. This is true, but no one wants to give up part of themselves and what makes them who they are. There has to be respect given to those who speak a language other than English because the truth is, being bilingual is a lot more convenient, interesting, and beautiful.

School is a very important part of a Latina girl's life. It is usually expected by her parents that a Latina girl will do one of two things: finish high school and continue through college, graduate, get married in her 20s, and settle down and support a family, or not continue in school after high school graduation and get married and have children. For example, when I was in the eighth grade, my guidance counselor (an older White man) called me into his office to talk about my future plans. When I told him I wanted to be lawyer, his response was "Well, I suggest that because you don't have well-developed skills, you reconsider your aspirations. . . . Don't your people like to have children? Perhaps that would suit you better." These expectations are not appropriate for all Latina girls. With this in mind, it should be clear how hard it is when a Latina girl who is raised here tries to break away from the "norm" to do what she wants and not what people think she wants. Yes, higher education should be an expectation. One that should be supported and encouraged by parents, teachers, and administrators. If appropriate for another individual, creating a family is fine. There is a whole world of possibilities and Latina girls should not feel that because of their financial, social, or any other type of status that these doors are closed for them. Everyone deserves the right to know that these doors are open and if a Latina girl wants to step through, she should have the chance to do so. It is the teacher's job to inform students as to what kinds of programs and assistance are available to help them achieve their goals.

There is always an issue with culture shock. I have lived in the city all of my life. During my sophomore year in high school, I attended an independent school in western Massachusetts. I arrived there in January and remained until June. Everyone was dressed in different styles, they spoke differently, and worried about different issues. To add to that, I was living on campus in the mountains. I had a hard time adjusting and I never felt like I was part of the community. My grades suffered and I did too. Now I am aware of what it is like to live away from home. (Hopefully, in college I won't have to go through it again.) I realized how much more comfortable I felt in the city. That is another aspect that many adults don't take into consideration nor believe exist. Beyond school life and home life, *street life* plays a big role in many Latinas' lives. Is it right for students to find it natural to be searched every morning and have police officers surveilling the halls when they arrive at school? You can no longer assume that gangs and violence only play a role in males' lives because on the street, gender specifications no longer exist. Things like female gangs are beginning to rival male gangs. Death, guns, and knives are not aware nor do they care if you are a boy or girl. Girls and boys are killing one another and they usually don't know why. The transition that we make from home to street to school and back to the street affects our sanity. These are among the important issues in many urban Latino youths' minds. You can hardly blame students for feeling resentment toward individuals who assume things based on the way they dress, the music they listen to, and the way they verbally express their ideas. People have to stop following stereotypes. People have to give importance to these issues that directly affect concentration, motivation, and participation. These are vital accoutrements to success in school. If a student cannot do these things because he or she is too busy thinking of how he or she is going to get home, then something is seriously wrong.

As I stated in the beginning of this chapter, we are living in a violent and frightening society. Teachers, I understand that many of these issues need a collective of strong people to address them, but if you as individuals attempt to make students feel that they are safe in your classrooms and that you do care about them, their daily lives, and their future, you have taken a step in the right direction. I don't know how else to explain it. Labels have to be thrown away. We cannot expect to all like one another or to agree with each other. Consequently, however, we are all human and we do have to live together. If we don't learn how to, we're going to lose more than my generation.

Shouldn't these be the basic concerns for educational reform? If not, then what are?

IV

NEW
CONCEPTUALIZATIONS
AND VISIONS

This section presents the different voices of university-based educators, students, and a school superintendent. Its project is to engender a critical theoretical and practical approach to education reform that has social change at its center.

In the first chapter, Ochoa and Espinosa (chapter 14) argue that the underachievement of ethnically diverse and low-income students cannot simply be blamed on the students or the schools, nor can it be remedied solely by educational interventions. Such achievement must instead be examined within the concept of public equity, that is, by analyzing the ways in which social class, political power, access to institutional decision making, and self-interest shape social policy and the allocation of resources. They present a public equity and critical pedagogy model for analyzing social and educational policy and practices that contribute to student disempowerment and present recommendations for action at the national, state, and city levels. What this model and their recommendations evince is a framework that connects schools and school reform to the social, political, and economic systems; assuring that these systems work in ways that nurture the human condition of youth—academically, socially, and politically, is a responsibility that each one of us can assume. The context and format of this intervention for you personally and you in concert with others is something that you should think about as you read this chapter.

In chapter 15, Negroni considers what it means to educate all of our children. Negroni, the superintendent of an urban Massachusetts school system (and the only Puerto Rican to ever hold this post in the state), asserts that there are four major transformations that are at the root of required systemic change: organizational, pedagogical, social and attitudinal, and political. As an administrator engaged in working toward these transformations, both in his own school district and in a New England-based organization of superintendents, Negroni offers a voice and perspective that is different from the students, public school and university teachers, and the advocates and community activists present in other chapters. His text makes clear that, although grassroots work for educational reform is essential, changes must also occur in the visions and actions of the administration.

Chapter 16 is mine. It delves into what it really means to make a difference in schools and challenges the reader to locate his or her own social visions and beliefs and examine the association between these visions and beliefs and his or her commitment and action. It calls for a revisioning of society and schools and a reworking of pedagogical practice so that democracy, equity, and justice are at the base. And it implores you, the reader, to take a stand in all of this.

The substance of the chapter comes from Dominican, Puerto Rican, Chicana, Mexican, and Haitian adolescents and a South American Indigenous student. These students talk about what is wrong and what has to change in schools and, in so doing, craft an authentic framework and direction for school and classroom-based transformations – a framework and direction that are relevant to real life. Revealed in their words is a deep and critical awareness of the ideological and social issues that frame school policy, pedagogy, and relations; also present is a spoken as well as unspoken demand that we become more cognizant and socially aware as adults, and that we assume responsibility. This last chapter of the book should not leave you complacent.

The final piece of the volume is a poem written by Sandra Marcelino, who, at the time she wrote it, was 14 years old. Sandra's words exuberate self-respect, dignity, and strength: a willingness to stand up, speak out, and to struggle with stolid commitment and conviction. As educators, activists, advocates, students, and parents interested in educational and social change, should this not be at the center of our individual and collective practice and vision?

As you read the different chapters here, you may want to consider the following guiding questions:

- How do the authors similarly and differently envision educational and social change? How do your own views compare to those presented?
- What are the practical contexts, implications, and possibilities suggested or implied by these visions? Do any challenge or support your own work?
- What conceptualizations and visions do you take from the chapters here? How do these visions tie into other chapters or ideas that you have read in this text? How can these visions be made reality in your school or community? What will be your role in the change struggle and process?

14

Beyond Educational Reform: Public Equity and Critical Pedagogy

Alberto M. Ochoa
Ruben W. Espinosa

The 100 largest urban school systems in the United Statse contain 20% of all K-12 African American students; more than 45% of all Latino/Hispanic students, and 45% of all Asian students. These urban school districts have a substantial impact on the human capital of the nation (Action Council on Minority Education [ACME], 1990; Hill, 1993). Within the communities of these urban districts, one finds significant student disempowerment. Most of these students are poor and lacking the skills to succeed in school and in the workforce. Specifically, these urban districts have a student dropout rate of more than 40%; have more than 70% of the students reading, writing, and computing below grade level; have physical facilities that are overcrowded and dilapidated; have significantly large numbers of limited English proficient students; have the majority of the least experienced teachers; have budgets that are complemented by state and federal compensatory funds; have within-district school budgets that are unequal, with the majority of the ethnically diverse schools receiving less base funds than majority White schools; and have a curricula that is remedial/compensatory in nature (ACME, 1990; Edmonds, 1979; Espinosa & Ochoa, 1992; Haggstrom, Blaschke, & Shavelson 1991; Hudson Institute, 1987).

Within the context of major ethnically diverse demographic and workforce trends, this chapter discusses the need for a model of public equity and critical pedagogy for analyzing social and educational policy and practices that contribute to student disempowerment. Specifically, an overview of public equity and educational reform is discussed. A public equity model and approaches for

179

analyzing the model are presented. In addition, recommendations within the context of a public equity approach are made for our national, state, county, and local governments, public agencies, and labor and businesses. Such recommendations are presented as areas that need immediate attention to curb the dramatic underachievement of our low income and ethnically diverse youth.

In the 1990s, 85% of the new workforce entrants will be women and persons of ethnically diverse backgrounds (African American, American Indian, Latino/ Hispanic, and Asian). These are the groups that presently have limited school success and representation in the jobs of the postindustrial era—in oceanography, the space industry, bio-engineering, and telecommunications. Furthermore, 65% of the jobs in the 1990s will require 1 to 4 years, or more, of college (Hudson Institute, 1987). The agenda of our national educational reform has been to address this issue (Asayesh, 1993). Yet, all indicators point to continual failure. In California, with two major educational reforms, AB65 (1977) and SB813 (California Legislative, 1983), more than 75% ethnically diverse students continue to achieve below Grade 3, 6, 8, and 12 levels. The Hudson Institute, in its *Workforce 2000* report, states, "Minority workers are not only less likely to have had satisfactory schooling and on-the-job training, they may have language, attitude, and cultural problems that prevent them from taking advantage of the jobs that will exist" (p. 5).

These conditions are projected to become more dismal if we fail to address our political, social, and education public equity responsibility. Such responsibility calls for public policy and support that nurtures the development of youth to acquire the skills needed for the workforce of the postindustrial era.

Public policy that perceives the needs of disempowered youth from a deficit position can also contribute to the present condition of underachievement, crime, and human dependency on government. However, if public policy and services are designed to change the causes of disempowerment and nurture the development of the human condition, then the quality of our democratic society will truly provide equal opportunity for all.

DISCOURSE ON PUBLIC EQUITY
AND EDUCATIONAL REFORM

In the late 1970s and 1980s, a number of educational reforms were initiated in response to the need for our nation to prepare youth for the informational economy. Subsumed under these reforms was the increasing awareness to address the lack of educational achievement of low-income and ethnically diverse students (Cuban, 1990; Elmore & McLaughlin, 1988; Hill, 1993; Honig, 1985; Kliebard, 1988; Slavin, 1989).

Examination of the literature on educational reform during these periods, whose focus range from classroom teacher-centered instruction (Cremin, 1988; Goodlad, 1984) to centralizing and decentralizing authority to govern schools (Katznelson & Weir, 1985; Kearns, 1988), suggests that such reforms have had little impact on the large urban centers of our nation (Cuban, 1990; Guthrie, 1987). Although the initiation of educational reform to show concern for underskilled youth is popular and ongoing, few reforms have ever been effective and/or implemented. Cuban (1990) argued that it is important for policymakers, educators, researchers, and administrators to understand why reforms are rarely effective. Such understanding calls for pursuing problems that match the school context and solution—through the understanding of national economic shifts and the skills demands of the workforce; public policy directed at enhancing the skills of youth; governance that implements high academic expectations; school structures that are conducive to learning; staff expertise that matches the student needs; curricula that is designed to prepare youth for the postindustrial informational society, and social support for work–study that connects youth to the world of work and exposure to career choices (Cuban, 1990; Haggstrom et al., 1991; Ravitch, 1993; Tyack, 1974).

Related to the research literature on inequity in schools, is the role of research in understanding the dynamics of the conditions leading to inequality. The literature argues the position that the macro–micro focus of research and its interrelationships need to be reconceptualized. Macrostudies examine structural forces conceptualized at the societal level. Microstudies examine individual or group actions and responses to constraints imposed on social actors (De George, 1991). Such research calls for the understanding of inequality within the context of society, while also providing data on cultural elements, human actions, processes, and practices that contribute to inequality (Skuttnab-Kangas & Cummins, 1988). In the context of schools located in large urban centers in our nation, the need to examine macro- and microconditions contributing to and causing inequality becomes imperative.

The research literature on the mobilization of school resources also affirms that educational reform has failed, for the most part, to address the quality of schooling and equity issues that serve the needs of ethnically, racially, or culturally diverse youth. It is documented that the African American, Latino/Hispanic, Indochinese, and American Indian youth are more at risk in the third grade than the average youngster, and three times more likely to be a high school dropout (California Tomorrow, 1988; Espinosa & Ochoa, 1992; Ochoa & Hurtado, 1987; Rumberger, 1987). There are also reports that dominate the discourse on educational reform in which the issues of race, language, and gender are found not to be relevant in the analysis of school excellence (Hill, 1993; Kirst, 1989; Tetreult & Schmuck, 1985). Furthermore, we know that excellence means resources to improve the achievement of the top 30% of the students in our schools. To undertake research that will identify and document policy, practices, and programs that can improve the quality of life of our youth in the urban settings of our school communities, a public equity model is proposed.

PUBLIC EQUITY MODEL

Much of the research on the causes of poor academic achievement, high dropout rates, and unemployment has focused on the schools. A direct relationship has been established. Schools, primarily those with a non-White majority, have been labeled the cause (Catterall & Cota-Robles, 1988; Denton, 1987; Haycock & Navarro, 1988; Hill, 1993). But academic and social segregation in the schools is only another symptom of the more fundamental, pervasive societal inequities. Correlating symptoms with one another does little to explain, and ultimately to alter, the sources of the problem (Haggstrom et al., 1991; Oakes, 1985; Ochoa & Hurtado, 1987; University of California, 1989).

In 1988–1989, the California Department of Education reported that more than 50% of the students enrolled in schools in the state were members of ethnically diverse groups. Yet, for all grade levels, achievement scores of schools with a White majority were consistently higher than schools of all other ethnicities. Before the correlation between schools and various outcomes can be meaningful, the relationship between segregation and education needs to be understood.

Segregation was held to be unconstitutional in 1954 with the ruling in *Brown vs. Board of Education*. The Supreme Court found "separate but equal" facilities to be inherently unequal. With the advent of business and "magnet" schools, some desegregation has been achieved. But in California, 80% of the schools are not ethnically balanced. Why does educational achievement decline when the balance shifts to a nonmajority? And since the "minority groups" now comprise one half of the student population in a democratic society, why are these numbers not being translated into nurturing, supportive policy and programs for action?

Part of the answer can be seen in the wake of the government's response to the *Brown* decision. The ruling requires school districts to create and implement proposals for desegregating schools "with all due speed." As of today, most districts have not implemented such proposals, and many more have yet to even devise them. The lack of governmental enthusiasm and commitment was easy to read, and rendered the policy virtually meaningless. Further analysis to the answer lies in the distribution of power. Once federal and state laws are codified, policies and programs are developed by those with the mandate to do so. These policymakers are subject to pressure from various sources, including corporations, developers and other influential individuals, media, politicians, and special interest groups. For the most part, policymakers do not reflect the diversity of the community. Persons of color have limited access to the develop-

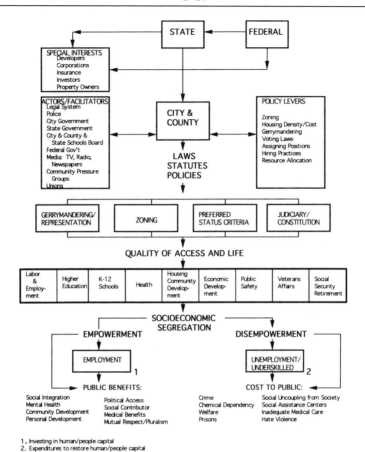

14.1.   Public equity model

diveristy of the community. Persons of color have limited access to the development of socioeconomic, political, and educational policy. For example, gerrymandering and redistricting are often used to maintain the status quo and political power. The result is a continuation of policies favoring those in power—most often a White majority or those with an economic power base. Figure 14.1 illustrates a top–down power base. The model depicts the interaction between governmental public policy and social institutions in addressing the quality of access and life of its citizens. Such interaction dictates social, economic, political, and educational policy that can both empower or disempower[1] the human

---

[1]*Empowerment* refers to the development of youth who will have the necessary academic and social skills to be productive members in a democratic society—socially, economically, and politically. *Disempowerment* is the absence of this condition.

condition. The model from top–down establishes the powerful role of the federal and state governments in directing social, economic, and political policy. Within its legal influence, the federal government establishes policy as to what states and communities must respect, support, and monitor. The federal government through civil rights policy, executive orders, and guidelines provides the minimal parameters for addressing housing, employment, social security, health, and other federal priorities. It is at the federal level that policy guidelines for implementing federal laws and policy are developed as distributed to states, counties, local governments, and schools. The state level becomes responsible for assuring compliance with federal policy. It is only when state policy and laws are stronger than those of the federal government that state laws are followed. However, if federal law is stronger, federal laws supersede state laws.

A major influential component of the public equity model is the role of special interest groups such as developers, corporate interests, insurance companies, investors, and property owners. Special interest groups directly influence what laws and policy are supported, with what degree of comprehensiveness, and degree of "reasonableness" and cost. The direct linkage between special interest groups and local, state, and federal government representatives is through political channels, campaign donations, and associational support.

The power of special interest groups is visible through the actors and facilitators of public policy who both establish and regulate laws. City and county representatives shape the political boundaries through gerrymandering; central zoning ordinances and the growth of the communities; promote preferred status criteria as to who needs to meet what criteria to have access to public positions, commissions, and boards; and regulate the judiciary system through appointments and regulations. These laws, regulations, and practices take the form of legislative committees at the state government level where thousands of bills are introduced to influence the quality of life of its citizens. These committees include labor and employment, higher education, K–12 public education, health, housing and community development, public safety, veterans affairs, social security, retirement, and economic development. In this public equity model, these nine major legislative committees decide the socioeconomic status and segregation in our communities.

The lower part of the model illustrates public equity disempowerment and empowerment. When socioeconomic and political policy is concerned with the nurturing and development of youth – public benefits are derived. The community is rewarded when youth acquire social competency and skills and become adults who are socially integrated into the community; become individuals who possess good mental health; are citizens who are concerned with their personal and community development; are active in our democratic process; are skilled and employed, and are contributors to the quality of life of the community; are recipients of medical benefits, and are persons who promote respect and diversity in our society. Public benefits are derived by the society when we invest in human capital.

When socioeconomic and political policy is driven by how our institutions need to restore the human condition, cost to the public for the restoration of human despair becomes the focus of concern. The community pays when individuals are unemployed and underskilled. Such a state creates problems in the form of crime, chemical dependency, welfare, the need for prisons, social uncoupling, individuals unable to pay for their medical care, hate, violence, and dependency on social assistance centers.

Empowering youth to succeed in our schools and society is the only choice of a responsible democratic society. To achieve this goal, the public equity model needs to be viewed from an open system theory approach. In his description of an open social system, Owens (1970) called for an organization (educational system) to interact with their environment (social, economic, political). In an open system, schools and educational systems are capable of facilitating their infrastructure (tasks, structures, technological resources, people) to respond to a variety of environmental contingencies, while maintaining a higher degree of integration among units/departments. Owens elaborated that school systems, as sociotechnical systems, are in constant dynamic interaction with social, political, and economic systems. In his analysis of Owens' work on open systems, De George (1991) provided examples of such institutional interaction.

> The "environmental contingencies" to which public school organizations may have to adapt are many. Public Law 94-142 on special education, the *Lau vs. Nichols* Supreme Court Decision of 1974, state laws regarding bilingual education or mandatory curriculum on drug and alcohol abuse, immigration patterns, which lead to increased enrollment of limited English speaking students in the schools, the public's dissatisfaction with public education and its perception of the need for educational reform—all these are examples of "environmental contingencies" to which the schools have had to adapt by making changes in their internal arrangements. (p. 5)

> Furthermore, State government may formalize aspects of educational goals by creating such things as minimum competency graduation standards or Congress can have an effect on school goals as seen in P.L. 94-142 or in Title VII of the 1968 Bilingual Education Act. In the final analysis, schools and school systems may choose to adapt to or to resist environmental influences. School desegregation and the elimination of discriminatory practices in student testing, grouping and tracking are examples of areas in which there has been resistance to external changes and maintenance of the *status quo*. (p. 6)

The public equity model calls for a community policy shift as to how we support and promote the development of low income ethnically diverse youth.

We can continue the present path of blaming the victim for their existing disempowerment. Or we can support and promote the development of youth through policy that is proactive and accountable.

APPROACHES FOR ANALYZING
THE PUBLIC EQUITY MODEL

In the operationalization of the public equity model, one needs to be cognizant of the approaches that can be used to perpetuate the deficit/blaming-the-victim perspective in addressing the development of our school communities. These perspectives blame the individual for the problems of school communities, while failing to account for the systemic conditions that perpetuate inequality. The research literature is rich in its documentation of how educational policy and practices can create inequitable distribution of knowledge, power, and resources (Apple, 1992; Bernstein, 1975; Giroux, 1981; Hill, 1993; Oakes, 1986; Scheurich & Imber, 1990). Three paradigms serve as a guide for differentiating how the public equity model can be used—the functionalist, interpretist, and critical theory approaches.

In the functionalist approach, the focus is on the technical knowledge and expert control by those in power positions. The decisions to address the needs of youth who are disempowered are made by those in expert positions who need to make the final decisions. In the case of education, the decisions on schools and curriculum are made by state and city politicians, with superintendents serving the interests of those in influential political positions. In this perspective, public schools are not part of the power center in the community and thus are dependent on the actors that formulate the interest on the community (Campbell, Cunningham, Nystrand, & Usdan, 1985; Feinberg & Soltis, 1985).

The interpretist approach rejects the functionalist perspective and calls for participation of all affected participants in any change effort. This approach insists on participatory involvement based on real power sharing (Feinberg & Soltis, 1985; Sarason, 1982). The implicit assumption of this approach is that participation alone gives adequate voice to diverse parties, while ignoring prior existing diversity of interest and power. In the context of education, although different sectors of the community are involved in policy decisions affecting youth, their voices are often advisory. The knowledge, power, and resources remain in the hands of those who control local and state governmental policies (Apple, 1982; Schumaker, 1990).

The critical theory approach takes the position that participation and the intent to share power is insufficient in democratic governance. This approach calls for equitable sharing of power and an analysis of how current ways or practices are grounded in the social context of the institution. Critical theory questions the framework of the way our lives are organized for us and examines human relationships in structural variables, namely, those of class, power, resources—as they relate to domination and repression. The critical theory approach seeks a systematic analysis of relationships between social, cultural, and political control (Feinberg & Soltis, 1985; Oakes, 1986; Rothberg & Harvey, 1993; Yeakey, 1987). With reference to the educational context, this approach moves away from blaming someone for the problem and seeks to identify the structural conditions contributing to educational inequality and access.

TOWARD A CRITICAL PEDAGOGY AND PUBLIC EQUITY

Since the beginning of mass education, the education of ethnically diverse persons has been characterized by two restricting problems—access to both schools and colleges and inequality. These decoupling conditions exist because racism, discrimination, hate, and violence are behaviors that directly impact ethnically diverse communities in their pursuit of equality and equal participation in a democratic society.

Furthermore, the available research on educational organizations document that our public schools are stratified institutions. Some students are provided with "high status" knowledge that yields social and economic control. Others are relegated to a second-class citizenship both within our K–12 public school system and in the larger society (Haggstrom et al., 1991; Kitchen, 1990; Oakes, 1985). Presently, our public schools continue to treat our ethnically diverse students as second-class citizens and fail to nurture their educational development.

Maintaining a free and open democracy demands that we actively pursue equity and excellence for ethnically diverse youth—two values that require resources, high standards, public policy commitment, and community activism.

The function of the public equity model is to analyze social and institutional relationships from a critical theory perspective. Specifically to examine structural variables—class, power, knowledge, resources—that create unequal conditions for low income ethnically diverse students. This section presents the problem, conditions, and solutions and alternatives that need to be taken by the federal, state, county, and local agencies and communities. The public equity analysis seeks a critical pedagogy process (problem solving that is systems-based) to develop human capital that will be empowered to be contributors rather than being dependent on social institutions for their quality of life.

Problem

Schools have a dismal track record in providing ethnically diverse and low-income youths with the necessary skills to have access to the world of work.

More than 40% of our ethnically diverse youth dropout of school, whereas another 30% receive a high school diploma with academic deficiencies that make them underskilled and underemployed. Of the remaining 30%, only 15% enter college, and about 5% eventually receive a bachelor's degree (Haycock & Navarro, 1988).

Underskilled youth become dependent on social and economic assistance and this disempowers them to become contributors to society. Disempowerment (see Footnote 1 for definition of disempowerment) is a condition that is visible as early as the third grade for ethnically diverse students. In responding to this disempowering condition, schools tend to begin to implement promising practices to arrest the underachievement of low-income, ethnically diverse students at the junior and high school level. Unfortunately, it is 6 to 8 years too late— after the problem of underachievement was created (National Commission on Excellence in Education, 1983; Rothberg & Harvey, 1993). The empowerment of youth is not a process that begins at the junior or high school level, but one that must begin before kindergarten with school–community interventions and public commitment.

Compounding the problem is the fact that the largest percentage of students who leave before graduation are Latino/Hispanic and African American. Research studies find that underachievement in the areas of reading and math for 80% of our students is detected as early as the Grade 3 (Espinosa & Ochoa, 1992; Haycock & Navarro, 1988).

In addition, the absence of a systematic school accountability process to determine instructional and school program effectiveness allows schools to perpetuate educational expectancy bands that justify low achievement and student disempowerment. Schools are expected to perform to the socioeconomic background of their students. School success is based on schools performing to their level of expectation (Arias, 1984; Rothberg & Harvey, 1993; Zachman, 1987).

The costs of leaving school are obviously high for the underachiever and also high for community and society, which must bear the financial brunt of the underskilled youth's inability to hold a job. Considering the tragic circumstances of dropping out, preventive action within the schools is not only desirable, but imperative (Catterall & Cota-Robles, 1988; Hill, 1993; Los Angeles Unified school District, 1985).

In addition, with respect to school structural conditions, ethnically diverse and low-income school communities are disempowered by their lack of adequate school funding, unpredictable year-by-year budgetary allocations and inadequate school facilities. This situation creates overcrowding, absence of capital improvement, diminishing educational and recreational space, delimiting classroom and support service space, harmful school safety, high number of inexperience and/or unproductive staff that address the needs of students, overloaded administrative responsibilities in managing the school site, and zoning conditions that allows for overcrowded school communities (Espinosa & Ochoa, 1984, 1992).

Conditions of the Problem

In predicting ethnically diverse student academic success or failure, one needs to examine how the school views the student's background, the sociocultural characteristics of the school community, and how it attends to parental community input and involvement. Student achievement is strongly influenced by the extent to which federal/state/county/local governments, businesses and labor, media, school boards, teachers, administrators, and community persons advocate for the promotion of student talents. In addition, one needs to acknowledge how public and educational policy can positively or negatively drive pedagogical approaches designed to develop student mastery of skills.

Without a doubt, the most prevailing issue facing the ethnically diverse community is the need for the development of a new attitude on the part of local, county, and state government that will not only accept, but promote the development of its youth. Yet, laws alone will not change behavior unless the majority of the population accepts that it is to their best interest to work in the empowerment of ethnically diverse youth. Equal opportunity can be legislated, but commitment to actualize such policies (that resides in the heart and minds of teachers and politicians) cannot be mandated. Thus, public policy hinders or promotes the necessary conditions to nurture our youth.

An example of public policy working against the interest of a community is visible at the local level in the establishment of zoning ordinances within a community. Zoning is intended to manage the amount and kind of growth of a community and to establish quality standards. In general, low-income communities have the least restrictive zoning that enable other communities to improve on their quality of environment. When a junkyard or industrial plant is located in such a neighborhood, its residents suffer from health risks, noise, and pollution. When a highway is constructed through the community, displacement and division occurs (University of California SCR 43 Task Force, 1989). The greatest harm is the self-fulfilling prophecy of government and schools toward the low-income ethnically diverse community—being of low income, its children are expected to underachieve and be underskilled. At the same time, we most acknowledge and recognize that we are part of the problem when we fail to exert our power of broad-based community participation that is guided toward bridging the home and school in the support of student achievement and holding local and county government accountable.

Political representation as dictated by gerrymandering has serious consequences on the quality of schools. School facilities, often overcrowded in the low-income communities, serve as a good example of who controls the resources. At the city level, politicians make calculated decisions on growth management.

Zoning regulations are passed to allow for only new single homes in the middle- and upper income communities, whereas apartment complexes with nonexistent recreational sites are authorized for the low-income communities. In a district facing growth, powerful development interests take over. The first priority is for schools to be built in the newer communities, while revitalizing older, and overutilized inner-city facilities that have significant numbers of underachieving and underserved students go unattended. Who has the power to make decisions about public equity becomes very important (Hill, 1993; Scheurich & Imber, 1990).

Also, most educational funding is tax based. Real property taxes and federal matching funds comprise a school's tax base. Inner-city and declining neighborhoods have a lower tax base and therefore receive a proportionable smaller amount of federal funds. Because of this, they have difficulty competing with schools in wealthier neighborhoods. The flight of affluent Whites to the suburbs further increases the tax base of the better schools, and with the greater share of federal funds, these schools continue to offer programs with superior resources.

Political influence, by different actors, also influences public equity. City council, for example, generally passes policy that will directly impact on the quality of facilities, space, and resources of a school community without notifying or discussing such policy with school district officials. This lack of articulation among public agencies creates inequality. The lack of coordination is between policymakers and those implementing policies. For example, very little attention is given to the relationship between schools and zoning policy. Rezoning by a city to allow for increased housing density does not precipitate a rezoning for school planning to compensate for increased student populations.

Thus, public policy concern with human capital/resources can empower or disempower student school success. For example, school achievement expectancies channel students into five respective curricular tracks—remedial, vocational, noncollege bound, college-bound, and gifted. These tracks are designed to address the characteristics and perceived needs of children as per zoning and housing density patterns, low-income status, language background of community, parental type of occupation, welfare incidence, and transiency. All factors have a direct linkage with federal, state, and local politics.

The problem of the underachieving ethnically diverse students is highly complex and interrelated with local, county, and state government policy, the values of people in leadership positions, the home, the student, the school, as well as organizational and structural factors that have a direct and indirect impact on the root causes of underachievement. Unfortunately, the focus of school policy toward ethnically diverse students, the orientation of major research studies, programs, and practices that seek to address the underachiever are narrow and based on a deficit model. As previously stated, this model blames the student, family, and sociocultural background of the student, ignoring public policy and organizational and structural school-related variables and conditions (Benne, Bennis, & Chinn, 1969; Espinosa & Ochoa, 1992; Oakes, 1985).

Solution and Alternatives

The type of schooling ethnically diverse and low-income students receive has powerful implications regarding the inception of their underachievement and the possible solutions. Present research has begun to examine policy issues and institutional and organizational conditions affecting disempowerment (Schumacher, 1990). For example, with respect to school size, research results suggest that urban elementary schools with more than 650 students, tend to be ethnically impacted, have the minimum base funds, and have large categorical programs and funding that have a negative bearing on student learning and motivation (Espinosa & Ochoa, 1992; Fine, 1991; Kirst, 1989; Venezky & Winfield, 1979). In general, the findings of the available research suggests serious concerns about the direction being taken by state, county, and local governments and educational institutions to develop effective programs for addressing the educational needs of ethnically diverse and low-income students (Kitchen, 1990; University of California SCR 43 Task Force, 1989).

To attain ethnically diverse human capital via communitywide collaboration and educational practices that yield educational excellence, the following recommendations are suggested for action at the national, state, county, and local levels. After each area of action, specific recommendations are made.

National, State, County, and Local Vision. Ethnically diverse and low-income youth need to be given the highest priority by all policymakers in promoting and establishing policies that are fair, just and that empower youth to be productive members of their communities.

- Local and county governments must form a new coalition that is proactive in investing in human capital that enables ethnically diverse youths to acquire motivation, knowledge, performance skills, community consciousness in actualizing their career choices.
- Employability dictates that schools, with the support of local, county, and state governments, prepare ethnically diverse youths with the skills needed in an informational technology that requires high-order skills.
- Empowerment of ethnically diverse youths calls for the collaborative involvement of educators, civic leaders, local, county, and state governments, social agencies, labor and businesses all working together in the investment of youth.
- A local, county, state government report should be issued annually to assess public commitment on the progress of preparing ethnically diverse youths for the world of work and/or higher education.

- Higher education, local, county, and state governments and the K–12 educational leadership should be involved annually jointly in addressing and articulating policy and practices to empower ethnically diverse and low-income youths to have access to higher education and career choices in the informational world of work.

Political Representation.   Imperative in the process of actualizing equity and excellence for ethnically diverse youths, is community activism in developing, nurturing, and preparing leadership in attaining school board representation.

- Training should be provided to community persons leading to the identification of a cadre of individuals (across gender) to be involved in higher order leadership development.
- A cadre of ethnically diverse community persons at the local and county levels, who would receive training to become school board members, should be developed.
- A Grassroot political networks in specific communities should be established for planning, implementing, and evaluating ethnically diverse board members campaigns.
- Action research on community efforts should be undertaken to effectively partake in the decision-making process of the community.

Access to Higher Education.   School districts must move from a policy of equal access of resources to a policy of equal expectations and equal treatment that yields an ethnically diverse labor force reflective of its community composition.

- School policy and personnel should view the background experiences of the students not as deficits, but as experiences to be used to develop concepts, literacy skills, and critical thinking.
- Testing and diagnostic assessment approaches should be used as tools for identifying the cognitive strengths and needs of students—in order to enrich their cognitive skills and to develop their intellect.
- It should be recognized that students learn at different rates, through different approaches and learning styles.
- Additive bilingual instruction and different types of curriculum programs should be provided, while maintaining high standards, core curricula, and expectations, to address the diverse academic and linguistic development of students.
- Educational curricula, school services, and staff must recognize and support cultural and linguistic uniqueness in the development of youth who are socially literate and responsible for the maintenance of democratic principles.

School Personnel Sensitivity and Staff Competence. Universities, undergraduate programs, and teacher education institutions need to be accountable for preparing and training school personnel who can demonstrate cross-cultural competence to address the pluralism of our school systems. Institutions of higher education must be accountable to preparing teachers, counselors, and administrators who can:

- incorporate the nature of pluralism and the diversity of the ethnically diverse community in the overall preparation of teacher candidates;
- demonstrate an understanding of the cultural, historical and educational significance of cultural and linguistic diversity;
- demonstrate knowledge of the application of sociocultural and linguistic diversity to cognition, learning, and schooling;
- demonstrate concrete applications and strategies for ethnically diverse classroom;
- demonstrate sensitivity in working with ethnically diverse parents as equal partners in the education of youth; and
- develop effective organizational school climate that facilitate and guide youth to achieve academically and to attain the necessary skills to enter careers and/or higher education.

Equitable Quality Resources. Ethnically diverse and low-income school communities must be provided with equitable fiscal, structural facilities, staff, and quality instructional programs that promote a pedagogically sound school climate.

- The *Serrano vs. Priest* standard of $100 per pupil base funds variation between schools should be applied as a new standard of school equity.
- Student attendance (ADA) should be matched to within-district equitable funding, school facilities, and staff to deliver pedagogically sound educational services.
- School utilization upper limits should be established at the elementary level not to exceed 650 students, with specified classroom and building capacity conducive to learning, student safety, and school climate.
- Long-term fiscal support on a 3-year cycle should be provided for impacted low-income school communities based on a funding formula and student growth pattern, to allow for planning and program implementation.
- Staff development resources should be identified to initiate a dropout prevention support team that can assist teachers, administrators, and counselors to develop effective intervention plans for underachieving ethnically diverse students.

Empowerment of Youth at the Preschool to Grade 8 Levels.   Ethnically diverse and low-income students must be provided with school interventions that are preventive in nature, carefully planned, addressing the core curriculum educational needs of students, and that prepares them for the world of work of the informational society.

- The early identification of academic needs as based on what standards students are expected to achieve at each grade level should be provided for.
- Instructional approaches that address the linguistic and academic needs of the student, and that create and ensure early school success at the preschool to Grade 3 level should be provided.
- A "mentor" teacher should be hired to teach at the most critical years of the student—preschool to Grade 3.

System of School Accountability.   Ethnically diverse and low-income school communities must be provided with an accountability system that is designed to provide its youth with the core curriculum that prepares them for the informational economy of the world of work, while addressing the prevention of early underachievement.

- Educational excellence should be mandated at every school, through a curricula that is driven by state core curriculum standards and highly challenging learning.
- Status-ranking expectancy bands must be eliminated and core curriculum expectations for all students established.
- Early underachieving prevention programs that begin at the preschool level and provide for the identification of needs, instructional intervention, and ongoing evaluation of the effectiveness of the intervention process should be established.

Parent Empowerment.   Provide training to ethnically diverse parents on home–school collaboration that will enable parents to monitor the academic achievement of their children and to collaborate with the school in their social and academic development.

- Parents should be trained in the most critical years of education—preschool to Grade 6—to address early parent intervention in the education of their sons or daughters.
- Parents should be given the skills to hold schools accountable for maintaining high academic expectations based on career choices for the 21st century.
- Parent-involvement programs should be established, requiring parents

to attend a minimum of one parent education class per quarter and one parent conference per semester.

- Train parents and school officials to collaborate in order to yield high aspirations, positive self-esteem, self-respect, and productive ethnically diverse youth who are proud of their language and culture and personal development.
- Train ethnically diverse parents to enable them to assist, motivate, guide their children at home in their social and academic development.

Careers and Jobs. Provide career job orientation at the K–6 grade level to begin to prepare ethnically diverse youth for the world of work.

- Early academic instruction needs to begin preparing ethnically diverse youth with fundamental communication, computational, and problem-solving skills that will be required by any employer.
- Multilingual competence for all youth must be promoted in order to connect our communities with the rest of the world through an English-plus policy and not English-only.
- Students needs should be matched with viable services and resources to enable them to be exposed to the core curriculum/world of work/career choices.
- Credentialed staff should be available and trained to meet the diverse academic and linguistic learning needs of students.

CONCLUSION

The findings of our previous research on achievement trends and inequitable resource allocation challenge the assumption that local communities and/or cities manage or provide public services in an equitable, fair, or reasonable manner. The concept of public equity demands an analysis of the ways in which social class, political power, access to institutional decision making, and self-interest shape social policy and the allocation of resources. The public equity model proposes discourse that can move our thinking from blaming people for their condition to an examination of the conditions faced by urban schools and communities from a macroperspective and permit all schools to provide equitable and sufficient educational services irrespective of students' economic, ethnic, racial, cultural, or linguistic characteristics.

A public equity model has been proposed, as well as recommendations for action, that begin to raise our consciousness as to our responsibility to assure that our social, political, and economic systems work directly with our schools to develop and nurture the human condition of our youth – academically, socially, and politically.

In the face of an egalitarian ideology, differentiated educational practices, economic and political inequality among different segments of society suggest the need to reexamine social policy and educational practices impacting negatively on low-income ethnically diverse youths. We face the commitment to reexamine the values of equity and excellence, and their implications to the social, economical, political, and educational institutions of our community. This reexamination of values must encourage a renaissance of hope in our community and of pride in ethnically diverse decisions as to what our destiny will be as we press forward to actualize equality, freedom, and democratic principles.

Although political forums and educational conferences advocate for sound and effective programs for all students, our communities must insist on sound, effective, efficient, and relevant preschool to university education. With the achievements of science and with the social commitment of educators and people to actualize our democratic principles, we must hold our communities accountable for quality education, specifically at the preschool to Grade 3 level and up to the university level. Finally, it is imperative that we intervene collectively, socially, and politically, on behalf of our youth in order to transform their social, economic, and political opportunities and quality of life.

REFERENCES

Action Council on Minority Education. (1990, January). *Education that works an action plan for the education of minorities.* Cambridge: MIT Quality Education for Minority Project.

Apple, M. (1992). *Education and power.* Boston: Routledge & Kegan Paul.

Arias, M. B. (1984, January). *The status of educational attainment of Chicano/Latino students.* Paper presented at the Stanford University Latino Conference, Stanford, CA.

Asayesh G. (1993). Ten years after a nation at risk. *School Administrator, 50*(4), 8–14.

Benne, K. D., Bennis, W. G., & Chinn, P. (1969). *The planning of change.* New York: Holt, Rinehart & Winston.

Bernstein, B. (1975). *Class, codes and control: Vol. 3, Towards a theory of educational transmissions.* London, Routledge & Kegan Paul.

California Legislature. (1977). *Assembly bill 65: Education reform of 1977.* Sacramento: Author.

California Legislature. (1983). *Senate bill 813: Hughes-Hart education reform act of 1983.* Sacramento: Author.

California Tomorrow. (1988). *Crossing the school/house border.* San Francisco: Author.

Campbell, R. F., Cunningham, L. L., Nystrand, R. O., & Usdan, M. D. (1985). *The organization and control of American schools.* Columbus, OH: Merrill.

Catterall, J., & Cota-Robles, E. (1988, November). *The educationally at-risk: What numbers mean.* Paper presented at the Stanford University Accelerating the Education of At-Risk Students Conference, Stanford, CA.

Cremin, L. (1988). *American education: The metropolitan experience, 1876–1989.* New York: Harper & Row.

Cuban, L. (1990). Reforming again, again and again. *Educational Researcher, 19,* 3–13.

De George, G. (1991, February). *Essential elements of bilingual administration* (Working paper). Washington, DC: U.S. Department of Education.

Denton, T. W. (1987). *Dropouts, pushouts, and other casualties.* Center in Evaluation, Development, Research.

Edmonds, R. R. (1979). Effective schools for the urban poor. *Educational Leadership, 37,* 15–24.

Elmore, R. F., & McLaughlin, M. W. (1988). *Steady work: Policy, practice, and the reform of American education* (R-3574-NIE/RC). Santa Monica, CA: Rand.

Espinosa, R. W., & Ochoa, A. M.. (1984). *Achievement and ethnicity: The impact of selected variables on student achievement for the California public schools, 1977–78.* San Diego, CA: San Diego State University, Social Equity Center/ College of Education.

Espinosa, R. W., & Ochoa, A. M. (1992). *The educational attainment of California youth: A public equity crisis.* San Diego, CA: San Diego State University, College of Education.

Feinberg W., & Soltis F. J. (1985). *School and society.* New York: Teachers College Press.

Fine, M. (1991). *Framing dropouts: Notes on the politics of an urban public school.* Albany: State University of New York Press.

Giroux, H. (1981). *Ideology, culture, and the process of schooling.* Philadelphia: Temple University Press.

Goodlad, J. (1984). *A place called school.* New York: McGraw-Hill.

Guthrie, J. W. (1987). Exploring the political economy of national education reform. In W. Boyd & C. Kerchner (Eds.), *The politics of excellence and choice in education* (pp. 25–47). London: Falmer Press.

Haggstrom, G. W., Blaschke, R., & Shavelson, R. (1991). *After high school, then what? A look at the postsecondary sorting-out process for a American youth.* Santa Monica, CA: Rand.

Haycock, K., & Navarro S. (1988, May). *Unfinished business.* A report from the planning committee for the achievement council, Oakland, California.

Hill, P. T. (1993). Urban education. In RAND MR-100-RC, *Urban America: Policy choices for Los Angeles and the nation* (pp. 1–25). Santa Monica, CA: Rand.

Honig, B. (1985). *Last change for our children.* Reading, MA: Addison-Wesley.

Hudson Institute. (1987, June). *Workforce 2000: Work and workers for the twenty-first century.* Indianapolis, IN: Author.

Katznelson, I., & Weir, M. (1985). *Schooling for all: Class, race, and the decline of the democratic ideal.* New York: Basic Books.

Kearns, D. (1988). An educational recovery plan for America. *Phi Delta Kappan, 69,* 565–570.

Kirst, W. M. (1989). *Conditions of children in California.* Berkeley: PACE, School of Education, University of California, Berkeley.

Kitchen, D. (1990). *Educational tracking.* Unpublished doctoral dissertation, San Diego State University, Claremont Graduate School, San Diego.

Kliebard, H. M. (1988). Fads, fashions, and rituals: The instability of curriculum change. In L. N. Tanner (Ed.), *Critical issues in the curriculum* (pp. 16–34). Chicago: National Society for the Study of Education.

Los Angeles Unified School District. (1985, Feburary). *A study of student dropout in the Los Angeles Unified School District.* Los Angeles, CA: Author.

National Commission on Excellence in Education. (1983, April). *A nation at risk: The imperative of educational reform.* Washington, DC: U.S. Department of Education.

Oakes, J. (1985). *Keeping track: How schools structure inequality.* New Haven, CT: Yale University Press.

Oakes, J. (1986). Tracking inequality, and the rhetoric of reform: Why schools don't change. *Journal of Education, 168*(1), 60–80.

Ochoa, A. M., & Hurtado, J. (1987). *The empowerment of all students: A framework for the prevention of school dropouts.* San Diego, CA: San Diego State University, Policy Studies Department, College of Education.

Owens, R. G. (1970). *Organizational behavior in education* (2nd ed.). Englewood Cliffs, NJ: Prentice-Hall.

Ravitch, D. (1993). Launching a revolution in standards and assessment. *Phi Delta Kappan, 74*(10), 767–772.

Rothberg, I., & Harvey, J. J. (1993). Findings and recommendations. In *Federal policy options for improving the education of low income students* (Vol. 1, pp. 1–68). Santa Monica, CA: Rand.

Rumberger, R. W. (1987, Summer). High school dropouts: A review of issues and evidence. *Review of Educational Research, 57*(2), 101–121.

Sarason, S. B. (1982). *The culture of the school and the problem of change.* Boston: Allyn & Bacon.

Scheurich J. J., & Imber, M. (1990, April). *School reforms can produce societal inequalities.* Paper presented at annual meeting of the American Education Research Association, Boston, MA.

Schumaker, P.(1990). *Critical pluralism: Evaluating democratic performance in the resolution of community issues.* Lawrence: University Press of Kansas.

Skuttnab-Kangas, T., & Cummins, J. (1988). *Bilingualism or not: The education of minorities.* Clevedon: Multilingual Matters.

Slavin, R. (1989). PET and the pendulum: Faddism in education and how to stop it. *Phi Delta Kappan, 90,* 750–758.

Tetreult, M., & Schmuck, P. (1985). Equity, educational reform and gender. *Issues in Education, 3*(1), 45–67.

Tyack, D. (1974). *The one best system.* Cambridge, MA: Harvard University Press.

University of California SCR 43 Task Force. (1989, April). *The challenge: Latinos in a changing California.* Report to Senate Concurrent Resolution 43.

Venezky, R. L., & Winfield L. (1979). *Schools that succeed beyond expectations in teaching reading.* Newark: Department of Educational Studies, University of Delaware.

Yeakey, C. C. (1987). Critical thought and administrative theory: Conceptual approaches to the study of decision-making. *Planning and Changing, 18*(1), 23–32.

Zachman, J. (1987). *A selected review of the literature on factors and conditions driving the high risk and dropout problem.* San Diego, CA: San Diego State University, Policy Studies Department, College of Education.

15

The Transformation of Public Schools

Peter J. Negroni

For the first time in this experiment called the U.S. democracy, educators are expected to do something never done before in history: Educate everyone. This new expectation—education for all—is occurring at a more curious time in history when the demographics in the United States are changing more rapidly than ever before. New Americans from many different countries are not of the previous immigrant backgrounds and countries. This new phenomenon has enormous implications for public schools. At the same time, poverty is increasing at an alarming rate in this country.

Combine higher expectations for all, the increase in poverty, a technologically complex society as well as the present economic downturn, and this country faces the most problematic historical moment for U.S. public schools.

How can educators committed to making the public schools work deal with all of this at the same time? Is there hope that we can solve some of the most complex issues ever to face this country? Can we afford not to be optimistic?

There is hope. Difficult times can provide doom and gloom as well as tremendous opportunity to forge a new social order with the schools as the focus of that order. A great deal of change by all in the United States, however, is required, particularly those employed in the public schools. Key to the transformation of the public schools is the understanding and respect for the United States' growing diversity by people who work in those schools. This is the enormous challenge before us today.

In the next decade, children will continue to come to school as they are today, increasingly brown and Black, certainly poorer and more than likely not ready for school. Parents will continue to send to school the best children they have—they will not keep the good ones at home. These are the children U.S. public schools will be responsible to effectively and appropriately educate. Educators clearly understand that the job is a difficult one. Poor children are, indeed, more difficult to educate than middle- and upper class children. However, when and where a community decides to transform its schools into effective ones that work for all children, it happens and will continue to happen.

The proof is in the success of hundreds of U.S. schools. Clearly, it is what the schools do in response to how children come to school and not how they come that makes the difference. It is the school's responsibility to teach the children they get to the best of the school's potential. This is the new paradigm: Teach children to the best of our potential and not to the best of their potential. We must embrace the notion that all children can and will learn and that, to a great extent, it is the school and not the children who will make the difference.

There are many schools in this country that are in the middle of a transformational process. Thousands and thousands of schools and educators have recognized the need for a transformation. These schools and educators understand that the results they are getting are not what they want and what this country wants. They understand that to get different results, they must change what they are doing. If they are satisfied with the results, then nothing should change. If they are not satisfied with their results, change must occur in order to get different results.

Of very great importance is that educators do not translate the need to change into personal failure. Too much time has been spent in this country trying to find someone to blame for the problems in public education. We cannot blame the educators, the parents, and, certainly, not the children for our problems. We must begin to concentrate on developing and implementing solutions to the problems that exist.

One of the major reasons for the condition in public schools today is steeped in the history of the independence of schooling. Initially, schools were set up on the hill separate and apart from the community—totally isolated. It is the job of the educator—the expert—to teach the children independent of everyone else. Today, the results of this thinking are quite evident. Educators are virtually alone and unsupported by the public. Americans have not made the connection between an effective quality of life in a community and the quality of public schooling in a community.

The complete and total interdependence of community, schooling, and democracy must be recognized by the United States as part of reform efforts. Our schools cannot be successful until the workers in them and the total community understand that interdependence. Of course, this is further complicated because 75% of the U.S. public do not have children in the public schools. The senior citizens and the childless families all ask "What's in it for me?" They must be convinced that their ability to effectively participate in this democracy is closely linked to the salvation of the public schools.

They also must be made to understand that we live in a changing society that can no longer survive with only some of its children being successful. All Americans must be convinced that these are the compelling reasons for the transformation of U.S. public schools into places that effectively educate all youngsters.

Once the need for change in U.S. public schools is accepted, the method and process of transformation must be addressed. The complexity of the situation and the interdependence of varied forces require four transformations to occur. In fact, these transformations must take place simultaneously for U.S. schools to be able to deliver the type of education necessary for a globally competitive and increasingly diverse democratic 21st-century United States.

These four transformations—organizational, pedagogical, social and attitudinal, and political—are at the very root of required systemic change. Although these transformations are discussed separately—a limitation of language—this is done more as a requirement for clarity than as a distinct separation of each transformation. All four transformations must be applied to the specific issues facing schools in a systemic change process. Until all of the constituents involved in the educational process take a broader perspective that enables them to see themselves working within a new paradigm, movement in the direction of real reform will be at a snail's pace.

The stress cannot be on saving and fostering present structures in school districts and education-related organizations. All must be willing to change. To reinvent schools, the rules, roles, and relationships of the past that have led us to where we are today cannot be kept and self-interest cannot continue. The failure to make this paradigm shift has been one of the major failings of our reform efforts in the U.S. public schools during the last 10 years. Currently, broad rhetoric for change on the part of education-related individuals and groups exist, but there is very little self-reflection and analysis of how to change. All of the evidence indicates that little change has taken place in U.S. classrooms.

If we are to transform our schools, we must naturally transform what is happening in our classrooms. The transformation of our classrooms requires enormous change on the part of U.S. public schools, particularly the employees, students, and parents. These changes are not the typical tinkering ones, but paradigm shifts that will have an impact on every part of U.S. life. There is no one solution or answer to the problem of transforming present policies, practices, beliefs, and structures. If this were so, identification and replication of a model in every school would suffice. The truth is that no one model answers the needs of every school. We must create the processes that will lead to the self-analysis, reflection, and inquiry necessary to create local solutions. In developing a process for change, people, predictably, will use as parts of their solutions existing models and programs to fit their needs. In order to make these changes, a capacity to manage this change must be developed. All of these transformations will require a new capacity to manage the changes required for successful implementation.

A word of caution must be issued about the four transformations and the time it will take to accomplish them. Americans are impatient people, who believe that once the problem is identified all that remains is to focus on solutions and the problem will be solved. That is why superintendents are often given 6 months to show notable improvement. Often, after 2 years, superintendents are sent packing, because they were not able to "fix" the school system.

The transformational process is long and hard. It requires a new approach that does not use old, tired ideas about change. It requires a focus on a vision of the future as the motivation for change. The transformational process is not about solving a few problems that have been identified as the impediment to change. It is about creating a new future, a new social order with the schools as the focus. The transformational process requires that the visions to which we aspire are based on a common belief system. Consequently, the organizational and pedagogical transformations cannot occur without the social and attitudinal transformation. This is why schools cannot be independent of the larger society and community. This is why the political transformation has to be connected to the other three transformations.

The work of transforming our schools will take time and nurturing and cannot be done by one person or one group. It is multidimensional. With intense managing and support, the transformation of our schools is possible and probable. Self-analysis and self-assessment both on the part of individuals and groups, creation of a broad community vision guided by a common belief system, agreed on and clearly defined strategies for realizing the vision – all lead to successful change.

AN ORGANIZATIONAL TRANSFORMATION

The present organizational model used in public schooling needs scrutiny to determine its effectiveness. Although the majority of U.S. educators would conclude our present structure is not an effective organizational model, they have done little to demand organizational reform. We are basically doing that which we have always done. We continue to organize our schools the same way they were when we went to school. The following questions must be asked: Do we use what is available in the research about teaching and learning to make adjustments in the way schools are organized? Do we ask why and what of everything we do in our schools? The answer is a resounding *no*.

Consideration of some of the organizational structures in schools reveals we are not using inquiry and analysis to reform our organizational patterns and structures. If we were, we would not continue doing what we are doing. The most familiar structures include the following:

1. a school calendar of 180 days;
2. a school day from 9 a.m. to 3 p.m.;
3. age-grade grouping;
4. subject concentration in secondary school;
5. scheduling practices;
6. 45-minute periods, 6 or 7 period days;
7. no built-in time in the day for staff interaction, staff development, school improvement;
8. no time in the day for working with parents and for other agencies;
9. Carnegie unit completion rather than performance as the basis for measuring success;
10. retention as a solution for failure;
11. lecture as the main delivery strategy;
12. one teacher for 20 to 30 students in an individual classroom;
13. teachers working totally independent of each other;
14. top–down governance structure command and control as an organizational strategy;
15. instruction organized around the principle of remediation;
16. children in rows and in lines one behind the other;
17. little choice on the part of teacher, student, or parent;
18. prescriptions for success;
19. acceleration as the exception;
20. tracking, on the increase since 1950, as an organizational strategy in spite of the volumes of research that challenge its viability;
21. schools organized around covering the content or material not around having the children learn the material
22. the complete separation of teaching services and support services;
23. a variety of social services other than teaching services provided in a fragmented manner: guidance, drug education, mediation, psychological screening offered without connection to each other or the outside world and other agencies servicing the youngsters.

Although these are 23 of the most obvious problems with our organizational structure, obviously dozens more exist. In examining each of these structures, a reason for their inception in the U.S. public school is evident. The amazing thing is not that each of these structures has developed, for each has a valid historical educational reason, but that teachers, students, and parents identify clearly and understand the limitation of the present organizational structures; and yet, these structures still survive.

One of the most serious problems in the public school system involves present local, state, and federal rules and regulations that lead to serious fragmentation. On the one hand, we tout our interest and support of new pedagogy; on the other hand, we insist on rules and regulations that make it impossible to implement this new pedagogy. The most glaring example of this in U.S. public schools is the Chapter I programs prior to the current reauthorization. Of course, there are literally dozens of examples where rules and regulations are impediments to implementing cohesive and nonfragmented programs that apply what we know about teaching and learning to instruction; however, there is none more guilty of fragmentation than Chapter I.

The study conducted by a panel commissioned by the U.S. Education Department points to all of the issues regarding Chapter I in a clear and concise manner. The recommendations are extraordinarily on target and probably 98% of educators agree with them; however, it will take years for these changes to be incorporated into the Chapter I program. Something is wrong when everyone agrees something is wrong, but little is done to change existing conditions. It is hoped that the reauthorization act will effectively deal with this issue.

Why is it that teachers, students, and parents can clearly identify organizational structures beyond my 23 that render public school operations almost obsolete? And yet, why can't they abandon these structures? Educators cannot continue to support ineffective organizational structures. Their detriment to the youth of the United States demands that the organizational transformation of our schools begin right now.

Concepts and structures that cannot be defended and explained in the organizational structure must be eliminated. At the same time, concepts and structures in the organization that work and are good for children must be reaffirmed.

In the evaluation process, the issue of what is taught must be considered. The U.S. public schools have been asked to teach the children more and more each year, whereas the time allotted for schooling has not increased. The schools are besieged by proponents of just about anything people feel is critical for children. From bicycle safety to instruction about AIDS, schools are asked to teach more and more. It is obvious that something must give if schools are to add to the curriculum. Drucker (1993), author of *Concept of the Corporation*, defined the need to make adjustments in what is done in any organization as "organized abandonment." For any organization to survive, he indicated, it must learn to abandon what is no longer useful for the organization. U.S. public schools must learn this principle of organized abandonment.

This will not be easy because each of the disciplines wants more time to teach. The great curriculum school wars are coming. The battle lines are being drawn and sides are being chosen. Unfortunately, the needs of the children are not the prime considerations in making decisions about what will be taught. Each group operates out of self-interest. Very often, special interest groups spend a great deal of time, energy, and money lobbying for their position. Of course, subject-centered educators themselves support their own specific interests. This can range from more mathematics to more counselors. The better organized the group, the more attention it receives from boards of education.

While each of these groups fights for a clear, defined piece of the pie, they forget to think about what is good for children. They forget that the real issue is how to organize schools so that additional time for their subject area or pet project is available. If we concentrated on creating an organizational structure that used what we know about teaching and learning to deliver instruction, there would be amazing results in the achievement of youngsters.

We talk about whole language, collaborative and cooperative teaching, student-centered instruction, and other new pedagogical approaches, but we refuse to recognize the organizational transformations required to effectively implement these new pedagogical approaches.

In addition, we do not model in our own analysis, reflection, and inquiry the pedagogical processes deemed important for use in the classroom. If these processes are good for students, why aren't they good for educators? In other words, if we believe reflection, analysis, and inquiry are the basis for learning in the classroom, then, we should apply these processes to adults in the institution as well as to the institution itself. It is conceivable that the institution called *school* that is in charge of learning does not see itself as the ultimate learner. Schools and school systems see themselves solely as teachers and not as learners. This is quite paradoxical and requires a broad shift in perspective that runs across all four transformations. However, most important is that schools make the transformation from teaching organizations to learning organizations. The noted author and scholar Senge (1990) said it best in *The Fifth Discipline*: "Perhaps your own orgànization is subject to crippling learning disabilities" (p. 18). Imagine the places in charge of learning—schools—with crippling learning disabilities.

The issue of what we teach in schools as well as viewing our public schools as learning organizations requires a great deal of attention and analysis in U.S. public schools. Educators and the public must come to some agreement. Although local control over the curriculum must be maintained, this country must come to an understanding about the broad expectations for our schools. Broad curriculum as well as broad assessment standards must be defined for the nation. In addition, the public school system must become the chief learning organization in the United States.

This problem of organizational transformation is difficult for any institution but much more complex for schools. First, in order to change or transform the organization, the fundamental theoretical framework on which our school organizations are built must change. In other words, the fundamental assumptions of educators must change. The problem here is similar to home improvement. To install a new kitchen, a period of time without a kitchen must be spent.

This period of time can be very painful. Similarly, educators cannot put up a sign in front of every public school that says, "Closed For Repairs." The schools must continue to operate while making the fundamental systemic changes that will lead to transformed schools.

Second, we must also consider that schools are very different than other institutions. They are much more than organizations that are instruments to create and achieve goals. Schools are communities that are infused by the common values of the people in them. Because decisions in the school must embody the values and commitment shared by all, the work of transforming the present structure of schools becomes an extremely complex and tricky business.

Third, this is further complicated by the fact that schools are presently organized around an industrial model rather than an informational model. Schools are traditionally organized to produce young people who are capable of working in isolation and taking direction. They are meant to produce young people who can relate to machines and not to other people. The role of the school today is such that it attempts to extinguish the natural desire of people to gather, be inquisitive, and interact. Schools are organized as places where learning is a private, psychological matter between teacher and learner.

The new world requires a total transformation of the organizational structure of schools. Schools must move to become places where the organizational structure and the pedagogical models stress the importance of producing students who have the following specific skills:

- higher thinking skills;
- ability to frame new ideas and problem solve;
- creative thinking;
- ability to conceptualize;
- adaptability to change;
- good human relations skills;
- ability to work in a team atmosphere;
- ability to re-learn;
- good oral communication skills;
- ability to negotiate, come to consensus, resolve conflicts;
- goal-setting skills coupled with motivation and know-how to get things done;
- self-assure and determination to work well;
- many and varied work skills, including office, mechanical, and laboratory skills; and
- ability to assume responsibility and motivate coworkers, leadership skills.

In order to develop these skills, the organizational norm must be transformed to one that recognizes and supports people who are able to work together and collaborate on problem identification, analysis, and solutions. Schools must be organized so that the needs of the students become the focus of the organizational structure. Therefore, how we use time in the structure must be examined, including the present practices of grade levels, scheduling, and time devoted to specific subject areas. The relationship between subject areas, content coverage, length of school day and school year, and subject matter taught, must all be thoroughly examined.

As the school's organizational structure is transformed, educators must also consider that schools are learning communities that have shared goals, values, and commitments. Unlike other institutions, schools are places that must focus on reflection and inquiry. Educators have a responsibility to define those differences for government and the public in general. In *Moral Leadership*, Sergiovanni (1992) very clearly identified the difference between schools and other organizations. Every decision made in U.S. public schools must be based on this new sense of schools as communities. We must act in such a way that we reaffirm our values as institutions. The goal is not to make a profit, but to educate youngsters so they can build and foster the U.S. democracy.

In 5 short years, it is probable that the organizational structure of today's schools will be dramatically different. Achieving the goal of education for all in an increasingly diverse society requires that educators move as quickly as possible in creating this new transformed organizational structure.

PEDAGOGICAL TRANSFORMATION

Pedagogy and organizational structure must be interwoven. Too often, meaningless changes are defined as transformation, but, in fact, are as useful as the reorganization of chairs would have been on the Titanic on that tragic day.

One cannot simply rearrange the chairs in a classroom into a circle and proclaim that this will help instruction. In U.S. public schools, historically, children have been asked to sit one behind the other and told to be still, be quiet, and never talk to each other. If the change constitutes putting the children in a circle and telling them to be still, be quiet, and never talk to each other, little has been done to change the results.

A growing body of evidence indicates that present instructional delivery models cannot survive if we are to meet the needs of a 21st-century world. This growing body of knowledge about the way people learn must and will strongly influence future pedagogy. These changes are not the traditional and faddish changes in methods and approaches. They are based on physiological evidence that recognizes the very complex functioning of the human brain. Scientific evidence verifies that different people learn in different ways and that educators, as the engineers of learning, are capable of adapting teaching styles to the learning styles of children. Only one tenth of what is already known is being used and the research continues to explode. This new knowledge will require an adjustment to the pedagogy, which will have a profound and lasting influence on each student as well as each school and how each will look in the future. The work of Gardner (1985) and others continues to shed new light on the issue of how we learn and the implications of such on how we teach.

The pedagogical transformation is not about a new method or approach. This transformation requires a revolution not an evolution. It will not come about as a result of legislation from the federal or state government or by imposing new or greater standards or new regulations. It will also be stymied if remediation is used as the philosophical and operational process to undo what has been done in the schools. The pedagogical transformation requires the liberation of the U.S. educator. It can only happen in conjunction with the organizational transformation. The children will require more time in school, but certainly not more time doing the same thing. If children are not to be exposed to the same thing, the teachers will have to act differently. This will not come easily and will require enormous effort on the part of teachers. Although some students seem easier to educate, for they seem to thrive on the practices of the past and do not become discipline problems in the schools, we must examine how we can better prepare these young people to live and learn together in a world that will continue to change and will continue to demand more from each of them. Teachers will need to provide additional time and should be appropriately compensated for their time. They will have to work longer days and longer years that provide ample time to interact, plan, and learn.

For the pedagogical transformation required for success in the next century, teachers and administrators are key. If they are not supported in becoming liberated, it simply cannot and will not happen. In the process, unions will not be an impediment if all understand that the social, attitudinal, and political transformations must take place at the same time. The pedagogical transformation must address the issue of what is taught, how it is taught, and how what is taught is measured. It must address the issue of individual needs of a community as well as the needs of this nation. Each community will have to determine what will be accepted as evidence that the expectations for the schools have been met.

It must also be understood that the expectation for results has dramatically changed in the last 10 years. This change in expectation must naturally change the pedagogy that is used in our schools. Although these new expectations will be defined in the next transformation, social and attitudinal, the impact of these expectations on pedagogy must be examined. The U.S. public school system has taken on a new requirement that has enormous implications for the pedagogy used in the classroom.

For the first time in the history of public education, educators are now expected to be successful with all of the children. Heretofore, the role of the U.S. public school was to decide who would go on to college and who would directly enter the world of work. This process begins as early as the first day the child enters kindergarten. Today, the new requirement of the school is to provide an effective and appropriate education for all children no matter how they come to school. The role of the school has changed to educating children to the best of the school's potential and not to the best of the child's potential. Educators, therefore, must behave as if all children can and will learn. Although this statement may sound very simple, it is not. This is the first time in history that society is demanding that all children be successful in school. This has placed an enormous shock on U.S. public schools because they were not ready for this new demand. The responsibility has been shifted to the school—this is an important if not critical shift in perspective.

The public schools cannot point to the children and say that some children come with so many problems that they cannot be educated. Educators, recognizing the problems and issues confronting children, must figure out how to solve those problems so that everyone can be effectively and appropriately educated. Recognizing that the present pedagogical models will not be acceptable, educators must combine what we are discovering about teaching and learning (pedagogy) with changes in organizational structure to meet the new requirement of teaching all children. As part of the pedagogical transformation, a shift from process to results must be incorporated. The emphasis cannot be on the number and quantity of programs developed, but on the results generated as measured by student achievement. The new pedagogy requires the belief that continuing improvement in student results is always the goal.

Once this goal is accepted, educators must seek and become proficient in the use of alternative teaching strategies. The methods of the past were not successful with all the students. The high dropout rate is not a new phenomenon. What is new is that now the expectation is to reduce if not eliminate the dropout rate because skilled individuals are needed for the new economy and for the continued survival of a democracy. Saphier of Research for Better Teaching provides a systematic analysis of teaching strategies in *The Skillful Teacher* (Saphier & Gower, 1987). The teacher who organizes the classroom and the presentation of material with distinct and varied methods will provide students with the essential instruction, reinforcement, and growth in a challenging and supportive environment for the attainment of skills.

Technology promises to play a very important role both as a tool to deliver the effective teaching and learning model as well as a vehicle for increasing the efficiency of information exchange. Technology can provide all employees in the school system with the information required to make effective and informed decisions about students that will lead to all students having access to equity and academic excellence. Classroom teachers need to investigate the role that technology might play in increasing the quality of teaching and learning in individual classrooms. Computers and other technologies are no longer "add-ons"; they are integral tools for preparing students for life in the 21st century. Technology provides immediate access to all kinds of information, accommodates different learning styles, and provides alternative classroom activities, promising to help educators meet national and local education goals. Technology can prove to be the greatest asset in linking the belief that all children can learn with the repertoire of instructional strategies and skills necessary to make the belief system a reality, thus, creating a school system that is effective for all children.

The new requirement that all students achieve has tremendous implications. The responsibility to change and acquire new skills exists both for management and teachers. Teachers must recognize that the skills they brought to teaching are no longer adequate. They must participate in professional development programs to acquire the new skills necessary to be successful will all children. The role of administration and management is to provide training and support for teachers to acquire these new skills. The teachers and administrators of the public schools of this country cannot simply say to the public that they do not have the new skills required to do the work of the new public school of the United States. They cannot simply indicate that they need training to perform the new task required of them and expect that the system is responsible to train them. They must become active partners in the process, and they must give their time and energy to acquire the new skills that are required for the pedagogical transformation. This must be a shared responsibility. None of the groups involved can walk away from that responsibility.

The pedagogical transformation is an enormous challenge for the teacher unions in the United States. By providing viable solutions that are reasonable and allow for this new training for teachers, teacher unions can become the champions of the pedagogical transformation. Teachers and administrators must work closely to identify the issues and develop and implement solutions. Neither can walk away from their responsibility to participate in the pedagogical transformation that will make the U.S. public schools effectively support economic and democratic development.

SOCIAL AND ATTITUDINAL TRANSFORMATION

The social and attitudinal transformation requires everyone in the community to understand fully the interdependence of school and community. One cannot have an effective quality of life in any community without effective public schools. Each community must form broad alliances with the following communities:

- business,
- religious,
- parents,
- human service providers,
- community agencies, and
- senior citizens.

These broad alliances are difficult and require major changes in social attitudes. The United States has not, as a nation, believed that schools should work as part of a larger and interdependent society. In fact, we have attempted to keep these structures in the community separate and apart. Recently, we have begun to recognize that we must work with the entire community if we are to successfully educate all children.

There still lingers, however, the notion among some educators that keeping these institutions separate and apart is in our best interest. For schools to be successful, however, the services provided for children must be fully integrated. There are several experiments in major U.S. cities that are successfully trying this new approach. Every community in this country—urban, suburban, or rural—must move in the direction of integrating services that support each other. This social and attitudinal transformation requires the development of child-centered communities where children and families have real value.

This transformation requires acknowledgment that the United States has moved from an industrial society to an information society, which is dramatically different from the industrial society, and requires major changes in social attitudes.

During the industrial society, the United States had a very defined set of expectations for the distribution of results. Society was controlled by a few people at the top (totally dominated by men) with most people in the middle working and taking direction from people at the top. Society had to take care of a small group at the bottom. This group would constitute "throw away people," the excess of human capital, who society did not need to be economically successful, but for whom a societal obligation was felt.

In moving into the information society, our expectation of the distribution of results must change. Present conditions in our country are moving us from a moral imperative to educate all to an economic imperative to educate all. U.S. business is facing a most critical challenge in the coming century.

Consider that U.S. industry will develop 16 million new jobs by the early 21st century; however, it will have only 14 million people to fill these jobs. Of these 14 million new entrants into the workplace, a majority will be female and/or minority. (The minorities or new immigrants will be different from those that came to early America and this presents a different problem.) This is a group that has historically been underprepared. A majority of these new entrants into the workforce will be high-risk employees.

How can a country that already will have a shortage of 2 million workers cope with at-risk employees not capable of productively entering the job market? Under these circumstances, U.S. business will not be able to survive. In addition, a majority of the 16 million new jobs will require skills far beyond those we expect of entrants into the workforce today. It is estimated that 50% of these new jobs will require a college degree; 75% will require at least 2 years of college.

Although U.S. industry today is spending between $30 and $40 billion on training efforts for their employees, this investment is not enough. The schools must produce a new kind of worker for the 21st century. This worker will need a new literacy and the ability to relearn and be adaptable. It is predicted that today's first graders will change jobs from 4 to 7 times during their lifetime. Up to 51 million workers may need retraining in the next 15 years; 21 million new entrants plus 30 million current workers.

The United States will no longer have an excess of human capital. Every citizen is needed as a productive and contributing member of society. The problem is that there is a looming mismatch between the needs of industry (the skills required of new workers) and the type of worker or student who is graduating from schools.

No discussion about the kind of skills students need to be successful in a democracy can be complete without an examination of the purpose of schooling. Is the role of the school to prepare youngsters to be able to enter the workforce after high school and perform the tasks required by the employer or is it to educate in the classical sense of the word so that youngsters once educated are capable of receiving further work-related training once employed? Should one group of students be prepared for work and another group for further education? At this time, this argument rages in our community and our schools.

The question, however, is wrong. The question is generated from an old paradigm, which is based on the belief that the purpose of schooling is sorting and selecting. All of our behavior from the very first day a child enters school indicates that it is our job to sort and select students in such a way that we define and, thus, limit the next step for each of them. All of the practices in public schools clearly indicate the belief that everyone has limits and that the job of the school is to define those limits so as to not cause anguish to the students or to the teachers trying to teach them. After all, if one believes that all students have limits that cannot be transcended, why would one antagonize students who just can't learn beyond those limits and frustrate teachers who are constrained from teaching them beyond their limits.

Although this may sound somewhat ridiculous, it is exactly how we have organized our schools for instruction. Most schools in the United States operate on the premise that children come to school with their ability predetermined by birth. Schools then sort youngsters by judgments about their educability. As one looks at the present practices and policies in schools today, one sees the natural outcome of such a belief system. It is only when the belief system about the impact of innate ability on learning is replaced with a new belief system that sees effort and development as the basis for instruction that the operational practices and policies that exist today also can be replaced. One must ask questions that will force an examination of the belief system and, therefore, the practices and policies in support of that belief system.

What is the purpose of French I or algebra? If one believes that the purpose of French I is to keep French I students from taking French II, then all students will never take French II. However, if teachers see their role as assuring that all French I students are ready to take French II, they will work at reducing variation among students to get them all to take French II. This, of course, is a new belief system that says all children can learn if they and their teachers believe they can and if they use their effort to lead to the students' further development. This naturally will require a new set of practices and policies that support this belief system. Jeff Howard, President of Efficacy Institute, has most thoroughly developed this theme in his work (see e.g., Howard, 1992; Howard & Hammond, 1985).

This shift in perspective that allows teachers to believe that high performance is possible for all children coupled with an instructional strategy system that provides teachers with the thoughtfulness and repertoire of skills needed to respond to the different needs of youngsters in front of them will generate achievement in youngsters beyond anyone's present imagination.

U.S. society and U.S. schools must change their expectation of the distribution of results. People who were traditionally not expected to succeed must now succeed if our economy is to survive. This requires a complete social and attitudinal transformation on the part of society and more specifically on the part of teachers. Again, the challenge has now become not teaching students to the best of their potential, but teaching students to the best of our potential. This new paradigm indicates that it is what we do in the schools in response to how the children come to school that makes the difference and not how they come to school. This transformation is possibly the most challenging and the most difficult for the U.S. public school to make.

The context in which to make this change makes this transformation difficult. Those in the schools are expected to teach more to more children. Although it is understood that this is the only way our democracy will survive, we also know this is a difficult task. Indeed, no other society to date has accomplished it. Our task is made more difficult because ours is a heterogeneous, pluralistic society unlike any other in the world. Our country is made up of different races and cultures with different values and perspectives on life. With the arrival of new immigrant groups, the United States is experiencing an increasing mosaic rather than the melting process that is often spoken of in the literature. Hodgkinson (1992), a demographer, pointed to the increasing new diversity in this country. Today, the United States is experiencing diversity that includes dramatically different cultures than ones that originally came to this country. This makes effective education for all more difficult than in homogeneous societies. Yet, this difference may be our biggest asset. It very well may be that this country of different cultures and races bound by a common goal called democracy is our greatest strength.

We have in this country struggled with our multicultural and diverse nature and have attempted to view our differences as part of our strength. As of yet, we have not been fully successful in using the diversity of our nation as the potential asset it can be. Educators have tinkered with multicultural and diversity programs as the answer to these problems, but with limited success.

A new approach taking hold in some school systems is called *inclusion*, which has great promise and is predicated on the fact that the ultimate goal of the public school system is to meet the social and educational needs of all students in the least restrictive environment. This goal calls for a nationwide retraining of administrators, principles, teachers, paraprofessionals, and parents and the development of new class structures that promote a single and inclusive system of education. The mission of our schools is to successfully provide instruction in an integrated environment through the cooperative utilization of all program services.

It is expected that every U.S. classroom will be involved in activities that will not only promote, but will facilitate inclusive education among all students. Such a vision and environment will make the public school motto, "Every child can and will learn," a reality. Inclusive education is a fundamental belief that considers each person an important, accepted member of the school and the community. Inclusive educators work to create a sense of oneness and belonging within the group; they celebrate diversity. The focus is on the positive, including respect and integrity for all people. There is hope among many that inclusion will become a nationwide foundation that will guide future dreams and decisions in our public schools.

- Inclusion focuses on everyone's abilities and possibilities – not on disabilities and limitations.
- Inclusion acknowledges that everyone has different skills, talents, and gifts to offer – no one has to be good at everything.
- Inclusion means a climate of acceptance is created – no one is rejected or left out.
- Inclusion means that all school staff, students, and parents work together as a team in partnership.
- Inclusion is characterized by gentleness, individualization, openness, and humor.
- Inclusion means talking openly about differences in a productive and positive way.
- Inclusion is a daily ongoing process – not just mainstreaming in lunch, art, music, and physical education.
- Inclusion is something that changes all the time. It is a series of small adjustments to meet the needs of the people involved.
- Inclusion is characterized by an attitude of problem solving to discover what is possible.

• Inclusion creates opportunities for people (adults and children) to learn and work together.
• Inclusion is a dynamic rather than static process.

No checklist or definition can capture the spirit or commitment to all children and youth inherent in this concept. This points to the need for the United States to develop inclusive schools where all community members participate fully and are valued by all. Inclusion is truly a process through which all children can develop the skills, attitudes, and experiences to be fully enfranchised members of society. Inclusion can and should be the focus of the U.S. public schools as we move toward the 21st century, for it exemplifies all of the transformations required to make our future a viable one for all people in our country.

POLITICAL TRANSFORMATION

This area of transformation has several parts and includes political change within the school construct as well as in government and society, in general. First, it is important to recognize that we live in a society that has had as its underpinning a strong middle class. This middle class as of late has not been replenishing itself. An analysis of our national birth rate indicates that the middle class has about an average of 1½ children per marriage. This means that the natural replenishment of the middle class is not taking place. By comparison, the birth rate for poor people is exploding.

The political question here surrounds the will of this country to educate those that it has traditionally ignored. Will U.S. society understand the political and economic repercussions and implications of not educating its poor? Will U.S. society support public education in urban centers when the people being educated do not resemble both in class and color the people controlling the economics of those urban centers?

The additional fundamental issue of equity and excellence must also be addressed within the political context. At present, where one is born, to a great extent, will determine the quality of education. There are communities in this country that spend $1,200 a year per child educating a child, whereas others spend as much as $18,000 per child. Although the issue is not money alone, how could anyone accept that there is not an inherent political inequality in this funding approach?

A political transformation is required at the local and federal level in the area of funding public education. We cannot continue to run away from this reality. This is the political issue of our times that must be confronted very soon in this country. Interestingly, referenda for education are the U.S. way; however, referenda are not required for bullets and tanks or for war. As a country, we must recognize that education is the national defense of the years ahead.

An additional political transformation that must take place concerns what is taught to children and how what is taught is measured. How we teach children was addressed in the pedagogical and organizational transformation. The United States must come to some political agreement on what the children are expected to know and how that knowledge will be measured. These two areas demand broad national attention and must be resolved politically.

Equally as important is that politically the governance of U.S. public education must remain at the local level. All attempts to nationalize education are filled with danger. However, in the area of funding for public education, the United States must develop a federal funding process that supports an equal education for all. This is one of the major areas of political transformation that must take place during the 1990s.

As a nation, we must develop a plan to improve education that includes financial support to deal with all issues that face our children. The appropriate distribution of money must be combined with adequate accountability so that money would not be wasted as is the case in so many federal programs. It must also include attention to all of the other issues that impact our children being able to learn. The United States must demonstrate that it loves and respects all of its children by providing them with all of the support they need to be successful in school. Will a government operated by people who do not look like its citizens see the importance of providing for the needs of its diverse citizenry. Evidence indicates that this has not been the case in the past. Will the fact that we can now prove there is an economic imperative to educate all as well as create child- and family-centered practices and policies make any difference to the people in charge? It has certainly not worked when we approach the need for change from a moral and social justice perspective.

Unequivocally, the single most critical issue in education today is one of equity. Does every child born in this country have equal access to an effective and appropriate education? The present system is such that if one is born poor, more than likely an inferior education will be received. The difference between what is spent on poor children and what is spent on middle- and upper class children is immense. Kozol's (1991) *Savage Inequalities* exposes these differences as the United States' shame. Moreover, the research clearly supports the implementation of early childhood programs that provide a firm foundation for continued development and academic achievement. Why not begin all schooling at age 4 and continue for 13 years? This change in the school entry age would not increase the number of years of K–12 education, but would provide education during those important formative years, and would allow students to end at age 17. Then, they can continue learning as an apprentice at a job or continue a postsecondary education. The changes in society and the workplace indicate that the worker of tomorrow must be capable in many skill areas and must have higher thinking ability. Beginning earlier and providing a continuum of educational opportunities will go a long way in addressing these new challenges.

We are at the crossroads of choosing to pay adequately for the education of all children regardless of where they live, the color of their skin, or the language they speak, or of choosing not to pay for equal education and losing our democracy.

The federal government must play a more intensive role in the funding of U.S. public education. The link between our economic survival as a nation and education has been clearly defined. The question is more how the United States can raise funds for accomplishing this task. A tax program that specifically raises funds for education is needed. Why not propose a U.S. mail education surcharge? Why not have a 15¢ education surcharge on every piece of mail with a higher scale for pieces of mail that cost more than $1? This education tax would affect every individual and every business in our nation. An equitable distribution plan for this money would also be easy to devise.

Another part of the political transformation is in the area of race relations. This country has attempted to deal with its pluralistic and diverse nation from a political perspective. Part of our history records a side that enslaved an entire race of people. Our educational system has been dramatically impacted by that part of our history. The U.S. public school still suffers from the practices developed during the slavery period that created different expectations for the races.

In addition to asking whether or not those who pay for education will continue to pay to educate those of a different color, a different language, and a different socioeconomic level, namely poor Black and Hispanic children, we now need to ask whether or not those who govern the educational process will continue to strive for those of a different color, a different language, and a different socioeconomic level, namely poor Black and Hispanic children. So far, too few have fought for equity and excellence for these students.

The performance of Black and Hispanic students since the 1970s has conditioned everyone, including their parents, that they are not able to perform similarly to White, middle-class children. It is going to take a very great transformation to have those who govern education – teachers, principals, administrators, school board members as well as the general public – to believe, to really believe, that poor Black and Hispanic students can be taught and will be able to learn as well as middle-class, White students.

What is it going to take to make that transformation? It will demand a different approach to the preparation of educators. It will require a different environment than what we now call school. It will require a new vision and a new belief system. It will require a major paradigm shift among Americans. It will require brave and bold leadership.

The transformation must be built one success on another, for we must see that our old "truth" is a lie. We have ample evidence that indicates poor Black, Hispanic, and female students can compete and achieve as well as anyone else. But until we actually "see it with our own eyes" and, then, believe it is possible for all, the transformation will be incomplete.

These transformations can take place in the United States if we understand and accept the following precepts:

1. More money for doing more of the same thing is not the answer. Money to advance the transformation of the public schools is absolutely necessary.

2. Children do not come to school the same way; however, it is our response to how they come that makes the difference. It is the role of the people in the school to provide students with highly challenging learning opportunities as well as present them with instruction that considers the learning style of the student. Success among students will inevitably follow.

3. The superintendent of schools must be the chief advocate for children and has the responsibility to lead the development of the community vision and assure its realization.

4. The present system of funding public education is inequitable and must be changed. Some children cost more to educate than others. Furthermore, where one is born to a great extent determines how much will be spent for education. It is in our best interest to educate them all.

5. The present model of education must be adjusted so that firsttime quality becomes the norm and not remediation as is presently the case. Thus, schools must change their focus. Education or schooling should begin at 4 years old for all youngsters. This can be done without spending additional money. All we would have to do is rearrange our present curriculum and keep children in school for 13 years—just begin 1 year earlier.

6. The relationship between the school, home, and community must be understood and internalized. Schools need the community and the community needs the schools. They cannot exist independent of each other. It is the responsibility of the home and the community to provide support to students.

7. Our goals must be realigned with our curriculum. What do students really need to know for the 21st century? It is insane and silly to teach well what these students cannot use. Every community must ask itself what do we want our children to know? What will be accepted as evidence that they have learned? How can what they have learned be measured? Multidimensional assessments must be developed to accomplish this task.

8. Schools and classrooms and the way they look and are organized must change dramatically. They must be organized around the interest and needs and not around the interest and needs of adults. Enough is known to do this right now. Although there is an abundance of research on how children learn, not one tenth of what is known about learning and teaching has been implemented.

9. Technology as the key to the future must be emphasized. Not even one tenth of the power of technology is currently being used. We must move from the chalkboard to the electronic board. We must integrate learning areas around the technology that exists.

10. The principle of organized abandonment must be learned. Abandon the things that have not worked for a long time, such as age-grade grouping, retention, tracking, standardized tests, the Carnegie unit as a process and not a product unit; abandon the present system of scheduling, particularly at the high school level; abandon specific student to teacher ratios and let teachers decide what is necessary, appropriate, and effective.

11. Our schools must be transformed from places where people are told what to do, to places where students, parents, teachers, and administrators identify the issues and provide the solutions as well as invent the processes that will be used to implement and manage the changes necessary to meet their goals. These constituencies must be able to exercise control over their own destiny. The classroom and school is the unit of change and as such local governance must be promoted, encouraged, and maintained. With this control and power will come increased accountability. As the staff is empowered, they will be able to greatly influence learning. This should naturally lead them to commanding higher salaries and status.

12. Choice as a school reform device must be used with great care lest we create new inequities for a segment of our population or as a divider of the haves and have nots.

13. Massive professional development programs are needed at the school level. They must be planned and implemented by teachers and administrators.

14. Additional time is needed in the school day where teachers can plan together around the issues that confront them. Schools must become the units of change where teachers see the interdependence of what they teach and how they work and support each other.

15. Everyone in the United States must understand the seriousness of our work and the interdependence of the quality of life in our community and the quality of our schools. As a nation, we must understand the relationship between quality education and the salvation of our democracy.

Educators will be able to effectuate the transformations described. Through U.S. educators, a positive vision of a future United States can be defined. Vision is not with respect to a vision statement—a statement that one writes and puts away to be shown to visitors when they ask about your vision statement. Vision is something people carry with them at all times, something that is part of the heart and mind. It is the compelling reason for our work. It is in effect a snapshot of the preferred future. Educators will have a difficult time educating all of the children for a complex and demanding future until every child in this country can see him or herself in a snapshot of their preferred future as a contributing member working side by side with individuals who may not look like them—a snapshot that shows them as productive and effective citizens in this great democracy.

The educators of U.S. schools have an awesome task. This task has placed educators in what is possibly the greatest opportunity any one group of people have ever had in the history of this country. The United States is poised for its greatest failure or its greatest success. U.S. educators have been placed in an enviable position. They will decide the fate of the great U.S. experiment called *democracy*. The United States cannot and will not survive without an educated populace. What a challenge! What an opportunity!

REFERENCES AND BIBLIOGRAPHY

Block, P. (1991). *The empowered manager: Positive political skills at work*. San Francisco: Jossey-Bass.

Bonstingle, J. J. (1992). *Schools of quality: An introduction to total quality management in education*. Alexandria, VA: Association for Supervision and Curriculum Development.

Caine, R. N., & Caine, G. (1991). *Making connections*. Alexandria, VA: Association for Supervision and Curriculum Development.

DePree, M. (1992). *Leadership jazz*. New York: Currency Doubleday.

Drucker, P. F. (1993). *Concept of the corporation*. New Brunswick, NJ: Transaction.

Elmore, R. F., & Associates. (1991). *Restructuring schools: The next generation of educational reform*. San Francisco: Jossey-Bass.

Gardner, H. (1985). *Frames of mind*. New York: Basic Books.

Hodgkinson, H. L. (1992). *A demographic look at tomorrow*. Washington, DC: Institute for Educational Leadership.

Howard, J. (1992, December). *The third movement: Developing Black children for the 21st century*. Lexington, MA: The Efficacy Institute, Inc.

Howard, J., & Hammond, R. (1985, September). Rumors of inferiority. *The New Republic*.

Kozol, J. (1991). *Savage inequalities, children in America's schools*. New York: Crown.

Lane, J. J., & Epps, E. (Eds.). (1992). *Restructuring the schools: Problems and prospects*. Berkeley: McCutchan.

Lezotte, L. W. (1989, August). Base school improvement on what we know about effective schools. *The American School Board Journal*.

Lezotte, L. W. (1989). *Strategic assumptions of the effective schools process*. Okemos, MI: Effective Schools.

Lewis, A. (1989). *Restructuring America's schools*. Arlington, VA: American Association of School Administrators.

Marzano, R. J. (1992). *A different kind of classroom: Teaching with dimensions of learning*. Alexandria, VA: Association for Supervision and Curriculum Development.

Miller, J. A. (1992, December 16). Chapter I panel calls for radical set of revision. *Education Week*, pp. 1, 23.

Miller, J. A. E. D. (1993, February 24). Study joins a chorus urging chapter I reform: New tests, flexibility for schools proposed. *Education Week*, p. 1.

Peters, T. (1987). *Thriving on chaos: Handbook for a management revolution*. New York: Alfred A. Knopf.

Presseisen, B. Z., et al. (1990). *Learning and thinking styles: Classroom interaction.* Washington, DC: National Education Association Professional Library.

Saphier, J., & Gower, R. (1987). *The skillful teacher.* Carlisle, MA: Research for Better Teaching.

Sarason, S. B. (1991). *The predictable failure of educational reform: Can we change course before it's too late?* San Francisco: Jossey-Bass.

Schlechty, P. C. (1991). *Schools for the 21st century: Leadership imperatives for educational reform.* San Francisco: Jossey-Bass.

Senge, P. M. (1990). *The fifth discipline: The art & practice of learning organization.* New York: Doubleday Currency.

Sergiovanni, T. J. (1992). *Moral leadership: Getting to the heart of school improvement.* San Francisco: Jossey-Bass.

Shedd, J. B., & Bacharach, S. B. (1991). *Tangled hierarchies: Teachers as professionals and the management of schools.* San Francisco: Jossey-Bass.

Stevenson, H. W., & Stigler, J. W. (1992). *The learning gap: Why our schools are failing and what we can learn from Japanese and Chinese education.* New York: Summit Books.

16

Making a Difference: Social Vision, Pedagogy, and Real Life

Catherine E. Walsh

What does it mean to really make a difference in schools? Who should be the actors and what should be the substance of educational change? What does educational change and making a difference signify and suggest at the school building and classroom levels? And, where do you, the reader, stand in all of this? In other words, how do you answer these questions? What do you believe about the current state of education and how do you envision possibilities, directions for change, and why? What is the association between your beliefs, your visions, and your commitment and action?

Questions like these are important because they require us, as readers, to consider the practical educational significance of our own hopes, visions, and beliefs, in addition and in relation to those that are presented by this text's authors. They require us, in other words, to ground education reform in real life and to locate ourselves within this scenario.

As the chapters in this text have hopefully made clear, the work to reform education cannot be left solely to legislators, policymakers, or others who have neither a vested interest nor an inside perspective on why education is failing the majority of urban youth, bilingual students, and students of color. Educational change and social change go hand in hand. Students, communities, advocates and activists, teachers, and other concerned citizens must assume an active voice and role in shaping, directing, and pushing the change, change that has a different social vision of schools and of society at its center.

This chapter elicits such a vision. It is directed to both practicing educators and to others who are now or plan to someday be involved in schools. It is focused not on a cleansed, imagined, or nonproblematic social world but on the REAL. Its project is to address why real life has to become a much more central part of pedagogy and of schooling.

The chapter draws from my perspectives as well as the perspectives of Puerto Rican, Dominican, Haitian, and South American Indigenous students in the northeast and Mexican and Chicano students in California on how schooling and pedagogy might make a difference. The intent is to make clear that if educational reform and pedagogical transformation are to promote social change they must take into close account and, in essence, derive from students' social realities. This does not mean merely renaming the educational "core," refashioning educational assessments, or re-establishing educational standards, benchmarks, or goals. It does not mean adopting the right buzzwords (e.g., *school-based management, empowerment*) nor does it mean simply assuming the direction of new and improved instructional methods, models, approaches, strategies, and tools. Although curricular/instructional initiatives are certainly needed, taken outside of the social context, none will make any appreciable difference. This is important to highlight because education courses, workshops, articles, and texts may lead one to think they do. But if this is so, why even after numerous instructional innovations, is the educational achievement of our schools, particularly urban schools, a continued failure?

As the chapter reveals, teaching and learning cannot be examined as separate from the people—the teachers and students—they involve or from the social environment these people study, work, struggle, love, and live in. The concept of *pedagogy* as I understand it, incorporates this social aspect. It is more than teaching or the imparting of knowledge; it is the interaction of the teacher, the learner, and the knowledge they together produce (Lusted, 1986).

In order to make a difference, schools, educational programs, administrators, and teachers must grapple with what it means to prepare students for a social world that is clearly unequal—a world in which race, ethnicity, and class largely determine one's options and possibilities at birth and in which schools tend to produce compliant consumers rather than critical thinkers and citizens. This means that before we begin to make changes in teaching practice, we must carefully and critically think about the social context of this teaching—the social context and reality of the school, of ourselves, and of the other educators within, of students, their families, and communities.

REVISIONING SOCIETY AND SCHOOLING

It is easy as teachers to get caught up in the everyday demands of classrooms and schools, having neither the time nor the energy to step back and reflect on one's individual and collective work and the broader contexts and conditions that shape and frame it. Attention is to the intructional activity—the recipe—that will get one through tomorrow rather than to theoretical musings about the complex place of teaching and learning in an unequal social world. To paraphrase a teacher:

> Reflection always seems like a luxury, time taken out from real work. In thinking about it, it almost seems that schools intentionally keep reflection out. That way there is less questioning, less chance of teacher and student resistance. (Walsh, 1995, p. 81)

As educators, thinking and rethinking about what we believe, what we do, and how and why we do it (reflective thought) is important because it helps reveal pedagogy's human and productive elements. In other words, it helps make clear that as teachers we are not neutral transmitters of knowledge – that our personal, social, and cultural beliefs, values, and backgrounds and our teaching are intimately connected. Central to this process of reflective thought is an examination of our own understandings and vision of schools and society. Whether we consciously think about it or not, we all do have our own, and to some extent, shared, understandings and visions.

Probably underlying the understandings and visions of many is a shared belief that we live in and are preparing students for life in a democratic and just nation. It is the concept of democracy – that is, meaningful participation in the decision making that affects our lives – and the notion of justice (fair, equitable, right) that attracted, and continues to attract, many immigrants, possibly some of our own relatives, to this country. Stories of their "success" have been engrained in our minds and in texts – they are the stories that are told, remembered – while the equally real and prevalent stories of prejudice, discrimination, and failure remain hushed, forgotten, unspoken. The dangerous memories of African peoples, of indigenous, of those of Aztlan and of peoples of U.S. colonies like Puerto Rico further contradict our historical "democratic" and "just" roots; their present-day realities provide evidence that in the United States, democracy, justice, and equality are only partial, at best.

Certainly, the current and rapidly spreading anti-immigrant sentiment nationwide further provoked by California's Proposition 187 and recent Congressional initiatives including the "Contract on America" is illustrative of the continuous battle over power, representation, and participation. Immigrants are blamed for societal problems ranging from welfare abuse, increase in crime, to the country's state of illiteracy and disunity (Louie, 1994). Actions by the 1995 Republican-majority Congress to limit legal immigrants rights including public assistance serve as examples of the increasingly visible and organized White hegemony. Yet, even before the 1995 elections, the anti-immigrant, anti-minority agenda was underway. In the 1994 Congressional session, new legislation regarding undocumented immigrants was introduced almost every week. Like the Republicans before them, Clinton's "democratic" administration showed governmental preference for Eastern Europeans and Cubans over Haitians; for many months, the concern for the violence and repression in Bosnia took precedence over that in Haiti. A direct relationship between skin color, U.S. policy, and populace concern/interest is one that continues to be fairly constant.

The English-only movement, as Louie (1994) pointed out, has been riding on this recent wave of anti-immigrant sentiment, "using tactics from high profile, misleading advertisements in mainstream publications such as the *New Yorker*, the *New Republic*, and *USA Today* to sophisticated 'grassroots' lobbying efforts" (p. 1). In their Spring 1995 issue, United Airlines in-flight magazine ran a full-page advertisement for U.S. English, the largest national English-only organization with over 600,000 members. State referendums to make English the "official" language, rampant during the late 1980s but generally dormant during the early 1990s, are back; as Mauro Mujica, chairman of U.S. English stated in his United ad, "we're at the forefront of legislation on a state by state level. To date 19 states have passed official language bills. We're going to be busy this year." As of Summer 1995, two more states had made English the official language. In late January 1994, the Arizona State Superior Court ruled Arizona's English-only law constitutional, contradicting an earlier Federal Court decision. Several English-only bills are pending in the nation's Congress. What lies behind English-only initiatives is not a desire for more supportive ways to help newcomers adapt or become participating citizens, nor is it more or better access to English as a second language (ESL) classes (for which there are waiting lists of 3 or more years in many large cities). Fear, racism, and xenophobia are at its root. As Crawford (1992) stated, "the English Only movement serves to justify racist and nativist biases under the cover of American patriotism" (p. 3). Bred within and supported by the English-only and anti-immigrant movements, are inequitable policies and practices that are neither just nor democratic.[1]

In order to find out more of who is behind the English-only movement and what its real goals are, Brugge (1994) became a member of U.S. English.

> My mailbox was choked with solicitations from the American Immigration Control headquarters, the Heritage Foundation, Federation for American Immigration Reform, Made in the USA Foundation, and Jack Kemp. I received a Citizen Opinion Survey on the "New Nationwide Plan to 'Multiculturalize' America with such distorted questions as, "Do you believe it is necessary to purposely try to lower some students' self-esteem to strength the self-esteem of others?" Finally, I received a membership card for the Republican National Committee with my name emblazoned on its plastic face!

Further evidence for the shakiness of democracy, justice, and equality is provided in our nation's schools. There, the contradictions between the promise

---

[1]For a detailed, critical analysis of the English-only movement, see Macedo (1994).

and the reality of schooling are unmistakable. It is as if students of color, many of whom speak a language other than English at home, are kept behind a fence, their full potential unleashed, their full participation denied. An examination of test scores, retention data, dropout, push-out, and school completion rates, college enrollments and attrition, employment and salary statistics among other areas, indicates that for these students, now the new majority in California and in many U.S. cities and schools, education is neither democratic, a great equalizer, or adequate insurance for civic inclusion. The fact, for instance, that White high school dropouts are still more likely to get jobs than Latino or African American high school graduates, that college participation rates for Latinos have actually declined (Matthews, 1991), that federal, state, and local reform efforts including the Goals 2000, are virtually oblivious to the reality that White, native English speakers no longer form the majority school composition, and that nationwide, 88% of the teaching force and an even higher percentage of school administrators and school board members are monolingual English-speakers and White, raises serious questions about this nation's commitment to and concern about the future. It also illustrates the pervasiveness and height of the fences that, if we are to make a difference, must be brought down.

Efforts like the Clinton administration's 1994–1995 plan to add 10 million more police and build more jails or New York City's Spring 1994 police-run crack down on truants (Fainaru, 1994) represent repressive responses to the manifestations of the nation's and the schools' social ills. Why is so little attention put to working with the systemic problem? Why, in the case of schools, for example, is money and attention not put into addressing why large numbers of youth feel there is nothing for them in our school systems? To deconstructing rather than building more fences?

The growing inequities in society and schools, the not-so-distant experience of South Central Los Angeles (differentially referred to as a *rebellion*, an *uprising* or a *riot*, depending on one's race, social position, and/or political perspective), and the everyday, growing level of racial tension, conflict, and violence in communities and schools in large and small cities and even the suburbs speaks to the crucial need for educators to reconsider, redefine, and rework the social vision and the identity of the United States, as well as the nature and shape of its social and cultural institutions, particularly schools. It means that we cannot sit back any longer; it is time that we take things into our own hands.

Really becoming involved in the reshaping of our society and schools is difficult not only for the work it entails but because it challenges us to deal with uncomfortable, threatening, tension-producing concerns that are personal as well as social in nature. It necessitates a thoughtful consideration of our individual perspectives and positions including how they came to be as well as a thoughtful consideration of our pedagogy and practice in and out of the classroom. Such a process requires that as educators, we become more cognizant of the differences between our students and ourselves—racial, ethnic, cultural, economic, residential, and generational (growing up in today's world vs. when we were children)—of the overt and hidden ways that some students' voices are trivialized and denied, and of the ways that the policies, relations, and instructional, and language practices of our classrooms and schools reproduce the power and ideology of the broader society (e.g., see Darder, 1993; Foster, 1995; Sleeter & McLaren, 1995). It requires that we begin to question that which we do and how, why, and with whom do we do it. And it challenges us to create and construct different relations and pedagogies in our classrooms—ones that build on the knowledge, strengths, expertise, and realities that students bring with them, pedagogies that push students and educators to see the surrounding world with a more critical eye, and to take actions that will somehow make this world more equal, just, and democratic.

As *Voices from the Inside*, a study of teachers' and students' perspectives on schooling in California notes,

> It is a national paradox that a nation whose ideological roots are so profoundly democratic would structure an educational system that valued the teaching about democracy but not its practice. (Institute for Education in Transformation, 1992, p. 39)

What I am suggesting is that issues of democracy, justice, and social vision are at the base of our work as educators and, as such, provide a contextual framework for educational and pedagogical reform. In constructing a more personalized version of what democracy, justice, and social vision mean for you, I challenge you to think about the following:

- How do you understand the fact that despite more interactive instructional methods, bilingual education programs, and numerous educational "interventions," school success remains differential by race and ethnicity?
- What are the ways that race, class, culture, and power function in society in general and in your city, school, or school district in particular? What are problematic policies and practices? How can these relations, policies, and practices be changed? What can you do to change them?
- As educators, how can we promote learning environments that legitimize student voices that have been traditionally subordinated, suppressed, and silenced?
- How can we assure that "assimilation" is not the primary educational goal?
- What does it mean to create conversations among administrators, teachers, students, parents, and communities and to heal the divisions and ruptures in relationships?

- What does it mean to break with the taken-for-granted, the status quo, and to make a difference in instruction? What visions can you create and what changes can you design that promote real democracy, equity, justice, and transformation?

My intention in asking questions such as these is to provoke consideration of the seriousness, the complexity, and the personal and social nature of the task at hand. The problems of schools mirror the problems of society at large; as such, educational or pedagogical change cannot be considered in neutral, simple, singular, or individual terms but rather must be seen as replete with societal tensions, contradictions, and implications and tied to a broader goal, hope, vision, and struggle. Moreover, as Anyon (1995) stated, "schools cannot be fundamentally altered without making structural changes elsewhere in the social system, such as political and economic institutions" (p. 65).

Rosalba, a Mexican bilingual student and member of the Oxnard, California group, Students for Cultural and Linguistic Democracy (SCaLD), made the implications of the school–society connection clear:

> How can we talk about just changing schools? Schools reflect society. No matter what structural or instructional changes we put in place, they are always temporary. What we really need to be talking about is how to set up a system that cultivates something different.

STUDENT PERSPECTIVES

What does it mean and where do we begin as educators to cultivate something different? I am convinced that a meaningful and expert source for understanding the significance and substance of this difference are students—for they are the ones who potentially spend about 1,080 hours a year or about 13,000 hours in 12 years in the educational setting, observing what is going on and being the subjects and objects of teachers' instructional objectives, delivery, and assessments.

Several years ago I began speaking with bilingual high school students of color about their thoughts regarding schools, learning, and teaching and about how they think of schools, pedagogy, and teacher–student relations. This has evolved into a collaborative research project with students and several colleagues on identifying the changes that are needed in urban schools and working with students, educators, families, and communities to foster these changes. As opposed to studies that just document or use students' comments, experiences, and perceptions, this work has been directed at participatory forms of research and truly collaborative work that engages all of the participants in dialogue, critique, reflection, and action and in, so doing, helping students "hear their

own voices [and] see their own pedagogical power" (Fine, 1994, p. 12). Some of
the students cited here are part of this project, whereas others are students with
whom I have had the opportunity to work collaboratively with and/or listen to
in different contexts.

For the purposes of this chapter, I have grouped the students' comments
around four central themes: school environment, identity, language, and
teaching and curriculum. Woven throughout these themes and everpresent in
students' remarks are the expressed needs of respect, *cariño* (caring), family, and
acceptance and the expressed concern of real, everyday living.

School Environment

Educators have long argued the connection between educational environment
and learning. For many students of color and bilingual students, particularly in
city schools, the school environment is neither conducive to learning nor a safe
place for students (or probably for teachers). The comments of Sandra, a Puerto
Rican/Dominican student who was 15 at the time, pinpoint the dilemma:

> If you are planning to live in the real world, you have to deal with real people.
> People that are the same and people that are different from you. The schools that
> I've been in act as if the students, the teachers live in a glass bowl or bubble. It's like
> they don't know the real world is out there or, if they do, they don't care. (Sandra)

Michie, a Puerto Rican student in an alternative public high school, clearly
states the problems:

> Schools are too big. We don't feel safe. Students and teachers are bored. Nobody
> cares. . . . I receive alot of negativity from school officials. They're supposed to be
> there for my positivity. (Michie)

The violence of city streets carries over to the schools. As Sandra and then
Lenny who is Puerto Rican elaborate, well founded fears for one's safety are
constant:

> How can you study, think, put attention when you're always having to watch your
> back? Yeah, when you are in the classroom with the door shut maybe its ok but
> then you're thinking about what happens when the bell rings or who might be
> walking down the hall right now. It's not just high school you know. I worry about
> my little sister . . .
> *Tu sabes, hay veces que pienso en eso mucho* [you know, there are times I think
> about this alot]—how can we make city schools safe for learning? (Sandra)

> It's survival of the fittest. (Lenny)

Although the social tensions that permeate many students in school and out-of-school lives may seem overwhelming and out of control, environments can be created as Adriana, a Mexican student and member of SCaLD points out, that are supportive, safe, and caring.

> In Mr. T's class, *el ambiente es* [the environment is] different from the rest. All of me is there. He knows where we are all coming from 'cause he was there. He really cares about us, *mi gente*, and he stands up for us with the other teachers. He respects us and because of the way the class is, he makes us respect one another. It's different from the rest. It can be bad out there but *aqui adentro, es como estar en familia* [here inside, its like a family]. (Adriana)

The words of these students speak to the need to give more attention to the environments our schools and classrooms provide; to heed the fears, take into account the needs, and to creatively and responsibly consider how both as individuals and in concert with others, we might change the alienation, the symbolic and physical violence, the feeling that there is no connection to life outside, that nobody or only a select few, really care. Mercado (1993) speaks about "caring as empowerment." I wonder how many teachers or administrators feel any sense of caring from their colleagues, supervisors, the district, the system. Do you think the students feel any of it either?

Identity

The second theme is identity. As the students make clear, the conceptual complexity of identity and its subtle as well as overt exclusion in classrooms (including bilingual ones) and schools inhibits inclusion, learning, and participation. Adriana begins by challenging age-associated notions:

> From the time we enter school, how often are we asked: What do you want to be when you grow up? Even as a young child we are someone. We have an identity. The assumption is that education, age, being in the system will make you someone. I could say it all begins there, with those kinds of assumptions. (Adriana)

The fact that schools seldom recognize the dynamic, multiple, and complicated nature of identity is made evident by Sandra:

> My identity is me . . . it's my Dominican side and my Puerto Rican side, it's being female, it's growing up mostly here, in the city, and it's being a kid. . . . It is something that is not always the same. When I'm with my Puerto Rican friends I identify, think, act in one way. With Dominicans it's different. . . . Most of my friends until recently were African American. My identity when I'm with them is not the same identity as when I'm with Latinos. Teachers never see how complex it really is. It would be so nice to be in a school where I could just be me . . . where

there wasn't teacher pressure and peer pressure to be somebody else . . . where I didn't have to watch my back . . . where I could just learn and relax. (Sandra)

Rosalba, a Mexican student, and Adalberto, a Dominican, describe how schools ignore and exclude students' identities, their real real lives:

To be able to function in school you have to dehumanize, be an object . . . I've always been expected to leave myself, my family, my problems at home. We can't leave our lives, our problems, our family at home. It's always there, even when we read a book. It affects how we read—our perspectives and our understandings, our reading of it. (Rosalba)

Teachers think we come to school just to be with our friends, to fool around. They think we don't care about school, that we don't want to learn and study. We do but it's not so simple. When I'm in school I am also thinking about what happened last night, what I have to do today, the fight with my cousin, about other problems and worries. The teachers, they need to understand who we are. They need to understand that our lives are much more than just what they see and control in school. Our real lives are the family, our friends, the street, jobs, and all that we come with from before. (Adalberto)

What different understandings and visions of identity are raised by students here? What are they saying about issues of representation?

It seems that simply recognizing or naming language and cultural background, which is what many bilingual and multicultural classrooms tend to do, is not enough. In other words, assuming all "Latinos/as" are the same, that there is a singular label to describe who one is (e.g., Puerto Rican, Dominican, African American, Black) or that sharing these labels or speaking the same language necessarily implies unity is problematic. Identity is much more complex than this. The ways identities are excluded by teachers and in schools are similarly complex; through numerous subtle as well as overt forms, students are given the message that all of them cannot be present.

What I hear from students is a demand—a personal, collective, and pedagogical plea that their whole selves, in all their complexity and with all the baggage they bring, be recognized, respected, and be made an integral part of classroom relations and interactions and the learning and teaching process. Think about your own experiences now. Do your classroom pedagogies or the classrooms in which you have been really incorporate and emanate from the lived realities of students?

Marcela, a Chicana and member of SCaLD, argues that schools' exclusion of students' identities (or, I might add, teacher identities for that matter) is not simply an individual or pedagogical concern. Rather, it is tied to a broader social agenda:

Why do you think the system is structured the way it is? To keep control. People in power have to keep control of people. If people were to find their identity they could challenge, not accept those in power. So in school, our identities are intentionally played down, left out. (Marcela)

Could it be that issues of power and control are what are holding back real pedagogical and educational transformation?

If we are to make a difference, to promote and construct a quality pedagogical practice that treats students' backgrounds, experiences, knowledge, and lives as both valued and essential to learning how to live in and to make a better world, then we need to more critically consider the obvious and the not so obvious — the hidden ways identities are misunderstood, ignored, discounted, and deconstructed. This requires crossing the traditional boundaries of teacher and student, of unraveling social distance and personal unattachment, of making education and our educational involvement more than an 8 a.m to 3 p.m. affair.

It entails asking ourselves the same questions that one student posed to adults at a recent forum on school restructuring: "Do you really want to know what is going on with students? If you say yes, How far will you go to find out?"

Language

The third theme is language. Students here speak about the way speaking more than one language differentially frames their lives in school, at home, and on the street and they link language to other identity concerns. They also make clear the limited and often times assimilationist nature of transitional bilingual education programs. Roberto, an Ecuadorian Indigenous student who was learning English as his fourth language, highlights some of the intricacy and the frustration:

Sometimes people think the language you speak is who you are. That it's just that simple. I speak Spanish but it's my second language. They call me Hispanic even those in the [Spanish] bilingual program, but I'm Indigenous. I speak indigenous language — *quichua*. I tell them but they don't really listen or understand. They think it's the same, that it doesn't matter. (Roberto)

José, who is Dominican and attends school in a city that has not welcomed the growing Latino community, points out the programmatic contradictions and the anti-Spanish climate:

I'm in the bilingual program but my classes, they English. They say English what we need to get jobs. They say no Spanish with friends, in the halls. So why they call "bilingual"? Next year, no "bilingual," I go to "regular" program. (José)

In a bilingual program with a Haitian teacher that supports both English language development and native language use, Barbara emanates a linguistic and cultural pride. Her younger sister, however, has already internalized the view that English is better.

> I love speaking my Haitian Kreyol and now I also like speaking English. My little sister says "speak to me in English, no Kreyol." I say, "no I am happy to speak in Kreyol. You should be too." My teacher, she helps make me feel proud to speak both. (Barbara)

Sandra reflects on the limited, one-way nature of bilingual programs and on the dynamic nature of linguistic identification and communicative use.

> I don't understand why bilingual education can't be more open. The schools made me lose Spanish when I was little. I had to recuperate it back. Now I'd like to be in classes where I could use it—classes that recognize and respect all the different ways I can talk. . . . For those of us Latinas, Latinos, brought up here, codeswitching is real important. It says who we are. . . . Teachers still think codeswitching means you can't speak either language. They believe it has no place in school. . . . Does that mean we don't either? (Sandra)

Bilingual educators are generally well aware of the important role language plays in learning, self-esteem, and identity. Other educators may have a sense of the connection between language and identity or self-esteem; yet, the assumption that English academic proficiency and English academic proficiency alone is the ultimate educational goal, is what generally shapes and directs school and classroom language policies and instructional practice often times even within bilingual programs. Despite the cognitive and social advantages of bilingualism, the belief even among bilingual educators remains strong that English language proficiency is the bottom line. It is more common than not that the older students are (despite age of arrival) the more English is used and demanded in bilingual classrooms. It also remains common for younger children to reject and deny native language usage.[2] Outside of bilingual education, students' languages are seldom if ever included in instructional or in more socially oriented school settings (e.g., hallways, recess, cafeterias, or even in cooperative learning or small group discussions). The feeling is, as a student teacher recently expressed, that "the students could be talking about me and how would I know? Or worse yet, I could lose class control."

Even when the students' native language is used by the teacher, such as in bilingual classes, for example, it is most often the standard and variety of the teacher (not necessarily of the students) with all its attached culturally and

---

[2]For a detailed discussion of this denial, including elementary-aged Puerto Rican students comments see Walsh (1991b).

socially defined meanings, experiences, and ways of seeing and judging others. Moreover, this language use is generally understood and employed in ways that neither recognize nor support the fact that for many bilingual students, the natural conceptual process and communicative form is, as Sandra pointed out, not simply, for instance, Spanish or English but rather a fluid, back-and-forth movement that incorporates aspects and elements of both in their standard and nonstandard forms.[3] The comments of a Nuyorican teacher speak clearly to this issue:

> Schools try and close out that Puerto Rican part of me, of my students, and their parents. The African, Indian, white mix that we bring, the in-and-out mixing of Spanish, English, Black English, and street slang, our being born here but maintaining our difference, are things that most of them can't handle, including the bilingual staff who aren't Puerto Rican. We are US citizens, regardless if we are born here or on the Island. Our reality is not the same as the immigrants or refugees yet we are all referred to and treated as "Hispanics." (Walsh, 1995, p. 90)

What can be done to better incorporate the varied language and cultural resources that students bring? To not be fearful of or threatened by what we don't know or can't understand but to be open, curious, and more intentionally inclusive? To bring out, recognize, study, and understand the differences even within racial/ethnic groups that students bring? And, to expand, reshape, extend bilingual or multilingual learning beyond specific programmatic walls and structures?

Teaching and the Curriculum

Students' remarks here clearly call out for change—change in the ways that teachers and students relate and change in the content, substance, and method of instruction. Their messages are direct and to the point. They tell us to be cognizant of how social injustice is perpetuated in schools, classrooms, and texts, to be self-reflective, critical, and creative, and to be people not just teachers. They employ us to take a responsible stance, to stand up, to work to make a difference.

Adriana states the challenge:

> Look at the ignorance of most teachers—where is it coming from? They're comfortable. They think they've made the American Dream. But they are

---

[3]This is not to say that the standard variety of the native language and of English should not be taught nor is it to belittle the importance of English academic proficiency in U.S. society. Rather, it is to recognize that students with whom I have spoken strongly believe that giving place and space to students' wholeselves, including their language and cultural resources, can make a big difference in the learning and teaching process.

ignorant because they are centered in their self. It's uncomfortable for me to have to listen to them telling me what to do, how to act, how to learn and study. This kind of teaching is meant to really kill us. (Adriana)

Both Vanesca who is Dominican and attends school in Massachusetts and Rosalba who is a Mexican student in California indirectly reference the prevalent, underlying assumption that ESL learners are academically slow or deficient. The lack of academic challenges and the pushing students through to which they refer, are, unfortunately, not limited cases; such reality for ESL students is prevalent throughout the nation.

Some teachers treat you like they feel sorry for you, like you don't know nothin. They don't challenge you, they just pass you along. (Vanesca)

What they are giving me makes me feel stupid and I'm not. (Rosalba)

José and Roberto talk about how texts, curriculum content, and teacher behavior fail to appropriately reflect, incorporate, and represent the realities of the students in the classroom. Present in Roberto's remarks, is the intentional resistance and shutting out that follows:

I don't see myself in none of them books no matter they be Spanish. . . . The bilingual teachers, they ok, but what they teach and how they teach is boring. (José)

I get angry in my history class because it just gives one side—not my side—of the story. My indigenous people, it's like we don't exist, everything is from the white, the U.S. perspective. When I said that to the teacher, that I didn't agree, that there was more to tell, it brought me problems. Now, he keeps trying to use me as an example, to ask me questions, to put attention on me all the time. I hate this so I just don't talk. I say I don't know when he asks me. I stopped putting attention. (Roberto)

Being the experts that they are, students can offer us direction on how to change things:

The model needs to be like this—listen, speak to, work with students. Focus on real life situations, everyday life including issues, tensions (like drugs and violence), and current events. Teachers have to sit down and talk with you, ask your opinion, share about their own experiences and themselves. . . . They need to show respect to us as people . . . (Michie)

We shouldn't be taught what to think but how to think. . . . Being able to study things that relate to you make you more alive. (Marcela)

The teacher that I appreciate the most is one I had in fifth grade and she was White. She showed a real interest in me as a person. I remember she gave us an assignment to write about ourselves and then she brought us all to her house for lunch on a school day to read our papers. Getting out of the school, the class, we listened and talked in a different kind of way. I was surprised and impressed that she did that—that she wasn't afraid to let us see that other part of her, you know, where she lived, how she lived, the stuff she had on the walls. That was the first time I really thought about teachers as real people. (Sandra)

You need more teachers aware of where students are coming from and what they are about. (Frantz)

I would say the thing with the bilingual program, with ESL, it needs to be more than speaking English, more than teaching English. I mean I know English is important and they did a good job teaching it to me. But ESL, bilingual, it needs to be a two way experience. It's an opportunity for teachers to learn from students. . . . There's another part of the two way—that's the link that needs to get made beween different bilingual programs. It should teach Haitians how to get along with Hispanic students and let Hispanics learn about Haitians. It needs to pay attention to what goes on between students from different countries and also students from different countries and students from here. They think different but in ways they are also the same. Doing this is real serious for the future . . . (Didier)

Adriana reminds us that teaching and curriculum are intricately connected to the unequal social world in which we live. She brings us back to the need to explicitly link teaching and curriculum to real life issues, concerns, and needs, to students' communities, and to making a difference.

We need to deconstruct the Eurocentric model of curriculum. To look at the relation between power and knowledge in the classroom and within the curriculum, not only as teacher or student but as both—to understand how both teachers and students understand that relation. . . . About the way certain kinds of knowledge are taught to us, introduced to us. . . . About why everything is centered in an individual perspective, about self-interest. . . . About how we could be using knowledge to understand what's going on in the world and in our own communities. (Adriana)

CONCLUSION

Education reform for social change necessitates transformations in pedagogical practice. Such transformations must begin at the personal level. As an educator, an educator-to-be, or as someone concerned about the present and future of our nation's schools and classrooms, what messages did you take from these students' voices? What questions do their words pose for you? How do they challenge your beliefs, your fears, your practice? If you are working in a classroom now, what might your students say about you as a person and as a teacher, about how they feel in your classroom, about issues of identity and language, and about your teaching and the curriculum? Are you willing to ask them?

Educational change at the classroom level has been traditionally considered within the parameters of what teachers and students do and how and with what methods or tools they go about doing it. In other words, attention is most often to the instructional method or approach, to identifying appropriate materials and texts, to student–student and teacher–student interaction, to grouping, and to assessment. In bilingual classrooms, language – time in the native language and time in English – can be added to the list. In few cases, is emphasis given to the pedagogically related complexities, demands, tensions, and concerns of real, everyday living in a society that is neither socially just, equally accessible, or inclusionary in practice, policy, or nature. Also not generally considered is the ideological and pedagogical significance as well as the social implications of the instructional approaches. As I have discussed in detail elsewhere, humanistic, meaning-making approaches like that of whole language, for example, can work to deny the social, racial, economic, and linguistic inequities in society by treating all experience as neutrally lived and equally accepted (e.g., see Walsh, 1994, 1991a). If pedagogical change is to be linked with real life and with social change, such denial is a problem.

I believe that as educators our job is to make a difference in society, in schools, and in students lives, to know that we can make a difference and to help students see that they can make a difference, too. As such, I believe that we need to look critically at the instructional approaches we call our own, to move beyond simplified notions of language, and to give space and place to students' whole selves and whole lives with all their problems, tensions, conflicts, and complexities.

There are numerous ways to break with the status quo, to begin to refocus, rethink, and extend the teaching and learning process with social justice and transformation in mind. To not leave you totally overwhelmed, I will name just five:

1. We need to collaboratively study with our students the real-life sub-stance of their lives, their problems or dilemmas, their language, and their thought and construct active, creative ways to make these realities the knowledge base from which other learning emanates and evolves.

2. We need to more critically consider how content can make present multiple perspectives, lenses, and voices including the historical and present day perspectives, lenses, and voices of students' communities. In addition, along with students, we need to be clear about and broaden

the lenses through which we read, see, and understand the surrounding world.

3. We need to ask who is and who is not represented in the classroom and the school, in the curriculum, in language usage and forms, in the social relations and then work toward more inclusive representation.

4. We need to think about whether and how our schools and classrooms encourage or discourage critique. In other words, are students (and teachers) encouraged to question, to think "critically" rather than to passively accept knowledge, information, policies, practices, and relations as given?

5. Finally, we need to work collaboratively and collectively with colleagues and with students in the development of pedagogies that engage us as learners, that promote "civic" responsibility, and that encourage positive action for change in classrooms and schools, in individual lives, in communities, and in the society.

These are the questions, possibilities, and challenges I leave you to ponder. Nelson Mandela, the president of South Africa, has said: "Education is the most powerful weapon you can use to change the world." It is time as educators that we become more cognizant of the power that is produced, reproduced, and wielded in and by schools, of the ways schools disempower teachers, students, parents, and communities, how they limit the potential and possibilities of those of color. And it is time, that individually, collectively, and as a profession we stand up—to the taken-for-granted, to mediocrity, to the status quo, to become personally enaged, to use education to begin to change things.

Real education reform is not something that gets done by reading books or articles, writing papers, or sitting in legislatures, offices, or classrooms. It is not the new catchword or the new fix nor is it something that one can be only casually committed to. Real educational reform deals with real peoples lives, it has the potential to make or break individuals, to mold and shape a future citizenry, to construct, bit by bit, a more just and democratic society.

As you finish this chapter and this text, I ask that you heed the multiple voices, experiences, struggles, and visions within, not as stories to be filed or even words to be recalled—but as lessons to learn from, questions to ponder and pose, and catalysts to trigger a personal connection, a social commitment, and an active involvement.

REFERENCES

Anyon, J. (1995). Inner city school reform: Toward useful theory. *Urban Education, 30*(1), 56–70.

Brugge, D. (1994, Summer). English only: Part of the right wing. *Unity Organizing Committee National Membership Newsletter*, pp. 6–7.

Crawford, J. (1992). Editor's introduction. In J. Crawford (Ed.), *Language loyalties. A sourcebook on the official english controversy* (pp. 1–8). Chicago: University of Chicago Press.

Darder, A. (1993). How does the culture of the teacher shape the classroom experience of Latino students? The unexamined question in critical pedagogy. In S. W. Rothstein (Ed.), *Handbook of schooling in urban America* (pp. 195–222). Westport, CT: Greenwood.

Fainaru, S. (1994, April 7). NYC begins crackdown on truants. *Boston Globe*, p. 3.

Fine, M. (1994). Chartering urban school reform. In M. Fine (Ed.), *Chartering urban school reform. Reflections on public high schools in the midst of change* (pp. 5–30). New York: Teachers College Press.

Foster, M. (1995). African American teachers and culturally relevant pedagogy. In J. Banks & C. McGee Banks (Eds.), *Handbook of research on multicultural education* (pp. 570–581). New York: Macmillan.

Institute for Education in Transformation. (1992). *Voices from the inside. A Report on schooling from inside the classroom*. Claremont, CA: Claremont Graduate School.

Louie, T. (1994, Spring/Summer). The fight for language rights continues. In *English Plus News* (pp. 1, 3, 6). Boston: Massachusetts English Plus Coalition.

Lusted, D. (1986). Why pedagogy? *Screen, 27*, 2–14.

Macedo, D. (1994). *Literacies of power. What Americans are not allowed to know*. Boulder, CO: Westview.

Matthews, F. (1991, January 31). Special report: Recruitment and retention. *Black Issues in Higher Education*, 8–47.

Mercado, C. (1993). Caring as empowerment: School collaboration and community agency. *Urban Review, 25*(1), 79–104.

Sleeter, C., & McLaren, P. (Eds.). (1995). *Multicultural education, critical pedagogy, and the politics of difference*. Albany, NY: SUNY Press.

Walsh, C. E. (1991a). Literacy as praxis: A framework and introduction. In C. E. Walsh (Ed.), *Literacy as praxis: Culture, language, and pedagogy* (pp. 1–22). Norwood, NJ: Ablex.

Walsh, C. E. (1991b). *Pedagogy and the struggle for voice: Issues of language, power, and schooling for Puerto Ricans*. Westport, CT: Bergin & Garvey.

Walsh, C. E. (1994). Engaging students in their own learning: Literacy, language, and knowledge production with Latino adolescents. In D. Spener (Ed.), *Adult biliteracy in the United States* (pp. 211–237). Washington DC: Center for Applied Linguistics and Delta Systems.

Walsh, C. E. (1995). Critical reflections for teachers: Bilingual education and critical pedagogy. In J. Frederickson (Ed.), *Reclaiming our voices: Bilingual education, critical pedagogy, and praxis* (pp. 79–98). Ontario: California Association for Bilingual Education.

Myself

Sandra Marcelino

Yes, I do dance to a different beat.
and
Yes, I do eat wonderful different foods
and
on some occasions I may dress a different way,

but . . . if I have to be someone else to be your friend . . .
then something must be wrong.

I am myself and therefore will stay myself.

Why am I angry?

Because you are asking me to forget what I represent.

What's that?

mi cultura—oiste? mi cultura.
I represent a culture so exquisite that I don't know where to begin

o mi familia
Is it our family oriented society in which we all live?
or
mi musica
Is it the fast paced dances which we do
when we want to celebrate or just to enjoy ourselves?
or
the exotic foods which we serve at our dinner tables?
or
our beautiful language which we speak?
or . . .
is it *all* these things combined

plus people of all ages, shapes, sizes, tones and shades?

Yes . . . I think so . . .
all those things make me happy to be me.

Why call me names? Why make fun of me?

I'll be even stronger . . .

Radical Educational Reform, Critical Pedagogy, and Multicultural Education: Selected Readings and Resources

Books and Articles

Ada, A. F. (1988). The Pajaro Valley experience. Working with Spanish speaking parents to develop children's reading and writing through the use of children's literature. In T. Skutnabb-Kangas & J. Cummins (Eds.), *Minority education: From shame to struggle.* Philadelphia: Multilingual Matters.

Anorve, R. L. (1989). Community-based literacy educators: Experts and catalysts for change. *New Directions for Continuing Education, 42,* 35–42.

Anyon, J. (1995). Inner city school reform. Toward useful theory. *Urban Education, 30*(1), 56–70.

Apple, M. (1993). *Official knowledge, Democratic education in a conservative age.* New York: Routledge.

Apple, M. (1995). *Education and power* (2nd ed.). New York: Routledge.

Bartolome, L. (1994). Beyond the methods fetish: Toward a humanizing pedagogy. *Harvard Educational Review, 64*(2), 173–194.

Berlowitz, M. (1994). Urban educational reform. Focusing on peace education. *Education and Urban Society, 27*(1), 82–95.

Bigelow, B. (1988, Winter). Critical pedagogy at Jefferson High School. *Equity and Choice,* 14–19.

Brady, J. (1995). *Schooling young children. A feminist pedagogy for liberatory learning.* Albany, NY: SUNY.

Browder, L. H. (1992). Which America 2000 will be taught in your class, teacher? *International Journal of Educational Reform, 1*(2), 111–133.

Bryk, A., Easton, J., Kerbow, D., Rollow, S., & Sebring, P. (1996). *Democratic participation and organizational change. The Chicago School experience.* Boulder, CO: Westview.

243

Crichlow, W., Goodwin, S., Shakes, G., & Swartz, E. (1990). Multicultural ways of knowing: Implications for practice. *Journal of Education, 172*(2), 101–117.

Cummins, J. (1989). *Empowering minority students.* Sacramento: California Association for Bilingual Education.

Darder, A. (1991). *Culture and power in the classroom: A critical foundation for bicultural education.* New York: Bergin & Garvey.

Delpit, L. (1988). The silenced dialogue: Power and pedagogy in educating other people's children. *Harvard Educational Review, 58,* 288–298.

Delpit, L. (1995). *Other peoples children: White teachers, students of color, and other cultural conflicts in the classroom.* New York: New Press.

Edelsky, C. (1991). *With literacy and justice for all. Rethinking the social in language and education.* Philadelphia: Falmer.

Fine, M. (1989). Silencing and nurturing in an improbable context: Urban adolescents in public schools. In H. Giroux & P. McLaren (Eds.), *Critical pedagogy, the state, and cultural struggle.* Albany, NY: SUNY Press.

Fine, M. (1991). *Framing dropouts. Notes on the politics of urban high schools.* Albany, NY: SUNY Press.

Fine, M. (Ed.). (1994). *Chartering urban school reform. Reflections on public high schools in the midst of change.* New York: Teachers College Press.

Fingeret, A., & Jurmo, P. (1989). *Participatory literacy education.* San Francisco: Jossey-Bass.

Frederickson, J. (Ed.). (1995). *Reclaiming our voices. Bilingual education, critical pedagogy, and praxis.* Ontario: California Association for Bilingual Education.

Freinet, C. (n.d.) *Cooperative learning and social change. Selected readings.* Available from Our Schools/Our Selves Education Foundation, 1698 Gerrard St. East, Toronto, Ontario M4L 2B2.

Freire, P. (1970). *Pedagogy of the oppressed.* New York: Seabury.

Freire, P. (1977). *Education for critical consciousness.* New York: Continuum.

Freire, P. (1985). *The politics of education: Culture, power, and liberation.* New York: Bergin & Garvey.

Freire, P. (1996). *Teachers as cultural workers. Letters to those who dare to teach.* Boulder, CO: Westview.

Giroux, H. (1983). *Theory and resistance in education: A pedagogy for the opposition.* New York: Bergin & Garvey.

Giroux, H. (1988). *Teachers as intellectuals. Toward a critical pedagogy of learning.* New York: Bergin & Garvey.

Giroux, H. (1991). Democracy, border pedagogy, and the politics of difference. *British Journal of the Sociology of Education.*

Giroux, H. (1992). *Border crossings: Cultural workers and the politics of education.* New York: Routledge.

Giroux, H. (1993). *Living dangerously: Multiculturalism and the politics of difference.* New York: Peter Lang.

Giroux, H., & Aronowitz, S. (1995). *Education still under seige.*

Giroux, H., & McLaren, P. (Eds.). (1989). *Critical pedagogy, the state, and cultural struggle.* Albany, NY: SUNY Press.

Graman, T. (1988). Education for humanization: Applying Paulo Freire's pedagogy to learning a second language. *Harvard Educational Review, 58,* 433–448.

Gutierrez, K., & Larson, J. (1994). Language borders: Recitation as hegemonic discourse. *International Journal of Education Reform, 3*(1), 22–36.

Hooks, B. (1989). *Talking back: Thinking feminist, thinking Black.* Boston: South End.

Hooks, B. (1995). *Teaching to transgress. Education as the practice of freedom.* New York: Routledge.

Horton, M., & Freire, P. (1990). *We make the road by walking. Conversations on education and social change.* Philadelphia: Temple.

Institute for Education in Transformation. (1992). *Voices from the inside. A report on schooling from inside the classroom.* Claremont, CA: Claremont Graduate School.

Jennings, J. (1994). *Blacks, Latinos, and Asians in urban America. Status and prospects for politics and activism.* Westport, CT: Greenwood/Praeger.

Kanpol, B. (1994). *Critical pedagogy. An introduction.* Westport, CT: Bergin & Garvey/ Greenwood.

Kanpol, B., & McLaren, P. (Eds.). (1995). *Critical multiculturalism. Uncommon voices in a common struggle.* Westport, CT: Bergin & Garvey/Greenwood.

Kohl, H. (1994). *"I won't learn from you" and other thoughts on creative maladjustment.* New York: New Press.

Kreisberg, S. (1991). *Transforming power: Domination, empowerment, and education.* Albany, NY: SUNY Press.

Kretovics, J., & Nussel, E. J. (Eds.). (1994). *Transforming urban education.* Boston: Allyn & Bacon.

Ladsen-Billings, G. (1994). *The dreamkeepers: Successful teachers of African American children.* San Francisco: Jossey-Bass.

Ladsen-Billings, G., & Henry, A. (1990). Blurring the borders: Voices of African American pedagogy in the U.S. and Canada. *Journal of Education, 172*(2), 72–88.

Lee, C. D., Lomotey, K., & Shujaa, M. (1990). How shall we sing our sacred song in a strange land? The dilemma of double consciousness and the complexity of an African centered pedagogy. *Journal of Education, 172*(2), 45–61.

Levine, D., Lowe, R., Peterson, R., & Tenorio, R. (1995). *Rethinking schools. An agenda for change.* New York: New Press.

Loewen, J. (1994). *Lies my teacher told me: Everything your high school history textbook got wrong.* New York: New Press.

Macedo, D. (1994). *Literacies of power. What Americans are not allowed to know.* Boulder, CO: Westview.

MacLeod, J. (1995). *Ain't no makin' it. Aspirations and attainment in a low-income neighborhood* (expanded ed.). Boulder, CO: Westview.

McCarthy, C. (1990). Multicultural education, minority identities, textbooks, and the challenge of curriculum reform. *Journal of Education, 172*(2), 118–129.

McCarthy, C., & Crichlow, W. (Eds.). (1993). *Race, identity and representation in education.* New York: Routledge.

McLaren, P. (1989). *Life in schools. An introduction to critical pedagogy in the foundations of education.* New York: Longman.

McLaren, P. (1995). *Critical pedagogy and predatory culture. Oppositional politics in a postmodern era.* New York: Routledge.

McLeod, A. (1986). Critical literacy: Taking control of our own lives. *Language Arts, 63,* 37–50.

McLaughlin, M. W., Irby, M., & Langman, J. (1994). *Urban sanctuaries. Neighborhood organizations in the lives and futures of inner-city youth.* San Francisco: Jossey-Bass.

Meeroff, P., & Sklar, H. (1994). *Streets of hope. The fall and rise of an urban neighborhood.* Boston: South End.

Meir, D. (1995). *The power of their ideas. Lessons for America from a small school in Harlem.* Boston: Beacon Press.

Mercado, C. (1993). Caring as empowerment: School collaboration and community agency. *Urban Review, 25,* 79–104.

Mohanty, C. (1994). On race and voice: Challenges for liberal education in the 1980s. In H. Giroux & P. McLaren (Eds.), *Between borders. Pedagogy and the politics of cultural studies.* New York: Routledge.

Miller, J. (1990). *Creating spaces and finding voices. Teachers collaborating for empowerment.* Albany, NY: SUNY Press.

Muñoz, V. (1995). *Where "something catches". Work, love, and identity in youth.* Albany, NY: SUNY.

National Coalition of Advocates for Students. (1988). *New voices. Immigrant students in U.S. public schools.* Boston: National Coalition of Advocates for Students.

Nieto, S. (1992). *Affirming diversity. The sociopolitical context of mulicultural education.* New York: Longman.

Noguera, P. A. (1995). Preventing and producing violence: A critical analysis of responses to school violence. *Harvard Educational Review, 65*(2), 189–212.

Olsen, L. (1994). *The unfinished journey: Restructuring schools in a diverse society.* San Francisco: California Tomorrow.

Park, P. (1988). Breaking out of culture: Critical education for the silent minority. In G. Okihiro (Ed.), *Reflections on shattered windows: Promises and prospects for Asian American studies.* Tacoma: Washington State University Press.

Park, P., Brydon-Miller, M., Hall, B., & Jackson, T. (Eds.). (1993). *Voices of change: Participatory research in the United States and Canada.* Westport, CT: Bergin & Garvey/Greenwood.

Peim, N. (1994). *Critical theory and the English teacher. Transforming the subject.* New York: Routledge.

Perry, T., & Fraser, J. (Eds.). (1993). *Freedom's plow: Teaching in the multicultural classroom.* New York: Routledge.

Peterson, R. (1991). Teaching how to read the world and change it: Critical pedagogy in the intermediate grades. In C. E. Walsh (Ed.), *Literacy as praxis: Culture, language and pedagogy.* Norwood, NJ: Ablex.

Poplin, M. (1993). Making our whole-language bilingual classrooms also literatory. In J. Tinajero & A. F. Ada (Eds.), *The power of two languages. Literacy and biliteracy for Spanish-speaking students.* New York: Macmillan.

Shor, I. (1980). *Critical teaching and everyday life.* Boston: South End.

Shor, I. (Ed.). (1987). *Freire for the classroom. A sourcebook for liberatory teaching.* Portsmouth, NH: Boynton/Cook Heinemann.

Shor, I. (1992). *Empowering education.* Chicago: University of Chicago Press.

Shor, I., & Freire, P. (1987). *A pedagogy for liberation: Dialogues on transforming education.* New York: Bergin & Garvey.

Simon, R. (1987). Empowerment as a pedagogy of possibility. *Language Arts, 64,* 370–382.

Simon, R. (1992). *Teaching against the grain. Texts for a pedagogy of possibility.* Westport, CT: Bergin & Garvey/Greenwood.

Sleeter, C., & McLaren, P. (Eds.). (1995). *Multicultural education, critical pedagogy, and the politics of difference.* Albany, NY: SUNY Press.

Slim, H., & Thompson, P. (1994). *Listening for a change: Oral testimony and community development.* Philadelphia: New Society.

Takaki, R. (1993). *A different mirror: A history of multicultural America.* Boston: Back Bay Books.

Torruellas, R., Benmayor, R., Goris, A., & Juarbe, A. (1991). Affirming cultural citizenship in the Puerto Rican community: Critical literacy and the El Barrio popular education program. In C. E. Walsh (Ed.), *Literacy as praxis: Culture, language and pedagogy.* Norwood, NJ: Ablex.

Walsh, C. E. (1987). Schooling and the civic exclusion of Latinos: Toward a discourse of dissonance. *Journal of Education, 169,* 115–131.

Walsh, C. E. (1991). Literacy as praxis: A framework and introduction. In C. E. Walsh (Ed.), *Literacy as praxis: Culture, language, and pedagogy.* Norwood, NJ: Ablex.

Walsh, C. E. (1991). *Pedagogy and the struggle for voice: Issues of language, power, and schooling for Puerto Ricans.* New York: Bergin & Garvey.

Walsh, C. E. (1993). Becoming critical. Rethinking literacy, language, and teaching. In J. Tinajero & A. F. Ada (Eds.), *The power of two languages. Literacy and biliteracy for Spanish-speaking students.* New York: Macmillan.

Walsh, C. E. (1994). Engaging students in their own learning: Literacy, language, and knowledge production with Latino Adolescents. In D. Spencer (Ed.), *Adult biliteracy in the United States.* Washington, DC: Center for Applied Linguistics and Delta Systems.

Walsh, C. E. (1995). Critical reflections for teachers. Bilingual education and critical pedagogy. In J. Frederickson (Ed.), *Reclaiming our voices. Bilingual education, critical pedagogy, and praxis.* Ontario, CA: California Association for Bilingual Education.

Weiler, K. (1988). *Women teaching for change: Gender, class and power.* New York: Bergin & Garvey.

Weis, L., & Fine, M. (Eds.). (1993). *Beyond silenced voices. Class, race, and gender in the United States schools.* Albany, NY: SUNY Press.

Wheelock, A. (1992). *Crossing the tracks: How untracking can save America's schools.* New York: New Press.

Young, I. M. (1990). *Justice and the power of difference.* Princeton, NJ: Princeton University Press.

Curriculum Resources

African American mosaic: A Library of Congress resource guide for the study of Black history and culture (Available through American On-Line Service).

Anti-Bias Curriculum. Tools for Empowering Young Children. By Derman-Sparks, L. (1989). Washington, DC: National Association for Young Children. (available through NECA, see organizational list).

Asante African-Centered Curriculum Guides (available from Peoples Publishing Group, 230 W. Passaic St., Maywood, NJ 07607. Tel (800) 822-1080).

The Asian American Comicbook. By Wen-Ti, Tsen. (1992). Boston: the Asian American Workshop. (high school or adult). (available through NECA, see organizational list).

Caribbean Connections: Classroom Resources for Secondary Schools. By Menkart, D. and Sunshine, C. (1990). (available through NECA, see organizational list).

Colonialism in the Americans. By Gage, S. (1991). Comic-book format for high school aged students. (available through NECA, see organizational list).

Dangerous Memories: Invasion and Resistance Since 1492. By Chicago Religious Task Force on Central America (1991). (available through NECA, see organizational list).

Educating for A Change. By Arnold, R., Burke, B., James, C., Martin, D., Thomas, B. (1991). Toronto: Between the Lines and the Doris Marshall Institute for Education and Action (see organizational list for address).

Literacy for Empowerment: A Resource Handbook for Community-based Educators. By Association for Community-based Education. (1988). Washington, DC: Author.

Making Meaning Making Change. Participatory Curriculum Development for Adult ESL Literacy. by Auerbach, E. (1992). Washington, DC: Center for Applied Linguistics and Delta Systems. (available through NECA, see organizational list).

Spinning Tales/Weaving Hope: Stories of Peace, Justice, and the Environment. Edited by Brody, E. (1992). Philadelphia: New Society Publishers. (available through NECA, see organizational list).

Teaching About Haiti. By NECA (1993) (available through NECA, see organizational list).

Rediscovering America/Redescubriendo America. By NECA (1992). (available through NECA, see organizational list).

Rethinking Our Classrooms. Teaching for Equity and Justice. By Rethinking Schools (1994). (see periodical list for address).

Rethinking Columbus. Teaching About the 500th Anniversary of Columbus' Arrival in America. By Rethinking Schools. (available through NECA, see organizational list).

Shadow of Hate Video and Text Kit By Teaching Tolerance (1995). (see organizational list for address).

What Changes are Needed? Latino Students, Parents and Educators Perspectives on Urban Schools. A video, manual, and monograph packet. (1995). Available from N. E. MRC, Graduate College of Education, UMASS, 100 Morrissey Blvd., Boston, MA 02125.

Who Belongs Here? By Knight, M. B. (1995). A picturebook that engages young children in issues of immigration, racism and tolerance. Available from Tilbury House, 132 Water St., Gardiner, ME 04345. Tel (800) 582-1899.

Journals and Periodicals for Practitioners and Students

Colors
Four Color Productions, Inc.
2608 Blaisdell Ave. South
Minneapolis, MN 55408-1505
(612) 874-0494 Fax (612) 874-0086
A bimonthly journal of opinion by writers of color.

Democracy and Education
College of Education
210 McCracken Hall
Ohio University
Athens, OH 45701
(614) 593-4531
Quarterly publication with articles by classroom teachers on teaching for democracy.

Dollars and Sense
1 Summer St.
Somerville, MA 02143
(617) 628-8411
Easy to understand articles on the economy from a critical perspective.

Multicultural Messenger. The Voice of Cultural Diversity for Educators, Administrators, and School Board Members.
Peoples Publishing Group
International Multicultural Education Association
230 W. Passaic St.
Maywood, NJ 07607
(800) 822-1080 Fax (201) 712-0045
Monthly newsletter.

New Schools. New Communities. Voices for Educational Change
(Formerly *Equity and Choice*)
Corwin Press, Inc.
2455 Teller Rd.
Thousand Oaks, CA 91320
(805) 499-0721 Fax (805) 499-0871
A quarterly journal devoted to rethinking and redesigning whole-community and whole-school renewal and giving voice to the range of stakeholders.

New Youth Connections
144 W. 27th St. 8R
New York, NY 10001
(212) 242-3270
Monthly newspaper written by high school students.

Radical Teacher
Boston Women's Teachers' Group
PO Box 102
Kendall Square Post Office
Cambridge, MA 02142
Journal with critical education articles and teaching ideas.

Rethinking Schools
1001 E. Keefe Ave.
Milwaukee, WI 53212
(414) 964-9646 Fax (414) 964-7720

An independent educational activist newspaper published by teachers and educators that is focused on elementary and secondary school reform and issues of equity and social justice.

School Voices
People About Changing Education (PACE)
115 W. 28th St., Suite 3R
NY, NY 10001
(212) 643-8490
A quarterly newspaper for pro-equality educators, parents, and students of all races.

Skipping Stones
80574 Hazelton Rd.
Cottage Grove, OR 97424
(503) 942-9434
A multiethnic children's forum.

Taboo: The Journal of Culture and Education
Peter Lang Publishing
62 W. 45th Street
New York, NY 10036
(800) 770-5264 Fax (212) 302-7574
An academic journal for the study of teaching and pedagogy that focuses on the relationship between education and sociocultural context.

Teaching Tolerance
400 Washington Ave.
Montgomery, AL 36104
A free, biannual magazine on promoting tolerance in schools.

Teen Voices
PO Box 60009
JFK
Boston, MA 02114
A magazine by, for, and about young women.

Third World Resources
464 19th St.
Oakland, CA 94612
(415) 835-4692
Quarterly review of resources from and about the Third World for concerned educators and political activists.

United Youth
Teens as Community Resources, Inc.
100 Mass. Ave.
Boston, MA 02115
(617) 266-2788 Fax (617) 266-0388
A newspaper written by Boston youth.

National Organizational Networks and Resources with a "Critical" Perspective

ASPIRA Association, Inc.
1112 16th St., NW #340
Washington, DC 20036
(202) 835-3600
An organization focused on issues pertaining to Latino students and families including dropout prevention, mentoring programs, and increased parental involvement. Publishes resource materials and a newsletter.

Centro de Estudios Puertorriqueños
Hunter College
695 Park Ave.
New York, NY 10021
(212) 772-5689
A research organization dedicated to the study of linguistic, cultural, educational, and economic realities of Puerto Rican communities in the United States. Has available films and other audiovisual materials, publications, and a quarterly journal and is the founder of El Barrio Popular Education Program.

The Doris Marshall Institute for Education and Action
818 College St., No. 3
Toronto, Ontario M6G 1C8
An organization committed to popular education and social change. Publishes useful materials for critical educators.

Educators Against Racism and Apartheid
164-04 Goethals Ave.
Jamaica, NY 11432
Curriculum kits, newsletter, and other resources.

Educators for Social Responsibility (National Office)
23 Garden St.
Cambridge, MA 02138
(617) 492-1764
A national teachers' organization offering programs and curricula that help students become engaged in the world.

Escuela Popular Norteña
Box Y
Valdez, New Mexico 87580
(505) 776-8432
A folk school dedicated to building movement for fundamental social change and conducting political education against cultural, racial, sexual, and class oppression.

Fair Test
National Center for Fair and Open Testing
342 Broadway
Cambridge, MA 02139-1802
(617) 864-4810 Fax (617) 497-2224

A national center devoted to the elimination or reform of standardized testing at all levels of education. Publishes resources including materials for organizing testing reform and a newsletter.

The Highlander Research and Education Center
1959 Highlander Way
New Market, TN 37820
A folk school and now research and education center that has long been dedicated to workers' rights, leadership development and education for social justice.

Multicultural Education Training and Advocacy, Inc. (META)
240A Elm St. Suite 22
Somerville, MA 02144
(617) 628-2226
A national advocacy organization committed to the defense and promotion of the educational rights of immigrant and language minority students. Has published a handbook for immigrant parents rights.

National Association for Bilingual Education
1220 L St., NW, Suite 605
Washington, DC 20005-4018
(202) 898-1829 Fax (202) 789-2866
A research, professional development, and public education and legislative advocacy organization dedicated to the educational needs of linguistic minority students. Has a Critical Pedagogy Special Interest Group.

National Coalition of Advocates for Students and Clearinghouse for Immigrant Education
100 Boylston St., Suite 737
Boston, MA 02116
(617) 357-8507 (800) 441-7192
A networking, information sharing, advocacy, and policy analysis organization that also offers parents, teachers, and students information on legal rights, bilingual and multicultural education, student support services and other areas.

National Coalition of Education Activists
PO Box 679
Rhinebeck, NY 12572
(914) 876-4580
A multiracial organization of parents, teachers, activists, advocates, and students-working for fundamental educational reform. The coalition serves as a national informational network and clearinghouse, publishes a newsletter, and sponsors an annual conference. They also have resource packets on a variety of topics including tracking and ability grouping.

National Coalition for Parent Involvement
Box 39
1201 16th St, NW
Washington, DC 20036

Coalition of more than 30 national organizations that offers publications and referrals to local organizations.

National Committee for Citizens in Education
900 2nd St., NE, Suite 8
Washington, DC 20002-3557
(202) 408-0447
A national organization dedicated to expanding parents' and other citizens; access to public schools and public school reform. Publishes numerous resources.

National Council of La Raza
810 First St., NE, Suite 300
Washington, DC 20002
(202) 628-9600
A Latino civil rights organization offering policy analysis, advocacy, and information on issues of education, employment, housing, health, and immigration.

Network of Educators on the Americas (NECA)
1118 22nd St., NW
Washington, DC 20037
(202) 429-0137
A nonprofit organization of K–12 teachers, parents, and community members (with local affiliates) that works with school communities to promote pedagogy, resources, and cross-cultural understanding for social and economic justice in the Americas.

Oxfam America
26 West St.
Boston, MA 02119
(617) 482-1211
An international, grass roots development and advocacy agency focused on the needs and realities of oppressed communities. Has educational materials, photoexhibits, and other resources that can be used in the classroom.

People for the American Way
2000 M St., NW, Suite 400
Washington, DC 20036
(202) 467-4999
Promotes anticensorship efforts and documents censorship attempts in the schools.

Teaching Tolerance
Southern Poverty Law Center
400 Washington Ave.
Montgomery, AL 36104
(334) 264-0286 Fax (334) 264-3121
An educational project that provides educational tools related to achieving tolerance in a diverse society either free or at low cost.

Author Index

Subject Index

About the Contributors

Alma Flor Ada is an internationally recognized author of children's literature and teacher educator. She is the Director of Doctoral Studies in the International Multicultural Program at the University of San Francisco.

Tony Baez is an Assistant Professor with the Center for Urban Community Development at the University of Wisconsin, Milwaukee and a long-time community activist and advocate for educational and social change.

Teresa Barrientos is a New York City-raised Puerto Rican. She was a bilingual teacher and parent educator for many years in the Holyoke, Massachusetts schools and is currently studying to be a family counselor.

Doug Brugge is co-chairperson of Unity Boston, a board member of the Massachusetts English Plus Coalition, and teaches and does research at the Department of Community Health, Tufts School of Medicine. He has done research on youth and tobacco advertising and provides technical assistance to parents and teachers on indoor air quality in schools.

La Colectiva Intercambio is a group of Puerto Rican researchers and educators from the United States and Puerto Rico who, since 1987, have been involved in a formal collaboration and exchange based on a shared concern for the education of Puerto Ricans/Latinos and the need for a more critical research methodology to study and understand these students' realities. Members of the Colectiva involved in the writing of this chapter include Carmen Mercado, Pedro Pedraza, and Jorge Ayala from Hunter College; Marceline Torres and Miriam Perez from the New York City schools; Marie E.

Torres-Guzman from Teachers College, Columbia University; Luis Moll from the University of Arizona; and Ana Helvia Quintero and Diana Rivera Viera from the University of Puerto Rico.

Martin Espada is a Brooklyn-born Puerto Rican poet who has won numerous literary awards for his work. He has worked as a legal services and tenant lawyer in Latino communities and is currently teaching in the English Department at the University of Massachusetts, Amherst.

Ruben W. Espinosa is a Professor in the Department of Policy Studies in Language and Culture in the College of Education at San Diego State University. He is Codirector of the Social Equity Technical Assistance Center, coordinates an elementary bilingual emphasis credential program, and teaches in the SDSU and Claremont Graduate School Joint Doctoral Program. He has directed a national bilingual education center and has published in the areas of school finance, achievement trends, and staff development.

Georgette E. Gonsalves has advocated and worked in the field of bilingual education for more than 30 years. A graduate of Boston University, she has focused on education in Creole languages in the United States, Portugal, and the Republic of Cape Verde. She currently works as a bilingual resource specialist at the University of Massachusetts in Boston.

Peter Nien-chu Kiang is an Assistant Professor in the Graduate College of Education and American Studies Program at the University of Massachusetts, Boston where he teaches courses in Asian American Studies and multicultural education.

Suzanne Lee is a member of Unity Boston and the chairperson of the Chinese Progressive Association, a grassroots community organization that works to empower Boston's Chinese community. She recently became principal of the Baldwin Elementary School in Boston.

Eva Mack is a teacher at Milwaukee Area Technical College stationed in a community-based organization. She has been actively involved in the development of multicultural curriculum for adult education and in linking adult education to community empowerment and advancement. She has her master's in multicultural education from the University of Wisconsin.

Sandra Marcelino, a Puertorican Dominican, is currently a junior at the Cambridge School of Weston, Weston, Massachusetts. Striving to successfully graduate in Spring 1996, she hopes to pursue her interests in law, education, and the arts. She has attended mainly public, some parochial, and some independent schools. She lives life one day at a time but with a keen awareness of her future. "This is just the beginning, I haven't said all I needed to say."

Beatriz McConnie Zapater, a native of Puerto Rico, obtained her bachelor's degree in fine arts and master's degree in bilingual and ESL education from Boston University.

Since 1974, Beatriz has worked in the Latino/Puerto Rican community, teaching, designing, implementing, and evaluating educational programs for youth and adults. Since January 1993, she has been the Director of YOU for Greater Egleston (Youth Opportunities Unlimited) and of its core program, the Greater Egleston Community High School, a community-based alternative high school for neighborhood youth. Beatriz is also the author of two children's books, *Three Kings Day* and *Fiesta!*

Peter J. Negroni is a 33-year veteran career educator who spent 25 years in the New York City Public Schools. He is presently superintendent of the Springfield, Massachusetts Public Schools, a 25,000-pupil urban school system engaged in a broad systemic reform effort. Negroni has dedicated his life to the issues of equity for all as well as social justice and inclusiveness in American society.

Sonia Nieto is professor of Education in the Teacher Education and Curriculum Studies Department, School of Education, University of Massachusetts, Amherst. Her research centers on multicultural education, critical pedagogy, and the education of Latinos in the United States. Professor Nieto is the author of *Affirming Diversity: The Sociopolitical Context of Multicultural Education*, numerous journal articles and book chapters, and the co-editor of *The Education of Latino Students in Massachusetts*. Nieto has worked extensively with teachers and schools and has served on many boards and commissions with a focus on educational and social justice for all students.

Alberto Ochoa is a Professor in the Department of Policy Studies in Language and Culture in the College of Education at San Diego State University. He is Codirector of the Social Equity Technical Assistance Center, directs the secondary bilingual emphasis credential program, and teaches in the SDSU and Claremont Graduate School Joint Doctoral Program. He has directed national desegregation and bilingual education centers and has published in the areas of bilingual education, desegregation, achievement trends, and parent empowerment.

Camilo Perez-Bustillo is a civil rights lawyer, cultural organizer, translator, and essayist who is currently a Professor of Communication Studies at the Instituto Tecnológico y de Estudios Superiores de Monterey, State of Mexico campus. He was lead counsel for plaintiffs in the Florida case on behalf of Multicultural Education, Training, and Advocacy, Inc. (META) which he co-founded in 1982. Camilo has a long history of educational activism and advocacy with bilingual communities throughout the United States.

Roger Rice is an attorney and Co-executive Director of Multicultural Education, Training and Advocacy, Inc., a national legal advocacy organization. He has more than 20 years experience with legal and policy questions regarding public education throughout the United States.

Alan Jay Rom was staff counsel to the Lawyer's Committee for Civil Rights Under Law of the Boston Bar Association for 18 years. His work has focused on employment discrimination, voting rights, and education discrimination, particularly bilingual education, school desegregation, and public school finance. He served as co-counsel in the recently decided school finance case *McDuffy v. Robertson* (1993). He has also been actively involved in helping Latinos and others enforce their right to receive bilingual education in many communities in Massachusetts.

The Students for Cultural and Linguistic Democracy (SCaLD) is a collective of students and former students from Channel Islands High School in Oxnard, California. SCaLD's main goal is to rediscover education for cultural and linguistic democracy and transform educational pedagogy to include emancipating curriculum from a critical, real-world perspective. Its members involved in the writing of the chapter for this text and their ages at the time include: Nick Crisoto, age 17; Adriana Jasso, age 18; Pedro May, age 20; Jose Luis Serrano, age 18; Ricio Soto, age 20; Marcela Sustaita, age 18; Minh Trinh, age 17; and Bill Terrazas, Jr., co-learner/educator.

Catherine E. Walsh is an educator/activist who, for over 20 years, has worked collaboratively with students, parents, educators, and community organizations in promoting educational and social change in the United States and Latin America. She is a faculty member in the University of Massachusetts Boston's Graduate College of Education where she also directs and coordinates several projects including the New England Educational Alliance for Equity in the Schools. She is a Federal Court-Appointed Monitor in several school districts and the author of a number of books and articles in the areas of critical pedagogy, literacy, language, and bilingual/multicultural and urban education that have been published in the United States, Canada, and Latin America.